INDIAN FOREIGN POLICY

INDIAN FOREIGN POLICY

Mukesh Kumar Singh

ANMOL PUBLICATIONS PVT. LTD.
NEW DELHI-110 002 (INDIA)

ANMOL PUBLICATIONS PVT. LTD.
Regd. Office: 4360/4, Ansari Road, Daryaganj,
New Delhi-110002 (India)
Tel.: 23278000, 23261597, 23286875, 23255577
Fax: 91-11-23280289
Email: anmolpub@gmail.com
Visit us at: www.anmolpublications.com

Branch Office: No. 1015, Ist Main Road, BSK IIIrd Stage
IIIrd Phase, IIIrd Block, Bangalore-560 085 (India)
Tel.: 080-41723429 • Fax: 080-26723604
Email: anmolpublicationsbangalore@gmail.com

Indian Foreign Policy

First Edition, 2011

ISBN 978-81-261-4544-7

PRINTED IN INDIA

Printed at Mehra Offset Press, Delhi.

Contents

Contents

Preface

The Indian Republic in the first five decades of its existence maintained a strategic autonomy in the conduct of its foreign policy despite a much more limited national power profile and economic profile than that exists today. Today, when India is economically vibrant and strong and has been able to amass sizeable conventional and strategic assets, India to its citizens seems strategically tied down in adding muscle to the conduct of its foreign policy. Adding muscle to India's foreign policy does not imply war mongering or military adventurism. Adding muscle to India's foreign policy implies that India's national security interests are accorded a paramountcy in the conduct of foreign policies to the exclusion of the personal predictions of the Indian Prime Minister and his proximate foreign policy advisors. It also implies the existence of political will to secure India's national security interests. The period 2004-2009 has witnessed a bartering away of India's national security interests.

The major part of India's foreign policy failures in this time span and the distortions that willingly or unwillingly have seeped into India's foreign policy (2004 – 2009) have resulted from policies or lack of policies generated by the predominance given by India's current Prime Minister to the "United States Factor" in our policy formulations. Co-attendant with the primacy given to the "United States Factor" in India's foreign policy formulations during 2004-2009 has been the "parallel track" of "Pakistan-appeasement policies" out of deference to United States Pak-centric strategic sensitivities.

—Author

1

Historical and Domestic Factors in the Shaping of Indian's Foreign Policy

Crossing the Rubicon: The Shaping of India's New Foreign Policy

P.V. Narashima Rao's predecessor Rajiv Gandhi tied India's nuclear disarmament with US and other nuclear powers. He was calling for total abolition of nuclear arms. But the world changed when Rao became the prime minister, he inherited an economy that was nearly broke, there was no Soviet Union to support, and the US fresh from its gulf war victory was strutting as the only super power of the world. In 1992, the UN security council passed a resolution stating that proliferation of nuclear and other weapons of WMD is a threat to international peace and security. US and other western nations were warning India, the list topper among the countries likely to acquire nuclear weapons that it has to face the wrath of the entire international system if it did not fall in line.

P.V. Narashima Rao and his principal secretary J.N. Dixit, understood that the moment of nuclear reckoning was at hand. They knew they had to summon all the intellectual guile to wriggle out of the situation. India could not have found diplomats more wily than these two. Bush senior asked India to join a conference of five nations with US, Russia, China and Pakistan to discuss nuclear nonproliferation in the subcontinent.

Negotiating framework proposed by Bush was deeply offensive to India's sense of standing. Not only would the conference concentrate on getting India and Pakistan to behave on the nuclear issue, but their conduct was going to be supervised by Washington, Moscow and Beijing sitting at a higher table. The ultimate insult was that China, which India saw as an equal, was to become a guarantor of peace and stability in the sub-continent. This was a China that, India knew, helped Pakistan acquire nuclear weapons. In no way was India going to accept such a set of negotiations.

In typical fashion, Narashima Rao was non-committal pointing to the political difficulties at home, he said that he would prefer to discuss the problem in detail with the United States bilaterally before he could join multilateral nuclear negotiations. It was agreed that bilateral nuclear talks would begin within few weeks.

Having found an escape route at a critical moment, Narashima Rao launched India on a two track policy-engage the Americans in a nuclear dialogue and prepare for conducting nuclear tests. The first was a visible track and the second invisible. Narashima Rao gave orders to the atomic energy establishment in Bombay to get ready for another round of nuclear test, but the scientists wanted time-at least 2 years. Meanwhile, the pressure from the United States was relentless. 'Buy me time' was the constant refrain from Narashima Rao to dixit. The foreign office bobbed and weaved and found every trick in the diplomatic book to avoid getting into multilateral negotiations on the nuclear issue. In the talks India invented arguments for expanding the multilateral negotiations framework to include every possible country from Israel to Japan.

By December 1995 India was ready for Pokhran-II. Narashima Rao had achieved the impossible. He had managed to fob off the various international pressure on India to close its nuclear option. The economy, formerly the weakest element in the country's portfolio, had turned around and was now an attractive feature that created the basis for a different relationship with the world. In addition he was ready to conduct nuclear tests and hence put India in a different strategic pedestal.

It's a different story that US found India's preparation for a nuclear test and Rao had to pull the plug on the supposed tests in 1995. But Raja Mohan agrees that PVN was the one who prepared everything for India to cross the nuclear Rubicon.

Indian Foreign Policy Orientation in the Twenty-first Century: Continuity and Change

It is a truism that the foreign policy of any major state will be predicated upon and shaped by its perception of what constitutes the core national interest as leavened by the principles and value systems that the state in question adheres to. The related extrapolation is that the national interest, desegregated into its principal constituent elements, viz: political, military and economic determinants, would have to be protected, nurtured and advanced, as the case may be, in a complex and on occasion contradictory manner. State itself as an entity is located in a definitive spatio-temporal context and this provides the backdrop against which individual states evolve distinctive foreign policies. The regional and global strategic systemic consequently becomes a referent that defines the contours of domestic foreign policy and the latter evolves in a dynamic manner. The temporal determinant acquires greater salience when we note that both the state and the systemic have their own transmutative trajectories in the long cycle of history.

This chapter seeks to examine the past evolution and current orientation of India's foreign policy (FP) and dwells in some detail on certain regions and countries. The chapter argues that there is an element of continuity and change that is discernible in India's FP and that this has been impelled by a combination of factors specific to the Indian experience. If FP is perceived as a 'strategy' to realize the larger national interest, a useful and succinct definition (for a word that has elicited a plethora of multi-disciplinary interpretations) is provided by John Lewis Gaddis who defines it as: "the process by which ends are related to means, intentions to capabilities, objectives to resources."

In relation to the process of evolving a FP, it may be added that the strategic culture of the state and its ruling/governing elite play a central role and this is very noticeable in the Indian case. India's strategic culture, as is the case of many other states, is a distillate of two ontological features-geography and history – filtered through the cultural impress of its ruling elite at any given point in time. As a civilizational-state (a characteristic it shares with China) there is an inherited, albeit burnished dominant narrative about the past even as it seeks to grapple with modernity in all its manifestations. To that extent, while independent India post 1947 sought to outline an appropriate FP, its genealogy goes back to the immediate and buried past – which in this case links the DNA of imperial British India with the tenets of the *Arthashastra* that goes back to circa 302 BC! Hence this chapter argues that there are certain elements of continuity by way of tangible objectives in India's FP that are inexorable and dictated by existential characteristics such as geographical location and size. These are further transmuted by contemporary politics and the constraints and opportunities exuded by the prevailing international strategic systemic.

This chapter is confined to the trends in the evolution of post-1947 Indian FP and its current orientation and the first significant articulation about India's objectives, interestingly, precede 1947. India which was coming out of the colonial yoke through the Gandhian path of 'ahimsa' (non-violence) had a set of nationalist leaders led by Pandit Nehru and in September 1946, while providing an outline of the interim government's objectives on the cusp of Indian independence, Nehru stated: "It is because of this expectation of an early realization of full independence that we have entered this Government and we propose to function so as progressively to achieve independence in action both in our domestic affairs and our foreign relations...as a free nation with our own policy and not merely as a satellite of another nation."

There is further elaboration of the Nehruvian vision of Indian FP and a few months after he became Prime Minister of independent India, he observed: "Foreign policies...are not just empty struggles on a chess board. Behind them lie all manner of things. Ultimately, foreign policy is the outcome of economic policy, and until India has properly evolved her economic policy, her foreign policy will be rather vague, rather inchoate, and will be groping."

There is a sense of prescience in Nehru's later articulation for the effectiveness of India's FP in the early decades – the objectives it may have set for itself – were not backed by adequate and appropriate national resources and capabilities. Hence many of the lofty aspirations were not realized, thereby resulting in the chequered nature of India's foreign policy effectiveness in the period 1947-62. However this paper argues that there is a core consistency by way of the security and strategic concerns that under grid foreign policy and in the Indian case, the linkages and departures with the policy of imperial British India are instructive. 19th century European geo-strategic rivalry among the major powers became the 'Great Game' (a la Arthur Conolly and not Rudyard Kipling) and the central objective of then ascendant Britain was to keep the Russian Bear from accessing the Indian Ocean through the Central Asian region. Historians aver that even the Mughal emperors had much the same unease about any Russian foray to the subcontinent and this geo-strategic chess-game informed much of the foreign policy of the then major powers.

Theoreticians introduced the 'heartland versus rim land' theory and the dictates of the continental power and the salience of maritime power. Post World War II, when the mantle of the dominant power had passed to the USA, the 'game' continued but with a different packaging – namely the containment of communism. The former Soviet Union was the new 'bear' whose advance was to be resisted and the global systemic evolved along the grid of bipolarity. Here one may introduce the co-relation between the foreign policy of individual states and the manner in which it is shaped by the compulsions of the global systemic. The proposition is that very few states barring the hegemon have the ability to conduct truly autonomous or independent foreign policies and the thumb-rule for all other states – to the extent they are relevant to the systemic – is that their manoeuvrability and space is shaped by the power. compulsions of the systemic. Bipolarity was the flavour of the Cold War decades and most of the world was divided along the East-West axis and their related military alliances. India, under Nehru, which had already anticipated this power block divisiveness had made its fundamental choice Non alignment. In his December 1946 speech, Nehru had already asserted: "We propose, as far as possible, to keep away from the power politics of groups, aligned against one another, which have led in the past to world wars and which may again lead to disasters on an even vaster scale."

Consequently the existential force of bipolarity and the postures of the two superpowers shaped the choices for the rest of the world – including the non-aligned group. India, as a nascent post-colonial state had its own internal consolidation to address as a first priority but its foreign policy, this chapter argues, flowed from an innate sense of how best to manage its more relevant strategic space. This was most succinctly summed up by the British High Commissioner to India at the time (1951) in a secret cable to London elucidating India's security-foreign policy orientation. Sir Archibald Nye opined that the Indian policy could be perceived as "operating in three concentric circles, the principles governing each of which bear little or no relation to the principles followed in the others."

This has been further interpreted as the innermost circle of contiguous states – viz: Afghanistan, Ceylon (now Sri Lanka), Nepal, Tibet and Burma – where it was perceived that India had 'vital' interests. The second circle included the rest of the world minus the four major powers at that time, namely the USA, USSR, UK and PRC. The second ring was prioritized as areas that were more relevant such as SE Asia to minimal relevance as say South America. Sir Nye added, even at that time, that Pakistan was a 'unique' case. The more detailed elucidation that followed suggested that the policies – security and foreign – followed by India were very different for each set of circles and that while the innermost elicited a kind of hard-nosed realpolitik approach *a la* Bismarck, while in the second circle, "Indian policy was characterized by anti-colonialism and support for nationalism, with perhaps a smattering of realism in Asian countries like Malaya and Iran, where India's interests were engaged." And with regard to the outermost circle, India's foreign and security policy posture was "to a great extent determined by her passionate desire to keep out of conflict and to stand aside from Great Power struggles."

This chapter argues that Indian FP was and is shaped by a set of three determinants – namely the external international systemic and the dominant strategic discourse and practice; the Indian perception about what constitutes the core national interest and the national resources and capabilities it can bring to bear to protect or advance this interest; and finally the cognitive perception of the ruling/governing elite at the time. Within this matrix, there is both continuity and change by way of specific trend lines and initiatives taken by India over a 60 year period – from 1946 to 2006. I would further aver that this entire policy response trajectory is to be located within the domain of India's distinctive strategic culture – which has also been evolving over this period.

Broadly desegregated, the trends in Indian FP may be divided in the temporal periods 1947-1962; 1962-1991; 1991-1998; and 1998-mid 2006 and refereed along the three elements identified earlier. The early phase from 1947-1962 was a period when nascent India was seeking to consolidate its identity as a free and independent state with the attendant mix of aspirations and anxieties and to that extent the immediate priority was internal and domestic. The aftermath of partition and the grapple with participative democracy when economic and fiscal resources were modest, consumed greater part of national funds and energy – but it would be fair to state that on the foreign policy front – the Nehruvian approach was followed. A degree of realism where India's vital interests were affected was one component, while issues such as de-colonization and support for freedom struggles comprised the other. On larger global issues such as nuclear weapons, a normative, humanistic approach was preferred and vis-à-vis the superpowers, nonalignment was the preferred stance. If the domestic ambiance and the persona of a leader like Nehru were two of the drivers, the ambiance of the external global strategic systemic as manifest in the early phase of the Cold war (post Cuban missile crisis in 1962, the author would argue, the Cold War entered a different techno-strategic phase) was the more significant determinant in shaping Indian FP.

The rationale for the creation of an independent Pakistan is beyond the scope of this chapter but suffice it to note that the reality of a Pakistan in August 1947 brought the Great Game DNA through the Cold War filter into the calculus of Indian FP. Pakistan's willingness to join the US-led military alliances such as the CENTO and SEATO during the 1950's and 1960's made it the problematic 'other' for India and a number of Indian FP initiatives including those relating to Kashmir were directly affected by this Cold War undercurrent. One may hypothetically aver that an undivided

British India would have perhaps adopted a different kind of FP orientation for there were no fundamental divergences with the US led Western alliance. Nehru himself had no special love for the ideology of communism so much so that India would have crossed over into the red camp in retrospect appear misplaced. On the international canvas, India acquired a certain profile that belied its nascent political pedigree and underdeveloped economic profile. This was evident in the Indian support to Japan immediately after Hiroshima, the Indonesian freedom struggle, the Korean and Indo-China wars, the mantle of Asian leadership et al. The brief 1962 Sino-India war punctured this self-image and is a major punctuation in the evolution of India's strategic culture, security perceptions and foreign policy orientation. Disillusionment and a rude awakening were the leit motifs of the trauma and humiliation of 1962 and this experience scarred Nehru personally and the Indian polity collectively. Bitter recrimination followed about the great Chinese betrayal and the invalidity of Asian solidarity on one hand and a realization that India's inherent national resources and tangible capabilities – in this case military – were woefully inadequate to underwrite the foreign policy contours that had been earlier envisioned. To go back to Gaddis, there was a mismatch between the objectives and the availability of resources. Post 1962 was a period of consolidation for India and Nehru died a broken man in 1964. His successors – Lal Bahadur Shastri briefly and later Indira Gandhi were wedded to the mantra of nonalignment on the global stage but introduced certain nuances in the practice of foreign policy. The external dynamic of the Cold War entered Asia through the Vietnam war and later the nettlesome issue of Cambodia. Both these events had considerable negative impact on India's relations with the USA and SE Asian nations– the focus of this chapter. In the post Nehru decades – that is from 1964 till the tragic assassination of Mrs. Indira Gandhi in 1984 – India engaged in two wars with Pakistan – in 1965 and 1971 – the latter leading to the birth of Bangladesh – and the 1974 Peaceful Nuclear Explosion, and here one notes a certain caution and assertiveness in Indian FP. The Indian disillusionment with the US and other western powers – such as UK (which in any case was becoming more and more dependent on the trans-Atlantic alliance and the US) in the aftermath of the 1962 war and the subsequent Chinese nuclear test in 1964 led to a gradual tilt towards the former USSR and in about a decade – from the mid 1960's onwards, the USSR emerged as India's major supplier of military inventory and a trusted friend over issues such as Kashmir when they came up in the UNSC. This tilt had its corrosive impact on India's relations with the USA and its allies – leading to what is often described as the 'estrangement' between the world's oldest and largest democracies – ironically when the values that were being contested in the Cold war were freedom and the threat to democracy. Subsequently the Soviet occupation of Afghanistan in 1979 and the Iranian Revolution brought the Cold War closer to India on its western flank and the estrangement with the USA was further enhanced through India's muted response over Afghanistan and the call for the Indian Ocean as a Zone of Peace among other foreign policy responses.

The period 1984 till 1990 was one of further consolidation for India under the stewardship of Rajiv Gandhi (this was the period when India embarked upon its Peace Keeping Operation in Sri Lanka) and some significant regional FP initiatives were pursued including a thawing of relations with China (which had gone into the deep freeze after the 1962 war) and improved relations with the USA. This was also a period when India's fiscal prudence was not as astute as it may have been and while on one hand there was a visible element of India's military capability being effectively enhanced – as perceived in the Indian Navy's expansion and the swift assistance to Maldives in November 1988 which was threatened by a renegade takeover – the macro economic and fiscal indicators were deteriorating. This was also a period of considerable internal turbulence for India and there was a quick succession of Prime Ministers and short-lived Central governments. Political instability was compounded by the terrorist assassination of Rajiv Gandhi and a very complex internal security environment. Apart from Jammu and Kashmir, the prosperous state of Punjab witnessed a rash of separatist violence that was finally quelled.

This was also the period when the Cold War was coming to an unintended end and Gorbachev's glasnost-perestroika and the rapprochement with the USA led to a dramatic turn of events. Overnight on December 8, 1991, the Soviet Union became 'former' and Russia emerged with a very different geography and political identity. Bipolarity was relegated to the pages of history and a very new global strategic systemic was born. Unipolarity – or so it seemed. The USA which had just led a very successful coalition in early 1999 for in Gulf War I – the War for Kuwait, was perceived as the sole hegemon with no challenger in sight – China was still recovering from the opprobrium of Tiananmen. It is the contention of this paper that while the end of the Cold War led to a complete review and re-orientation of the FP of most nations, for the global strategic grid was completely transformed, it was the equivalent of a double-whammy for India since the domestic situation was also undergoing considerable turbulence. PM Narasimha Rao assumed office in June 1991 succeeding two predecessors who had served for less than a year each. India's economic health was frail and the fiscal indicators were alarming with a balance of payment crisis looming. India's forex reserves were down to a few weeks. Thus the country was faced with an exigency wherein all three determinants that shape and influence FP were in a state of flux-namely the global systemic, national capabilities and resources, and a new leadership that was grappling with political, economic and social turbulence – the right-wing BJP party was gaining ground in India at the time.

India's major FP transformation came about in the Narashima Rao years (June 1991-May 1996) and much of it was impelled by the economic liberalization that Delhi was embarked upon. India's socialist command planning model and the license-raj permit economic and trade system gave way to a more liberalized approach and in many ways the Indian economy was freed from the politico-bureaucratic shackles imposed upon it for decades. The macro-results were very favourable. The inflexible Hindu rate of growth suddenly accelerated and this was also enabled to a great extent by deft financial planning led by then Finance Minister Dr. Manmohan Singh and the global techno-commercial wave related to the computer and information revolution. As Baru has noted: "after recording virtually no growth in the first half of the 20th century, the (Indian) economy grew at an annual average rate of 3.5 percent in 1950-80 and 5.4 percent in 1980-90 and 6.2 percent in 1990-2000."

Thus the economic sinews were strengthened under the Rao-Singh stewardship and I would argue that to achieve this objective, necessary changes were brought about to India's FP orientation. Trade and investment were accorded a higher priority as opposed to ideological positions and much of this is reflected in India's relations with the USA, ASEAN and China – the later focus of this chapter.

Relations with the USA

As noted earlier, the India-US relationship during the Cold war decades was described as one of 'estranged democracies' and this was largely due to the very divergent national security perceptions that the two countries had and consequently the security and foreign policies they adopted were often at variance to each other. In the early decades, India's policy of nonalignment was met with angry bewilderment by a US leadership that sought clarity from the world's largest democracy. However it merits notice that India's relations with the USA during the Eisenhower and Kennedy presidencies were relatively stable and it was only with the eruption of the Vietnam War that relations soured visibly. The Nixon years were particularly strained and subsequently India's 1974 PNE led to the creation of a very stubborn bone of contention. This was the legacy of the Carter years to a great extent, though in hindsight, it may be suggested that both Mrs. Indira Gandhi and her successor as PM, Rajiv Gandhi had very cordial relations with Ronald Reagan. It may be posited that the 1983 Cancun meeting between Mrs. Gandhi and President Reagan marks the beginning of the rapprochement between the two countries and that this is now poised to reach fruition in the Bush-Manmohan Singh agreement of July 2005.

With the end of the Cold War and the disintegration of the USSR, India had to re-order its relations with the remaining super-power and while Delhi was seeking to find the right balance, Washington was to be punctuated by the Clinton years – two terms from 1993 to 2000 – and an instructive overlap emerges. While the nuclear nettle continued to dominate the state level interactions (India had refused to sign the NPT and was outside of the global nuclear regime and it was the Clinton intent to 'cap, roll-back and eliminate' India's nuclear weapon capability), paradoxically, the Indian business and intellectual elite were building a robust relationship with their US counterparts. This was facilitated by India's cautious economic liberalization and the dynamic of globalization in trade and commerce where India's inherent affinity with the computer revolution proved to be an advantage at a time when the US economy was maximizing the opportunities provided by the IT revolution.

The India-US relationship was strained in the first Clinton term and much of this was evident in the CTBT debate in India. Ironically, the two countries that had been bitterly estranged over the nuclear issue – with the Indian 1974 test leading to the US introducing stringent nuclear legislation – actually co-sponsored the draft of the CTBT in the UN. This contradictory convergence ensued since both countries saw the CTBT as a leverage for advancing their respective interests – for India it was a means towards global disarmament, while for the US it was a means to place fetters on new nuclear powers. At the level of the global systemic, it is worth recalling that France and China joined the NPT only in 1992 and the US, post the Iraqi Scud scare of 1991 during Desert Storm, had a larger strategic objective wherein India was only a modest target.

However in the period 1993 to 1996, the CTBT debate within India became more animated impacting the India-US relationship. Various related developments including the Sino-Pak WMD cooperation pattern and the indefinite extension of the NPT resulted in a crystallization of India's posture on the nuclear issue. As more recent disclosures suggest – the Narashima Rao government had planned to conduct a nuclear test in December 1995 – but was deterred from doing so due to the adverse economic consequences. However, by mid 1996 the fault lines were visible when India distanced itself from the CTBT and the US and its allies pushed the treaty through in the CD and later at the UN. The official relationship was brittle both over the nuclear issue and terrorism but this was at odds with the economic ties. Two way bi-lateral trade that stood at US $ 5.68 bn in 1990 moved steadily to US $ 9.02 in 1995 proving the tenet that in the post-Cold war systemic, the market does not follow the flag.

Economic liberalization was paying dividends in the politico-diplomatic domain and very imperceptibly, India and the US were becoming cognizant of each other's complementary potentialities.

The year 1998 marks a defining moment in the evolution of India's foreign policy formulation. India's nuclear weapon tests established it as a state with nuclear weapons – SNW – as opposed to the NWS semantic of the NPT. This 1998 shift in India's security and foreign policies may be interpreted as an extension of the continuity and change paradigm, while allowing for the causal factors that brought about the transmutation. India had crossed the nuclear Rubicon but this was not sudden. True, a BJP-led NDA government headed by Atal Bihari Vajpayee was at the helm in Delhi but the intent to acquire nuclear weapon capability was discernible in the late 1980's during the Rajiv Gandhi years and was impelled by the determination that India was at a WMD disadvantage in the regional grid and that progressively, the international systemic was proving to be inimical to Indian interests. The author would argue that even if a non BJP party had headed the coalition government (a coalition at the Centre being one of the existential characteristics of Indian politics by about the mid 1990's due to the decline of the major national parties and the rise of regional parties with single state credibility such as the DMK, AIDMK and the TDP among others) the Indian government of the day would have acquired nuclear weapon capability by the late 1990's.

India-US ties plummeted to an all time low and Washington spouted harsh word denouncing India. The 1998 tests (Pakistan followed suit a few weeks later) were followed by what later turned out to be a false dawn of India-Pakistan amity as noticed in the Lahore pact of early 1999 signed by PM Vajpayee and PM Nawaz Sharief. Regrettably the Kargil War followed in the summer of 1999 and while India was caught by surprise by this Pakistani intrusion into Indian territory, the fallout of this limited war between South Asia's two nuclear armed neighbours was a strategic gain for Indian foreign policy. The global community took note of the restraint and extreme responsibility with which India conducted itself and The author would suggest that the end of this war which was negotiated by a dramatic meeting between US President Clinton and Pakistani PM Nawaz Sharief on July 4, 1999 (the US Independence Day) in Washington marks a turning point in the seemingly irreparably damaged India-US relations. This is reiterated by a perceptive analysis of the impact of the Kargil War from Washington. The Schaffers – Teresita and Howard – two former US diplomats with long experience of South Asia commented: "The United States saw the facts as India did, and pursued its own national interests. The fact that these coincided with India is not unique, but illustrates how, in a changing world, both countries need to look for opportunities where their agendas overlap.....Pakistan had started the (Kargil) problem by playing with fire; the remedy seemed clear: push Pakistan hard to end its provocation. India handled the situation with care and restraint; there was no reason to call for the usual reciprocating gesture."

The last phrase is significant for now Washington did not find it necessary to 'balance' its South Asian policy by admonishing India – a familiar pattern of the past. One may further aver that this marks the beginning of the de-hyphenation of US foreign policy as regards the subcontinent and this is taken to its logical conclusion by the Bush administration that was to follow the Clinton years in the White House. On the economic front, the bi-lateral trade continued to post modest but impressive gains and by 2000, this had further increased to US $ 14. 3 bn.

Post Kargil, there was a significant improvement in the bi-lateral relationship and the culmination was the very successful visit to India by President Clinton in March 2000. A broad statement of intent was agreed to by the two nations and the potential for a partnership between natural allies was the rhetoric of the day. However, the dark nuclear shadow loomed large and despite many rounds of talks between Indian Foreign Minister Jaswant Singh and the US Deputy Secretary of State Strobe Talbott, there was no satisfactory resolution. The US was keen to lasso India and bring it into some kind of nuclear restraint regime that would be similar to the NPT for non-nuclear weapon states, such as signing the CTBT and the FMCT but India remained firm in its refusal. Consequently there still remained a glass-ceiling to the potential of the bi-lateral relationship but the texture of cordiality was palpable – a welcome change from the bitterness that marked the earlier relationship. In January 2004, India and the US agreed to a new techno-strategic framework – the Next Steps in Strategic Partnership (NSSP) – that included hi-tech areas like nuclear energy, space and missile defenses. However this was at a preliminary stage and many US regulations and laws prohibited any meaningful cooperation in these sectors.

The arrival of the Bush administration with its very different world-view laid the foundation for dramatically altering the framework in which the US-India relationship was located. Even before the tragic events of 9-11, the Bush team signalled its intent to pursue a very different nuclear and missile path from that of the Clinton administration. The CTBT was rejected and the ABM abrogated and this removed two visible elements of discord between the US and India. Subsequently, in May 2005 Indian FP made an uncharacteristic departure when it was among the first major countries to cautiously endorse the new Bush strategic doctrine to go beyond the ABM and make missile defense the centrepiece of US nuclear strategy.

Relations with the Bush administration appeared to be poised for a definitive improvement but the enormity of 9-11 intervened. US security and foreign policies underwent a dramatic change and the US embarked upon its GWOT. It is pertinent that one of the first military actions taken by the US – the removal of the Taliban regime in Afghanistan – was in India's immediate security interests. The acknowledgement by the US that state sponsored or nurtured terrorism was a major security challenge for all liberal democracies was a vindication of the long standing Indian stand on the subject. The truly radical shift in the US-India bi-lateral relationship came about in the second tenure of the Bush administration beginning January 2005. A new government was in place in Delhi – the Congress-led UPA coalition with Dr. Manmohan Singh as the PM had assumed charge in May 2004. However, despite the presence of the Indian Left in the coalition, the essential continuity in India's FP orientation initiated by the NDA regime with the US continued. It was the US that initiated a major shift in the bilateral ties, when in March 2005, the new US Secretary of State Ms. Condoleezza Rice made India the first stop in her whistle stop-tour of Asia. On March 16, 2005 Ms. Rice met with Indian leaders in Delhi and alluded to the new salience being accorded to India in the Bush 2 foreign policy overhaul. The import of a significant but veiled reference to the need for the US and India to enter into an "energy dialogue" was perhaps not adequately understood at the time but this became more clear a few days later.

On March 25, 2005 the US State Department unveiled a new blueprint for restructuring US ties with India and asserted that it "will help India become a major world power in the 21st century"– and further added that it was aware of the implications of such a commitment including the military aspect. The determination to provide a robust defence and security underpinning to the March 25 statement was reflected in the landmark agreement signed between the US and India in June 2005. The new framework for India-US Defence Relations was signed by Indian Defence Minister Pranab Mukherjee with his US counterpart Donald Rumsfeld in Washington on June 28 and the scope of the agreement has the potential to positively recast the nature of the bilateral relationship. The two page document outlined an ambitious framework predicated on advancing "shared security interests." The preamble also added that this is derived from "a common belief in freedom, democracy and the rule of law."

India and the US identified their areas of convergence – namely the maintenance of security and stability in the region; defeating terrorism and violent religious extremism; preventing the spread of WMD and related material (AQ Khan episode); and finally protecting the free flow of commerce via land, air and sea lanes. To realize these objectives, it was added, the two militaries would work towards inter-operability and engage in combined operations – if required.

The last aspect aroused considerable disquiet in some quarters in India – particularly among the Left parties – and the anxiety seemed to be that India would become part of the next US military action – hypothetically against Iran or North Korea. This was perhaps misplaced for the exact reference reads as follows: "strengthen the abilities of our militaries to respond quickly to disaster situations, including in combined operations." It may be recalled that when the tsunami disaster struck in December 2004, the Indian relief response by the Navy, Coast Guard and the Air Force was noted with professional interest both regionally and by the US security establishment. The more important but ignored aspect of the Defence framework agreement is about the expansion of defense trade between India and the US. The document notes among its objectives: "in the context of defense trade and a framework of technology security safeguards, increase opportunities for technology transfer, collaboration, co-production, and research and development."

This section has the potential to facilitate India's growth and credibility in the defence production and R&D field. For India the long term challenge is not about buying a few squadrons of F-16s or more advanced fighter aircraft from the US but about acquiring the production and design skills associated with the US military-industrial complex. Indian foreign policy, it may be inferred, had internalized the tenet that any major power has to become militarily credible and this profile needs the assimilation of new technologies that currently only the US can provide.

However, in keeping with its cautious posture of not putting all its eggs in one basket and making haste slowly in its defence procurement relations with the US, India reiterated that it would continue to sustain its military supply ties with Russia – but observed that it needs to seek assistance in the new areas of military technology and the US is the logical choice in the years ahead. It is instructive that the US has opposed the supply of such technologies to China – which it sees as a future challenger – but is willing to provide the same to India.

The more formal endorsement to the improved nature of the bilateral relationship between Washington and Delhi is contained in the July 18, 2005 agreement signed during Dr. Manmohan Singh's visit to the USA.

The most significant aspect of this was the manner in which the contentious circle of the nuclear nettle was sought to be squared. US President Bush decided to adroitly convert the divisive nuclear issue from one of contestation to one of cooperation. The agreement noted that the US would recognize India as a nation with 'advanced nuclear capability':

- a euphemism for India's SNW capability
- and without compromising US commitment to nuclear nonproliferation, it would enter into a civilian nuclear cooperation agreement by effecting appropriate changes in existing US nuclear and related export control legislation. This was a very radical departure in US policy and India had reason to be more than satisfied with this breakthrough for it meant that the many technology denial regimes that it had been subject to since 1974 would be gradually lifted
- and in consultation with the other NSG members, it would be slowly brought into the ambit of global nuclear and hi-tech commerce.

Predictably there was a strong protest and rejection of this exceptionalism being provided to India by the Bush administration – most visibly from among the nonproliferation lobbies within the US – but there was a deeper consensus in the Beltway that a closer and nuclear-nettle-free relationship with India was in the abiding US strategic interest in the early part of the 21st century. Paradoxically, there was concern in India also that the fine-print of the new agreement with the US would lead to long term negative consequences including fetters on India's strategic an foreign policy autonomy but the UPA government stayed the course. Instructively, it was the personal political conviction of Mr. Bush and Dr. Manmohan Singh that brought about the requisite changes in the foreign policy orientation of the two states. This trend is in keeping with the formulation of this chapter, that a very significant factor of changes in foreign policy is the personal cognitive perception of individual political leaders, who with astute staff support – in this case the US State Department and the Indian MEA – can effect such changes in the face of conventional and received wisdom that prefers to maintain the status quo.

The July 2005 agreement was followed by a low key but successful visit of US President Bush to Delhi in March 2006 and the India-US nuclear deal – as it now being referred to – was kept alive by the political determination of the political apex on both sides. Down to the wire, is the off the record summarization of both July 2005 and March 2006 and at this point, while the Indian side has announced its separation of nuclear facilities plan, the

US side is engaged in bringing about the necessary changes to US legislation that would allow a fruition of the civilian nuclear cooperation agreement. As of end August, the draft legislation has been approved by the US House of Representatives and is awaiting the approval of the US Senate before it is reconciled. However, it is not a done deed and the passage of the nuclear cooperation agreement between the US and India may be termed as a complex work in progress that involves many players and constituencies.

Relations with ASEAN States

India has had very old ties with the SE Asian states that precede the formation of ASEAN as an entity and one set of linkages are civilisational. The spread of Buddhism and the rhythms of trade punctuated the medieval period. With the arrival of Western colonization, British India's policies were dictated by London and this pattern prevailed till the end of World War II. However in the modern period, post-1947, as argued in the earlier section of the chapter, India's foreign policy orientation towards SE Asia was an extension of the three determinants identified – viz: the domestic politico-strategic orientation; the perception of core national interests; and the international systemic. In the early decades, India was championing the end of colonization, support to nascent nations and the spirit of nonalignment and these determinants were applied to SE Asia. Hence there was unambiguous support to the freedom movement in Indonesia for instance. Similarly India provided assistance to the civilian government in then Burma and played a major role in the Geneva Accords and the related Indo-China International Commission of the mid 1950's.

However, the compulsions of the prevailing global security dynamic and the East-West confrontation gradually permeated the Asian canvas. The US was not very happy about the outcome of the Geneva Accord and what it perceived as a Sino-Soviet convergence and promoted an anti-communist collective security pact of the South East Asian nations. Consequently SEATO (South East Asia Treaty Organization) with its HQ in Bangkok was born in 1954 and by what may be termed an extreme oddity, Pakistan – despite it geographical location also joined the Philippines and

Thailand as part of SEATO. Predictably Nehru regarded SEATO as "harmful to Asia as well as the cause of peace."

Later on, the advent of the Vietnam war and India's own insular preoccupation after the 1962 war saw a dilution of India's relations with the SE Asian states – who themselves were at different stages of internal consolidation.

The Vietnam War and the estrangement between the US and India had its corrosive influence on India's ties with the SE Asian states who were also polarized along the bipolar grid. While the original five ASEAN states (established in August 1967) were aligned with the US in the containment of communism, others were tilted towards the socialist model a la USSR and or China. The mid 1970's turmoil in Cambodia which pitted China against Vietnam marked a defining moment of deterioration in India's relations with the ASEAN states. As one comment notes "India's support to Communist Vietnam and its recognition of the Vietnamese installed Heng Samrin government in July 1980, once again reconfirmed India's deep alliance with the Soviet Union and made her unpopular among the members of ASEAN."

The prevailing Cold War dynamic impelled India to a take stand that was at variance with that of the US and this animosity continued till the end of the Cold War. The early 1990's marked a major shift in India's FP overall orientation and under PM Narashima Rao there was a concerted attempt to improve the texture and tenor of relations with the ASEAN as a group. PM Rao was determined to increase India's economic space and opportunities and ASEAN with its proven trade-economic profile was a natural choice for Delhi. India embarked upon what is now called its 'Look East' policy in 1991 and this was consolidated by a series of high level visits by PM Rao to individual states. The pragmatism exuded by India and its economic liberalization program struck a chord of empathy in the ASEAN and gradually specific trade-commerce complementarities were arrived at. It is relevant that the Indian MEA Annual Report of 1992-93 noted that: "India decided to give a special policy thrust to its relations with the ASEAN."

India joined AEAN as a sectoral dialogue partner in 1992 and slowly became a full dialogue partner and was admitted into the

ARF – the security arm of ASEAN in June 1996. India's economic potential and performance and its military – particularly naval – capabilities were noted by ASEAN and gradually greater content was imparted to individual bilateral ties. Understandably, there was an asymmetry in ties with different ASEAN countries – who had increased in numbers progressively – that were evolving their own individual policies in relation to India.

The trade fallout was very positive and it merits note that after the ushering in of the Look east policy by PM Rao, the rate of growth of India's total trade with ASEAN over a 22 year period was impressive. In the period 1975 to 1997, India's growth of trade with ASEAN was 11.77 percent as against 8 percent with the world as a whole. Desegregated further, after the economic liberalization program, India growth of total trade in the period 1991-97 with the world was 9.95 percent while with ASEAN in the same period it was 18.15 percent. And among individual countries, with Indonesia alone, India's trade growth post liberalization registered a staggering 129 percent in the 1991-97 period.

India's nuclear tests of May 1998 altered ASEAN's perception of its western neighbour and though within the extended region, Australia was among the most vocal critics of this initiative, the inherent strategic balance that India provided apropos China was noted. The specific Indian military capabilities – naval and professional training in military schools – was acknowledged and slowly, there was the injection of greater military contact along the bilateral route. As an illustration of this facet, it is relevant that Indian naval ship visits to ASEAN ports (counted by individual ship and port index) increased as follows: in 1995 – ports 2 and ships 4; and in 2005 – ports 24 and ships 51. On the ASEAN side, total number of naval ship visits to India ports increased from 6 in 1998 to 19 in 2003.

In summary it may be opined that ASEAN's relations with India at the macro-level will be shaped by the forces of globalization on the trade and economic front. India's gradually improving indicators in this domain are being monitored by the relevant sectors within ASEAN which is going through its own internal transmutation through the ASEAN plus 3 and other initiatives such as the East Asia Summit formulation. On the strategic and security front, much will depend on the trajectory of US-China relations and the manner in which they impact ASEAN as a collective and on the specific interests of individual states. However, it would be reasonable to identify some immediate common concerns such as terrorism linked to radical Islamic jehadism, maritime threats such as piracy and pollution and natural disaster response capabilities. The ARF is a viable forum but India will, to my mind, keep a low profile and wait for ASEAN to arrive at an appropriate comfort level before it increases its security engagement with the region. India's relations with ASEAN have now acquired a level of satisfaction and exude promise for further mutually beneficial growth. India held its first annual Summit level meeting with ASEAN in 2002 and more recently Indian PM Dr. Singh participated in the 4th such summit in Malaysia in December 2005. This was followed by the first East Asia Summit where India was an invitee. PM Singh reiterated India's stance as regards ASEAN and noted: "We attach great importance to our relations with ASEAN, which constitute a central element in India's 'Look East Policy'."

Thus it may be inferred that from a tentative beginning in the early 1990's, India's foreign policy orientation vis-à-vis the collective of ASEAN is now more definitive and will be shaped by the larger global and regional framework as it unspools along the economic and strategic strands. Here the role of the US and China will be significant factors and India will nuance its own policies accordingly.

Conclusion

The Indian elephant, it may be surmised, is on the move and the early decades of the 21 st century hold considerable promise for India to realize its many potentialities and hone its latent capabilities in keeping with the dynamic of the century. By about 2030 or thereabouts, macroeconomic projections suggest that the world will be tri-polar with the US, China and India constituting the three nodes.

This exigency will have its own strategic ramifications. Consequently India's foreign policy is also adapting to the changing context – domestic, regional and international. The track record of the last decade – particularly since May 1998 has been encouraging and currently an emerging India is the flavour of the times. Much of this quiet confidence of how India will deal with the world at large is aptly reflected in a little noted but comprehensive overview offered by PM Manmohan Singh, which is being cited in some detail, for it offers very illuminating cues about the orientation of India's overall strategy and related external policies. Speaking to the apex of the Indian military at the annual Combined Commander's Conference in October 2005, PM observed: The end of the Cold War, increasing global interdependence and the trans-border nature of many threats have made strategic concepts developed in a bipolar world somewhat irrelevant. The United States is today the dominant economic, military, technological and cultural power. However, it can be anticipated that the European Union, Russia, China, Japan and India will consolidate their individual positions to play a global role. We must evolve a new paradigm of security cooperation relevant to an emerging multipolar world in which global threats obtain global responses. This is precisely what India has sought to do. We have entered into strategic partnerships with the United States, Russia, Japan and the European Union and are pursuing strategic cooperation with China. Today, nations are engaged simultaneously both in competition and cooperation........, our (Indian) strategy has to be based on three broad pillars. First, to strengthen ourselves economically and technologically. Second, to acquire adequate defence capability to counter and rebut threats to our security, and third, to seek partnerships both on the strategic front and on the economic and technological front to widen our policy and developmental options.

With this in perspective, India too is reciprocating positively to overtures of other major players in the global balance of power. No doubt this involves sophisticated bargaining with each of them. It is unrealistic to expect nations to act for altruistic reasons. International relations are in the final analysis, power relations. This balance of power politics in international relations is more sophisticated than during the Cold War era. We must learn to deal with this new reality and plan our long-term security based on a proper appreciation of these evolving trends. Consequently, we should develop friendly interactive relations with as many major powers as possible.

India's world view and its own orientation to the external as enunciated in 2005 bears strong resemblance to what Nehru had outlined in the early years after India attained independence. Friendly and mutually productive relations with all the major powers without being drawn into any kind of 'alliance' that would fetter India's autonomy remains the lodestar that provides continuity to India's evolving foreign policy.

The dynamic of change is evidenced in the manner in which India's own capabilities and resilience has been enhanced. After almost 60 years, India may have arrived at the appropriate harmonization of its resources and objectives as it strategizes to pursue its core national interests.

India's Foreign Policy Distortions (2004-2009): The United States Factor

Introductory Observations

The Indian Republic in the first fifty years of its existence maintained a strategic autonomy in the conduct of its foreign policy despite a much more limited national power profile and economic profile than that exists today.

Today, when India is economically vibrant and strong and India has been able to amass sizeable conventional and strategic assets, India to its citizens seems strategically tied down in adding muscle to the conduct of its foreign policy.

Adding muscle to India's foreign policy does not imply war mongering or military adventurism. Adding muscle to India's foreign policy implies that India's national security interests are accorded a paramountcy in the conduct of foreign policies to the exclusion of the personal predictions of the Indian Prime Minister and his proximate foreign policy advisors. It also implies the existence of political will to secure India's national security interests. The period 2004-2009 has witnessed a bartering away of India's national security interests.

The major part of India's foreign policy failures in this time span and the distortions that willingly or unwillingly have seeped into India's foreign policy (2004 – 2009) have resulted from policies or lack of policies generated by the predominance given by India's current Prime Minister to the "United States Factor" in our policy formulations. Co-attendant with the primacy given to the "United States Factor" in India's foreign policy formulations during 2004-2009 has been the "parallel track" of "Pakistan-appeasement policies" out of deference to United States Pak-centric strategic sensitivities.

In the process, India can be said to have abdicated its much prized "strategic autonomy" (not to be confused with nonalignment) in its foreign policy formulations. In another sense, it can also be said that India has diluted its aspirations to become a global power. The centre of gravity of the global balance of power has shifted to Asia. India along with China are the two prominent stakeholders and determinants of this shift in the balance of power.

While China has leveraged this shift to her advantage, India's foreign policies has not leveraged this shift in India's favour. On the contrary, India's current foreign policy has led it to seemingly emerge as more of a United States satellite or camp follower. Rhetorical flourishes by United States political leaders and officials will not impart global power status on India. India has to earn its global power status by standing firmly on its own legs, build its strengths and demonstrate its strategic autonomy globally and regionally, and firmly demonstrate fortified by Indian nationalism, that it has the will to use power to secure India's national interests.

This point is contextually relevant to the examination of the impact on India's foreign policy formulations of the "United States Factor". This chapter intends to examine the main theme under the following heads:

- The "United States Factor" in India's Foreign Policy (2004-2009): No End Gains
- Indian Prime Minister's "Foreign Policy Romanticism" with United States Reminiscent of Nehru's Romanticism with China.

- Peace with Pakistan: An Elusive Mythical Obsession of India's Prime Minister
- China's Containment was Implicit in Evolution of US-India Strategic Relationship: United States Now Shirks from it

The "United States Factor" in India's Foreign Policy (2004-2009): No End Gains The US-India Strategic Partnership much hyped in 2000-2001, including by this Author, now stands reduced to a "strategic relationship" only. That too is alive only in South Block corridors.

India's expectant hopes attending the advent of evolving a US-India Strategic Partnership focused on multiple aims. At the core of these aims were (1) India's rise to global power status with a US impetus (2) Strategic downsizing of Pakistan and limiting its "spoiler-state" role in South Asia (3) Joint US-India convergence in coping and managing of the growing military rise of China. Post 9/11 and now Post Af-Pak Policy unveiling it should be clear to all right thinking Indians that the United States global and regional agenda in South Asia is not in consonance with India's strategic expectations from the United States. The United States agenda is in contradiction to India's national security interests and India's national aspirations.

India's supine foreign policies during 2004-2009 in accommodating United States strategic sensitivities "at all costs" has landed India in a position where there are "no end-gains" for India by according a primacy to the "US Factor" in India foreign policy formulation. The above assertions stand fortified by the following manifestations:

- Proximity to United States has not contributed to lessening of India's threat perceptions emanating from Pakistan and China. United States has not contributed at all in this direction.
- United States strangulating hold over Pakistan has not been exercised to prevent Pakistan's proxy war and terrorism against India nor has the United States diluted the Pakistan-China strategic nexus
- United States till today has not supported India's candidature for the United Nations Security Council as a

Permanent Member. It indicates US reservations on the emergence of India as a global power.

- United States has revived or shortly will revive pressures that indirectly aim at capping/rolling back India's nuclear weapons arsenal.
- Strategically, the United States has only conceded the vast empty expanse of the Indian Ocean to India to extend its influence. The United States has not conceded that India is the predominant regional power in South Asia and that Pakistan must adjust its delusionary strategic mindsets accordingly.

Increased Indo-US military-to-military contacts are no index of a thriving US-India Strategic Partnership. One is now constrained to term it as a US-India Strategic Relationship. The United States has held itself back from adding enhanced strategic and political contours to the US-India relationship. The most striking deduction from the above analysis is that India's foreign policy (2004-2009) has been strategically misconceived and ill-advised in making the "United States as the "Central Pillar" of India's foreign policy."

Indian Prime Minister's "Foreign Policy Romanticism" with United States Reminiscent of Nehru's Romanticism with China

One would not be far wrong to term the Indian Prime Minister's "Foreign Policy Romanticism" with the United States as reminiscent of Nehru's similar romanticism with China. The results of the later were a great military setback for India.

It is not to suggest that the United States will attack India like China did. But an Indian monochromatic foreign policy focused on United States has brought distortions in India's present foreign policies, foreclosing many of its wider options afield, particularly India foreign policy towards Pakistan. Military setbacks can accrue to India by United States continued military build-up of Pakistan and thereby affecting the India-Pakistan Military Balance. It is strategically strange that while the United States increasingly harps on the strengths of its Strategic Partnership with India, it concurrently keeps building Pakistan's conventional military capabilities. Even a non-commissioned officer of the Indian Army would point out that it is a puerile US argument that it's provision of combat fighter aircraft and long range maritime surveillance aircraft fitted with anti-submarine weapons to Pakistan are intended for augmenting Pakistan's anti-terrorism warfare capability.

The Indian Prime Minister has failed in his foreign policy approaches to the United States to demand strategic 'quid-pro-quos' from the United States in relation to the adjustments and compromises he has made in Indian foreign policies to accommodate US strategic interests on Pakistan.

Peace with Pakistan: An Elusive Mythical Obsession of India's Prime Minister

Peace with Pakistan is a desirable objective for India's foreign policy. But the timing of peace and resumption of composite dialogue with Pakistan has to be decided by India's assessments and readings of the contextual security environment and India's national security interests.

The timings of such a process cannot be dictated by the United States to synchronize with the timings of its strategic overtures to Pakistan to serve US strategic interests. It does not require much imagination for anyone to assert that the United States and India have serious strategic divergences over Pakistan. Additionally, has the Indian Prime Minister and his advisory team ever asked themselves the question as to why the United States constantly preaches to India on peace with Pakistan?

India despite repetitive Pakistani acts of terrorism against India has exercised restraint. Even today India stands aloof and strategically not taken advantage of the growing civil war within Pakistan. Then why does the United States resort to peace sermons to India on India-Pak peace knowing fully well that these need to be given to Pakistan only. Further, in the past, and even now, Kashmir-mention is used as a strategic pressure point against India by US political leaders.

Sharm-al-Sheikh was a direct manifestation of the "distortions" that the "United States Factor" has induced in India's current foreign policy formulation. The Havana Agreement 2006 was the earlier manifestation. In both cases the "Indian foreign policy troika" of the Prime Minister, the National Security Adviser and the Foreign Secretary were the moving spirits behind these infamous appeasement concessions on terrorism to Pakistan, acting in duress under US pressures. Does it behave a country of India's size and potential to succumb to external pressures?

Fortunately, the force of Indian public opinion pressured the Congress President to make the Indian Prime Minister to retract from Sharm-al-Sheikh concessions to Pakistan. That does not lessen the gravity of the Indian policy establishment succumbing to external pressures especially over Pakistan.

Peace with Pakistan will continue to be an elusive myth till such time some Indian political leader emerges who can recognize that the only way to restrain Pakistan is to follow the US model against Russia in the Cold War.

Further peace with Pakistan will accrue when Indian Prime Ministers ensure that India's war preparedness at all times is so high that coupled with Indian Prime Ministers demonstrating the will to use power, these two realities existentially deter Pakistan from provoking India and indulging in military adventurism against it.

Indian Prime Ministers down the line have not grasped the fundamentals of why peace with Pakistan will remain an elusive myth. The onus of bringing about India-Pakistan peace lies squarely on United States shoulders and not on India's shoulders.

The United States has consistently invented and re-invented Pakistan's strategic utility for US national security interests. Pursuant to this fixation, it has armed and re-armed Pakistan substantially and encouraged it to box much above its strategic weight.

Peace with Pakistan will therefore continue to be elusive till such time United States re-calibrates its South Asia policies with Pakistan removed from the centrality it occupies in US strategy.

China's Containment was implicit in evolution of US-India strategic relationship: United States now shirks from it democracy and shared values were not the bed-rock of the advent of US-India's strategic partnership. The bedrock of this evolving strategic relationship was an implicit understanding and strategic convergence that China's rising military power needed to be contained for mutual strategic benefits. American strategic literature of the preceding decade and even in this decade is alive with discussions to this end.

The American stress on joint exercises and enter-operability with the Indian Armed Forces was surely not for disaster management purposes. The underlying intent has surely been a possible China contingency. Recent and latest United States foreign policy trends indicate that the United States is no longer imbued with a China containment strategy. Nothing could be more blasphemous for Indian ears than the latest US proposal of a G-2 (US and China) combine to control global affairs. The underlying content is not only economic but also a strategic compromise that the United States seems to be making with China.

Further, India's Prime Minister and his team are seemingly unaware that it is a cardinal tenet of United States strategic policies that no single Asian nation emerges as the predominant power. To that end United States would continue to play more of a role of a "balancer" rather than side with India to offset China's military rise.

India's Foreign Policy Options (2004-2009) Foreclosed by "United States Factor" Primacy

India will now begin to strategically pay for its foreign policies or lack of foreign policies during the period 2001-2009 arising from giving a misplaced primacy to the "United States Factor" in its foreign policy formulations. In respect of India's main threat adversaries, namely Pakistan and China, India's foreign policy options stand foreclosed because of the "US Factor".

The Indian Prime Minister with all his proximity to the United State has failed to prevail and convince the United States to restrain Pakistan's proxy war and terrorism against India. Contrarily, the Indian Prime Minister is being pressurized to suffer Pakistan's intransigence for the cause of greater American strategic good. The United States constantly changing priorities in its foreign policy stances towards China makes it an unreliable partner of India to deal with its China threat.

In relation to Pakistan, the close relations of India with Iran were a counter weight. In relation to China, the longstanding

Russia-India Strategic Partnership was an effective counter-balance and restraint. According primacy to the "United States Factor" in India's foreign policies during the period 2004-2009 led to a strategic downgrading of India's foreign policy priorities towards Iran and Russia. Earnest hard work would be required now to resurrect these relationships.

With aspirations to emerge as a global power, India's foreign policy cannot be converted into a US-centric mode. If the United States resorts to "balancing" India by use of Pakistan and/or China then Indian political leaders must learn to 'balance' the United States with an equally strong strategic partnership with Russia. Prime Minister Manmohan Singh for years did not attend the Shanghai Cooperation Organization Summit meetings. It sent wrong signals to Russia.

In the same vein, it needs to be pointed out that this Government should desist from making India's military inventories totally reliant on the United States. There is a danger that this Government for political reasons may place the multi-billion dollar order for 126 combat fighter aircraft for the Indian Air Force on the United States. By such a decision, in one single stroke, India would be mortgaging the cutting edge of India's offensive capabilities to the mercy of a Pak-centric United States.

Concluding Observations

In earlier views, of this author, a point that repeatedly stands made is that India cannot afford to emerge as a global player despite the United States or in opposition to it. The opposite is also true that no global power has ever helped another aspiring power to emerge as a global power.

This stands true for the United States and India too. The United States may, and one repeats may, assist India to emerge as a "global player" but it will never assist India to emerge as a "global power" on equal terms with USA. The years 2004-2009 have been "wasted years" in terms of India's foreign policy formulations and its conduct. The overwhelming reason was that India's foreign policy troika" comprising the PM, NSA and the Foreign Secretary made the United States as the "Central Pillar" of India's foreign policy. The resultant effect was that India stood disconnected from its proven traditional friendly partners. It is high time, that with no end-gains having accrued from such foreign policy fixations, India's foreign policy is re-calibrated and strong connectivities re-established with India's proven friends. An aspiring global power like India needs to have multiple foreign policy connectivities to provide flexibility of options. India's Prime Ministers need to emulate China. If the United States today talks of a global G-2 combine of USA and China to manage global affairs, it is because China has followed the dictum of a "mailed fist in a velvet glove." and leveraged its national strengths to propel its rise on the global stage.

India's New Foreign Policy – the Journey from Moral Nonalignment to the Nuclear Deal

The Geopolitics of Energy in South Asia, Dr. Marie Lall (ED)

'For 20 years no one called me. I had to make all the calls. Since we started talking about a nuclear deal, I have not had to make any calls. Everyone wants to speak to us because Bush wants to do a deal. India has become important.' (MEA official speaking about his postings abroad, anonymous interview, New Delhi 4th of August 2007) India is showing a new image of itself to the world and the world is recognising that today, India is indeed a country to be reckoned with. 60 years on, Jawaharlal Nehru's dream of India being recognised as a global power has never been closer. India always aspired global recognition, however for almost half a century India was seen as overpopulated, poor and irrelevant.

Although the hegemon in the South Asian region and a leader within the Non Aligned Movement this hardly mattered on the wider world stage. India's foreign policy in the first 45 years after independence was very flexible and reactive in nature. The global vision engendered by Nehru was based on moral supremacy and leadership of the developing world as well as economic self sufficiency at home. These moral principles focused largely on issues of superpower domination and anti-imperialism and were passed on from government to government till the late 1980s. However as the world around India changed these principles slowly became obsolete.

India's foreign policy formulation changed first under the United Front governments in the mid 1990s and then more radically under the BJP led NDA alliance in 1998. The backdrop to the changes were the economic reforms which had been started in 1991. India was opening up to the world and economic growth rather than self sufficiency became the major driver for international relations.

The realisation that foreign relations, energy policy and economic growth are linked has let to a new foreign policy formulation. New Delhi's priority today is to protect India's economic growth and foreign policy has been harnessed to create linkages with those countries that could provide energy security. This is because India sees that the only way it can maintain its' current position on the global scale is through its growth.

But India's new foreign policy formulation goes beyond securing oil and gas resources. Over the last few years India has been negotiating a nuclear deal with the US. This deal's main objectives are to help India's civilian nuclear power expansion as well as increasing business between the US and India. However this agreement goes well beyond energy security and economic growth. The most pertinent result of these negotiations is India's recognition as a nuclear weapon's state. With this recognition India achieves a large milestone towards global power status and fulfils Nehru's vision, albeit in a manner which could have never been imagined by India's first prime minister.

This chapter aims to draw together the nexus of energy, economic growth and the quest for global power status. It will give a brief background to India's foreign policy formulation before the economic reforms as well as how matters changed with the UF and the NDA governments. It will then analyse the role of energy in India's new foreign policy formulation, touching briefly on pipeline diplomacy before analysing the current negotiations around the nuclear deal.

The Construction of India's Foreign Policy

India's foreign policy evolved as a "dual" pattern, encompassing a global as well as a regional role. The two roles were run on a very different basis, as relations with India's neighbours were conducted on a much more realistic policy course as opposed to the moralistic international policy. The regional dimension was based on the fact that India was the hegemon in the region and would do everything to remain so.

The Non Aligned Movement (NAM) was created out of the desire to orient India's foreign policy towards the group of newly decolonized states, hoping to create a larger area of peace by fighting common dangers of imperialism and racialism together. Nehru wanted India to be the leader of the developing world, in this way carving out a global role for the country. The principle of India's leadership was to be based on moral rather than economic power. India's relations with the superpowers during the cold war were difficult as its non aligned status was never really accepted by the US who saw India as being in the Soviet camp. India's desire for economic self sufficiency also went against the grain of the concept of free market economy, which was being pushed by the western powers. On the other hand relations with the Soviet Union were cordial with substantial trade and barter trade underlying the relationship. However India never subscribed to the communist world's ideology, trying to combine a socialist economy with a democratic system at home. India refused to be apart of any defence pact or to take sides against either the western powers or the communist bloc.

Nehru believed that these idealistic broad concepts used in global policy formulation could also be used at the "micro-level", subject to some minor adjustments. Later, after Nehru's death this was dropped, making place for a more regional, realistic and forceful policy first under Indira Gandhi and later under Rajiv Gandhi, especially with regard to the South Asian region. The main incident, which established India as a regional power, was the creation of Bangladesh. 1971 was crucial for India's position in the region. The flood of refugees that poured into India had severe effects on the economy and on India's social structure. Out of economic and strategic necessity India trained, armed and then gave combat support to the Bangladeshi refugees.

India's regional priority has been to disallow the destabilisation of any neighbouring states by any internal or external forces. This includes the monitoring of ethnic conflicts on the borders in the

North East, Bhutan or Sri Lanka, and the promotion of regional cooperation. There are of course many obstacles to regional cooperation, paramount India's size and position as a hegemon, but it is also understood to be the only possibility for political and economic stability in the region. Nevertheless the regional part of the policy formulation was always rather ill defined and generally "reactive" in nature. The main emphasis was on establishing a security zone against possible threats from China.

The Chinese factor has been a sore point in India's foreign relations. Although China is a neighbour, it cannot be counted as part of the South Asian region, geographically set apart by the Himalayan mountain range. India and China are natural rivals and the relationship has been problematic over the years including border issues in Kashmir, India's North East, the status of Tibet and Sikkim. Nehru's political understanding involved advocating a policy of friendship, avoiding the isolation of newly communist China. In this way he hoped to establish a "normal" world order where Indo-Chinese cooperation would lead the newly independent countries of the third world. Throughout this time India upheld China's issues at the UN and recognised Taiwan as part of China. When in 1950 China asserted its authority in Tibet, Nehru exercised restraint. In 1954 the two countries signed an agreement on Tibet which proclaimed the "Panchsheel" doctrine, the five principles of peaceful coexistence.

The Indian humiliation of Oct./Nov. 1962 at the hand of the Chinese armed forces, made the nation realise that its relatively unarmed foreign policy towards China had failed to provide the necessary security and that idealism was no substitute for realism. India felt it was threatened by both its immediate neighbours, Pakistan and China, neither of which subscribed to nonalignment, and therefore a modern defence force had become necessary.

This section serves as a reminder how India's global and regional foreign policies were formulated prior to the economic reforms and to underline how until the early 1990s India's international foreign policy was idealistically oriented. India's national interest was seen both regionally and globally in solely in political and ideological terms with hardly any economic component.

The Changes After the Economic Reforms and under the BJP

The 1991 economic reforms saw the birth for a new role for international economic and trade relations. India suddenly had to engage with the post cold war world and reassess its foreign policy priorities. The opening up the economy to international players also meant that foreign relations had an economic dimension and trade became a foreign policy tool. Leaving *swadeshi,* economic self-sufficiency behind and engaging in international trade was India's new way forward. The Congress government under Narashima Rao initiated economic reforms, however worried that the economic pain of free trade and privatisation would hit the poorer section of India's society and increase the already large disparities. After the Congress lost power, the United Front governments under Deve Gowda and I.K. Gujaral started to focus more on foreign policy and foreign relations. In part this was due to India coming to term with its first coalition government where consensus on domestic affairs was not always forthcoming. The I.K. Gujaral peace moves towards Pakistan were a direct result of this-as were Deve Gowda's economic interest in South East Asia and the *'Look East'* policy with a clear vision for India's North Eastern states.

The 'look East' policy was a part of India's re-assessment of its role in the wider region, for the first time looking at Southeast Asia as a neighbour which mattered politically and economically. As India was looking for new markets and relations with the US still had not warmed up, a strategic decision to focus on Southeast Asia was taken. Closer cooperation with ASEAN was seen as a new priority, as it became increasingly clear that due to frosty relations with the neighbouring countries, SAARC was not going to be a huge success in terms of multilateral trade.

The BJP's vision was one of a multipolar world in which economic relations were going to be crucial. Regional policy became of prime importance, especially with regard to improving trade and improving the situation in India's border states. In part the BJP's moves towards Pakistan have to be seen in this light, but more so its' increase interest in the North East, which included starting a peace process with various insurgency groups as well as improving relations with Myanmar. There seems to have been an inherent understanding that the region could not be developed without international cooperation across the border. The BJP's foreign policy priorities have not been that different to that of Congress – i.e. to be and remain the regional hegemon with global power aspirations. However the BJP realised that the post cold war world needed a different approach based on trade and not on Nehruvian morality and righteousness. The BJP, unlike previous Congress governments also saw that there are direct links between foreign policy formulation and domestic policy, especially in the economic realm.

Despite the fact that the BJP had campaigned on an anti economic reforms ticket, they continued and intensified the reforms after forming their coalition government called the National Democratic Alliance (NDA). India's opening up saw the rise of multinational corporations, which resulted high growth with limited infrastructural development. The businesses – mainly multinationals, but also some large Indian firms gained better access to the Indian government in the 90s. Their agenda was focused on increased open markets and more trade, internationally as well as regionally. Indian businesses have always been aware that Indo-Pakistani and Indo-Chinese trade could be huge. As a result trade lobbies formed and have become more powerful in the political realm in Delhi in order to influence the decision making process. During the Kargil war, there were reports that businesses in India and outside were lobbying for a quick solution so as to not loose the multinationals and so that trade would not be lost either. Consequently since the economic reforms, businesses have become a new type of political actors or are at the very least influencing political decisions.

As a part of this new strategy, relations with the US, Israel and Myanmar were all revived. These were countries India aspired to keep away from for various reasons: the US for its imperialistic global bullying strategy, Israel for its war against the Palestinians and Myanmar for its undemocratic government in light of the 1990 elections. The 9/11 war on terror changed relations with the US for good. India saw in this an opportunity to ally itself with the US and portray the Kashmir problem as a part of the war on terror. The US was seen as a powerful economic ally holding the purse strings of various international funds. An agreement with Israel on the same basis meant that India could buy arms it would never had access to before. Peace or a dialogue about peace with Pakistan was seen as essential. Peace meant that India would finally be seen as an economically safe region for international investment. It also meant that the BJP would then be able to focus on internal changes. The government finally decided to tackle the China factor for the first time. India has for decades seen itself threatened militarily and economically by China. Disputed border issues have not been tackled as successive governments feared opening up 'Pandora's box'. However with China's increasing economic might in the region, India needed to improve relations and increase trade quickly. Finally the recognition of Tibet was exchanged against the recognition of Sikkim, a significant step in the move away from moralistic foreign policy vis-à-vis a neighbour.

These changes have '[...]to be understood as a larger re-orientation that has taken place since the end of the Cold War' where the US has come to dominate international politics. The Nuclear threshold was crossed by the BJP with the tests in May 1998 and showed the world that India would take on a more realist and pragmatic orientation. It was defended to Parliament with the statement: 'it is India's due, the right of one-sixth of human kind'. The gamble paid off as it brought a closer engagement with the US.

What this section wants to emphasize is that the aims of all governments, including that of the BJP, have been the same as Nehru's – to make India a major world power. India has always been suspicious of US neo-imperialist designs, however engagement with the US was seen as a key element in defining India's future. The NDA was able to make the link between improved economic growth, willingness to reform and improved international standing.

Consequently since the 1991 reforms, but especially under the NDA government India's foreign policy formulation has been conducted on the basis of trade and power priorities as a mechanism to hegemony. At a larger level, this move fits in with globalisation and the increasing power of business in government policy formulation, not only in Asia but in the world at large.

The Current UDA Government – borrowing from the BJP

In May 2005 the BJP led NDA alliance lost the elections to the Congress led UDA coalition. Immediately after the elections the Indian stock markets dipped. There was a general sense of unease with regard to India's new government's external support by the communist party and the fear that both domestic and foreign economic policy would change.

However within a few months it became clear that not only general economic policy would remain very much on the same track as the BJP had chartered, but also that the new government would further build on the new foreign policy relations which had been developed.

This was particularly but not exclusively the case for relations with the US and Myanmar. Energy security soon became a key government concept with a visionary Mani Shankar Aiyar at the helm of the petroleum ministry.

The Issue of Energy as a Pivotal Point

The geopolitics of energy has become of increasing importance as developing countries need to secure energy supplies in order to maintain economic growth rates. The volatility of the oil market has had severe repercussions on developing countries as price hikes lead to less competitive productivity and an increase in trade deficits. This is particularly a risk for India and China who do not meet their own needs with either domestic oil or gas supplies. As a result relations with states who can provide the well needed gas and oil is seen as central to India's new foreign policy. But it is not only the hydrocarbon rich states which are of importance, as any pipeline would have to cross India's immediate neighbours with whom relations have been at best cordial, and often quite a lot worse. Both on India's eastern flank relations with Bangladesh need to be improved as well as on the western border where peace with Pakistan needs to be secured in order for the energy supply to be secure and uninterrupted. So the issue of energy goes beyond traditional trade and economic relations and has wide-ranging effects on economic growth, peace negotiations and regional power status. The need for energy also ties in closely with the issues linked with the globalization of these countries as multinational energy corporations become the true players on the Asian markets with economic and political consequences which cannot be entirely foreseen at this stage.

India's Current Energy Needs

As mentioned above, India's current energy needs are largely dictated by the rise in economic growth. To sustain such growth (estimated between 7% and 8% pa, with the aim of increasing it to 10% pa) India has to secure energy resources quickly. The energy needs are also linked to India's population explosion. India's growing population is expected to reach 1180 million by 2010, 1362 million by 2020 and 1573 million by 2030 – i.e. a more than 50% increase in less than 30 years. India has stepped up the exploration for natural gas within its own borders; however it is becoming increasingly clear that large amounts of gas will need to be imported from abroad.

In February 2005 the Indian government approved plans for talks with six countries on the construction of gas pipelines that would pass through Iran, Afghanistan, Pakistan, Myanmar, Bangladesh and Turkmenistan. This new 'pipeline diplomacy' was seen as a key foreign policy priority as India's energy requirements are rising quickly. The Petroleum and Natural Gas Ministry was permitted to hold talks with the above mentioned countries to secure natural gas supplies. India produces only half the natural gas it uses and it imports 70 per cent of its crude oil. Then Petroleum and Natural Gas Minister Mani Shankar Aiyar confirmed that three pipeline projects were being discussed, including a pipeline running from Iran through Pakistan, one from Turkmenistan through Pakistan and Afghanistan, and a third from Myanmar (originally planned through Bangladesh). All transit countries would be paid high transit fees, making the projects worthwhile for them.

The Issue of Energy

However oil and gas are not the only energy priorities India is focusing on. The Kirit Parikh report focusing on energy security was completed at the end of 2005 emphasized the need for India to diversify its energy resources and to focus on development in all fields, including the nuclear field. At present, the Atomic Energy Commission (AEC) in India is only producing about 3000 MWs of energy. Despite toiling with this effort for almost 50 years, this current output still only represents less than 3% of its total power. Although the AEC does estimate that nuclear sources would generate some 63,000 MWs by 2032, a study of the organization's past record shows that this target is unreliable and unrealistic. Nevertheless, nuclear energy provided a source of clean energy for the heavily polluting India. In fact, India was no stranger to nuclear facilities. In 1956, it had the first nuclear reactor in Asia outside the USSR. However, with the 3 decades of sanctions against it, India lost out on key developments in the international nuclear industry.

The nuclear energy option is seen by India as a long term option as the highly technological development will take years to expand. India also realised that its indigenous programme would need western technology and more fissile material in order to be able to grow at a reasonable rate. Today the expectation is that at current growth rates and if the private sector in involved, nuclear energy could possibly provide 6% of India's energy consumption. This very low rate and the high expense begs the question why India would want to spend any time, money and energy to develop this sector. The role of 'the nuclear' in global power status however is central to being recognised as a power to be reckoned with. Despite India's nuclear tests in 1974 and 1998, such recognition had always eluded India. Since India was not a signatory to the NPT, it was effect seen as a nuclear pariah who suffered sanctions in retaliation for its 'unauthorised' and unilateral actions. In fact Indo-US relations suffered tremendously after the 1998 tests. Manmohan Singh has claimed that "this political impasse proved to be a thorn stuck in the throat of the relationship of both countries". In order to gain global recognition India needed to be recognised as a legitimate nuclear weapons state and in order to do this, relations with the US needed to be mended.

India's quest for a civilian nuclear cooperation agreement with the US has to be seen in light of India's quest not so much for energy and economic development, but a recognised role on the global stage of politics. This does not necessarily gel with the US's priorities or the US's reasoning on the deal, which hopes to bring most of India's nuclear facilities under international control in as short a time as possible. Nicholas Burns, US undersecretary of state for political clearly stated end of July this year that he expected 95% of India's nuclear facilities to be inspected by the IAE within 25 years. There is a feeling that India needs to be controlled and reigned in. The discrepancy of understanding between the two countries could in the long run lead to major problems.

Background

Besides the obvious benefits to their energy and nuclear industries, India also saw the civilian nuclear agreement as an opportunity to develop close ties with US. To India, closer ties with the US suited its changing strategic security policies given the rapidly changing geopolitical situation in the region and China's economic rise. Furthermore, cooperation with the US promised access to nuclear fuel and would place it among the elite group of recognized nuclear weapons states. A series of talks in 2000 between then US Deputy Secretary of State Strobe Talbott and then Indian Foreign Minister Jaswant Singh focused on a series of issues. However, any discussions about the nuclear issues between both countries faced a stalemate as the US insisted on a cap on India's fissile nuclear program.

It was thus left to a shift in US foreign policy to make the breakthrough. Attempts by the first Bush administration to achieve any significant progress proved futile. The problem lay in the presence of South Asian expertise in this administration who had a fixed mindset towards the region. In the nuclear cooperation context, these officials argued that any exception made for India had to be granted to Pakistan also. Given the proliferation controversy surrounding A.Q. Khan, the father of Pakistan's nuclear bomb and his proliferation network, any considerations of encouraging nuclear activity in Pakistan were immediately ruled out. Moreover, the administration was also littered with nonproliferation experts and advocates of the NPT. Even with such opposition, the strongest advocacy for any such cooperation between the two countries still came from within the US. This illustrated list of supporters included Stephen Cohen, Joseph Nye, Henry Kissinger and William Perry. It was the arrival of the second Bush administration in 2004 that brought along with it a new foreign policy team, which looked at Asia more imaginatively. This team recognized the emerging prowess of China's economic and strategic strengths. It also recognized that India had become too important a player in the Asian region and on the global stage for the US to continue to ignore it. India, it thought, could be a counter to the growing Chinese threat in Asia. After all, it made perfect ideological sense for the US as the oldest democracy in the world to partner India, the world's largest democracy.

Besides pitting it as an Asian balance of power, the US was also cautious of the growing relations between India and Iran, especially in light of closer cooperation between Russia, China, India and Iran between the late 1990s and 2005. The pipeline project proved to be a warning signal to the US foreign policy officials. They knew that if they did not get involved, relations between New Delhi and Tehran would deepen and this would be a threat to the US security interests. The US also saw India's presence outside the global nonproliferation architecture as a potential threat to its strategic interests, given India's vast and growing indigenous capabilities. This is despite the fact that the Indian government had established a rigorous export controls system and possessed an exemplary record of nonproliferation even though it was not a part of the international regime. The US did not feel that there were any assurances that these measures would be enforced consistently or effectively in perpetuity. From the Pakistani examples, the US had learnt that nonproliferation ultimately derives from inequalities between private and collective costs and benefits. Thus, in the event of high direct costs, the Bush administration felt that India could default. Indeed, economics did play a considerable part in the formulation of foreign policy in this case. Perhaps the least publicized benefit to the US deriving from the deal would be the direct access to the Indian civilian nuclear market for its nuclear technology companies. The promise of a large portion of the billion-dollar pie enticed the Bush administration and their political donors, many of who were energy companies. This would also help rectify the balance of trade deficit between the US and India.

Knowing full well that the improvement of Indo-US relations would be the defining success of the Bush term in office, the administration pursued achieving this objective aggressively. Washington also expected that transformed bilateral relations will facilitate the expansion of Indian power in a manner that ultimately will advance America's own global interests with respect to defeating terrorism, promoting democracy worldwide, contributing towards counter proliferation activities in the Indian Ocean and preserving a stable balance of power in Asia over the long term.

The nuclear deal has raised much controversy within both the US and India and also in international circles. This is mainly owing to the fact that India is not a signatory to the Non-Proliferation Treaty (NPT) and should not be allowed access to sources of nuclear fuel. However, under the agreement made two years ago, President Bush made a commitment to Prime Minister Manmohan Singh that the US would favour India in changing its nonproliferation and export control laws and policies also to garner their own domestic support in Washington. In return, the US wanted India to prove and to be accepted globally as a responsible owner of nuclear weapons, this despite India being a non-signatory to the NPT. In order to achieve this, India was asked to separate its civilian and military nuclear programs. In addition, it also agreed to place its civilian nuclear program under an international safeguards system as well as to support a variety of global nonproliferation initiatives. Further, India also agreed to extend its moratorium on nuclear testing. In committing itself to all of the above, India would assume the same responsibilities and practices as the acknowledged nuclear weapons states.

The Difference between the Indian and the US Perception

The biggest problem with the nuclear deal is the differences between the Indian and the US perception of what the deal means and what it aims to achieve. The following two lists show how both India and the US come from very different, possibly irreconcilable vantage points: The US wants to

- Bring India into the NPT framework
- Increased trade: the balance of trade deficit
- Use India as a counterweight to China's rise (Asian balance of power)
- Get Indian support for increased democratisation of the middle East
- Get Indian support in the anti Iran campaign.

The US will also get access to the Indian nuclear market which will help revive the US nuclear industry which has been dormant since the three miles accident in 1979. 'The US will also use the Indian human resource and India's scientific reactors and recycle them back to India.' Prasad in this article also believes that the US feels that sanctions did not work as India continued with the fast breeder reactor programme. The deal is a way of controlling, regulating and harnessing India.

India on the other hand wants:

- Recognition as a responsible nuclear weapons state
- Access to fissile material and latest nuclear technology
- US support with regard to Pakistan and the China-Pakistan nexus (Asian balance of power)
- Maintain its sovereignty in all aspects of domestic and foreign policy formulation.

The meetings between the US administration and the Indian government did not centre only on the actual deal, such as the one between Cheney and M K Narayan on the 22nd of July 2007. This points to the fact that the nuclear deal is part of a much larger agreement framework. The Indian press has been speculating about a security partnership, which possibly contravenes the sovereignty issue listed above.

Current Standing

On 3rd August 2007, the US and India unveiled the much awaited text of their agreed nuclear deal. The details of the 123 Agreement however revealed the extent of India's compromise with US laws in exchange for nuclear energy for civilian purposes. Both sides had reached a historic milestone in finalizing terms of the nuclear deal on 20th July 2007, marking the culmination of their two years of negotiation. Talks began in Washington on 17th July and were supposed to have lasted only 2 days but were extended for another day after failing to finalize some technical aspects of the operational deal. The agreement is to be valid for 40 years ad will stay in force for 2 additional periods of 10 years each. Each side can end the deal with 6 months notice at the end of 40 years or any subsequent 10 year period. Either side can terminate the deal mid term by giving a year's notice. Now India and US have to woo the Nuclear Suppliers Group to change their guidelines and to reach an agreement with IAEA on their safeguards. If these difficult obstacles are overcome, then President Bush has to ensure that Congress rule in favour of the deal before any implementation can be carried out.

Terms of Negotiation

The US has agreed in principle to provide nuclear technology and fuel to India for civilian use. In December 2006 the US Congress had approved a landmark ruling, the Hyde Act, which allowed US export of civilian nuclear fuel and technology for the first time in 30 years. India gets to have a civilian and military nuclear programme without being a signatory to the NPT agreement, this ending the 'nuclear apartheid' against India.

The detail revealed by the 123 Agreement on the 3rd of July includes the following points:

- The agreement will not to hinder or interfere with India's nuclear program for military purposes.
- US will help India negotiate with the IAEA for an India-specific fuel supply agreement.
- Washington will support New Delhi develop strategic reserves of nuclear fuel to guard against future disruption of supply.
- In case of disruption, the US and India will jointly convene a group of friendly supplier countries to include nations like Russia, France and the UK to pursue such measures to restore fuel supply.
- Both the countries agree to facilitate nuclear trade between themselves in the interest of respective industries and consumers.

- India and the US agree to transfer nuclear material, non-nuclear material, equipment and components.
- Any special fissionable material transferred under the agreement shall be low enriched uranium.
- Low enriched uranium can be transferred for use as fuel in reactor experiments and in reactors for conversion or fabrication.
- The ambit of the deal includes research, development, design, construction, operation, maintenance and use of nuclear reactors, reactor experiments and decommissioning.
- India can develop strategic reserve of nuclear fuel to guard against any disruption of supply over the lifetime of its reactors.
- Agreement provides for consultations on the circumstances, including changed security environment, before termination of the nuclear cooperation.
- Provision for one-year notice period before termination of the agreement.
- The US to engage Nuclear Suppliers Group to help India obtain full access to the international fuel market, including reliable, uninterrupted and continual access to fuel supplies from firms in several nations.
- The US will have the right to seek return of nuclear fuel and technology.
- In case of return, Washington will compensate New Delhi promptly for the "fair market value thereof" and the costs incurred as a consequence of such removal.
- Both the countries to set up a Joint Committee for implementation of the civil nuclear agreement and development of further cooperation in this field.
- The agreement grants prior consent to reprocess spent fuel.
- Sensitive nuclear technology, nuclear facilities and major critical components can be transferred after amendment to the agreement.

- India will establish a new national facility dedicated to reprocessing safeguarded nuclear material under IAEA safeguards.
- Nuclear material and equipment transferred to India by the US would be subject to safeguards in perpetuity.

The Issues

During the past 2 years, the deal was heavily scrutinized by all quarters. As a result many issues, both major and trivial, concerning aspects of the deal were raised. One source of agitation for critics of the deal has been its financing. There has been no mention yet of any details of proposed financing for the project. The government has also failed to address the concerns of reactor safety and waste disposal.

The greatest cause of concern however to Indian policy-makers is the effect this deal would have on the country's existing regime. Problems which remain are the fact that the agreement is governed by US law and the right of return of all materials. Article 2.1 makes it clear that Hyde act and other US laws, not international law will prevail: 'Each party shall implement this agreement in accordance with its respective applicable treaties, national laws, regulations and licence requirements concerning the use of nuclear energy for peaceful purposes.'

National security remains a priority of the Indian government and to commit to a moratorium on conducting further nuclear tests is seen as a compromise of their national sovereignty and national security. Since it is unlikely that the US will make an exception for India, New Delhi could face another round of sanctions should they conduct further testing in accordance with US laws. Although there was no clear mention of consequences of an Indian nuclear test, the agreement does indicate that either party could choose to terminate the deal prior to its expiration resulting from either party's serious concern about a changed security environment or as a response to similar actions by other states which could impact national security.

Critics argue that directly or otherwise, this clause effectively ends India's nuclear testing possibilities if it wants to avoid the termination of the pact. Opposition party, the BJP, led by senior leader Yashwant Sinha, has illustrated the main flaw of the agreement. According to him, the text of the agreement does state that issues not covered in it will be subject to national laws. This, he adds, refers to the Hyde Act, which was passed in December of 2006. The Act provides the US President with the discretionary powers to terminate the civil nuclear cooperation if India conducts a nuclear test. In fact the US can scrap the agreement at will (article 14(2) in an unequal deal as India's international safeguards are in perpetuity: 'The party seeking termination has the right to cease further cooperation under this agreement if it determines that a mutually acceptable resolution of outstanding issues has not been possible or cannot be achieved through consultations.' This puts India at the mercy of the supplier who holds all the leverage. Mr. Sinha concludes that the fundamental flaw lies in the fact that the US has provided unenforceable commitments in lieu of enforceable commitments from India. In addition to this, many in India saw the condition that US will continue to support their country's sourcing for fuel even after the deal is concluded as a continuous support from the Americans. However, the agreement provided a clause that allows the party seeking termination of the deal to cease further cooperation under the agreement if it deems that a mutually acceptable resolution of outstanding issues cannot be achieved.

The expectation of India to join in international efforts to sanction and contain Iran's search for uranium enrichment technology is also a difficult diplomatic and economic decision for New Delhi to make. Although not mentioned explicitly, Nicholas Burns and others from the US team have clearly stated that they are 'counselling India' not to engage with Iran. India did join the UN Security Council's resolutions to constrain Iran's nuclear quest, but the country is still dependent on the Iranians for oil and gas. However the reality of an Iran-Pakistan-India oil pipeline could be affected by the US anti-Iran policy. In relation to the requirement of reaching an agreement with the IAEA in perpetuity, India has been reluctant unless it is assured access to nuclear materials in perpetuity. However, India's attempts at negotiating this clause with the IAEA seem to be futile as the IAEA is a regulatory and not policy-making body.

The obligation of the US President to annually certify that India is conforming to the needs of the US legislation is viewed by many as an intrusion to its sovereignty. This again is specified under the Hyde act. Furthermore with the issue of continuity of the American leadership comes the question of consistency of its policy towards India. Adding to that, the subjectivity of such assessment built upon individual judgement, makes the uncertainty of the outcome even more obvious. Nevertheless, such concerns may be exaggerated. As President Bush has already proven through alternate language by agreeing to an "annual assessment" rather than a "certification", the US government can innovatively work their way around such small obstacles.

Although Manmohan Singh's administration heralded the deal as a negotiation victory for New Delhi, this was a rather premature analysis. Upon closer evaluation, terms of the agreement show that the US has very cleverly hidden key clauses in it that places India in an unfavourable position. The general sense of satisfaction in India surrounding the text of the 123 is derived from the agreement to petty details that New Delhi had been pushing for. The major component of the deal that has been much of the cause of a triumphant mood in New Delhi is regarding the reprocessing of spent fuel. Quoted in the Asian Age, A.N Prasad, a former director of the Bhabha Atominc Reseach Centre had said that 'India's three stage nuclear programme, which is geared towards harnessing thorium, is a prized jewel that cannot be sacrificed at the altar of politics.' As mentioned earlier, New Delhi had been pushing for an allowance for transfer of reprocessing or enrichment technology. Initial concerns from Washington were that this would allow India to divert nuclear material to its military program. However, under the condition that India's reprocessing facility be placed under special IAEA safeguards, the allowance has been made in the 123 for her to reprocess spent fuel. However Prasad makes the point that setting up a dedicated reprocessing plant will not make matters any better for the fast breed reactor.

Given the reality of the agreement on the ground and the different priorities of both governments it has to be remembered in New Delhi that this is not a two way deal: 'India is not selling something of critical interest to America in return for nuclear fuel or nuclear technology. India is a buyer. It is a one way transaction'. This of course makes the situation an unequal one, one which is heavily contested both by the opposition and the government supporting left parties.

The Opposition and the Left Parties

The BJP has argued that the 123 agreement compromises India's nuclear weapons programme and asked the government to put the next steps of the deal on hold. 'The BJP is of the clear view that this agreement is an assault on our nuclear sovereignty and our foreign policy options. We are therefore, unable to accept this agreement as finalized.' The controversy rage principally around the lack of definition of the word 'action' which the BJP feels could be interpreted widely by the US to include anything it perceives not to be in its national interest, including for example India's ties with Iran. The Left parties at first decided to consult scientists first and come back with a reaction a few days later. They have now publicly demanded that the deal be rejected and that it be brought to parliament for review. They have also demanded the constitution be altered to allow international deals to be reviewed in parliament so that every MP can vote for it and suggest amendments. Manmohan Singh has rejected these calls saying that the deal has been agreed and it will not be brought back to the study table.

Reaction in the US

Despite the overwhelming political support the nuclear deal has had in Washington, a large segment of the US press has been critical. The main argument lies in the fact that India is not a signatory to the NPT and is being rewarded for bad behaviour and that this is bad news when dealing with countries such as Iran or North Korea. The Economist argues that although China's increasing strength is at the heart of the deal, it will be decades before China represents a threat big enough for the US to make such a concession to India and that breaking the nonproliferation regime is both dangerous and unnecessary. The press does admit that the US will gain economically as India will engage in military equipment and possibly nuclear trade, but it also warns that the US should not expect to buy India's undivided loyalty.

Reaction in Pakistan

Relations between India and Pakistan could be profoundly altered as India is seen as being given preferential treatment despite Pakistan's cooperation with the US in the war on terror. In fact Pakistan's first reaction to the announcement was to warn the US of a potential arms race. Strategic stability is threatened as India will be able through the nuclear deal to develop larger amounts of fissile material for nuclear weapons. The Bush administration has dismissed Pakistan's claims as India's reprocessing of US nuclear fuel would take place in a separate facility under IAEA safeguards. It is possible that the deal will help Pakistan to seek a closer alliance with China to balance the new geopolitical reality in South Asia.

Effect on China

There has been a hardening on the Border dispute in Arunachal Pradesh. China is a major player in the nuclear suppliers group and is worried how the deal will impact on them. China is further worried by the quadrilateral for democracy which includes India, the US, Australia and Japan and which it sees as anti-Chinese. The quadrilateral is due to hold naval exercises in the Bay of Bengal in the first week of September 2007 with Singapore. Nuclear submarines, aircraft carriers, destroyers and frigates will participate and it is coined the largest exercise since the end of the cold war.

As the quote at the beginning of the paper illustrates, the nuclear deal is a central facet in India's new foreign policy formulation. Officials from various ministries in Delhi who were interviewed last week explained that the administration is aware of both the advantages and the drawbacks of the agreement. Greater cooperation with the US will not only bring in big business, it will change the geopolitical balance in Asia. India will have to be guarded not to do the US's bidding in the region and to retain an independent foreign policy.

In fact the discrepancy between US and Indian aims with regard to the deal and any further cooperation is bound to bring diplomatic conflict in the not too distant future. The US press already is heralding the deal as one sided whereby the US is portrayed as not receiving anything in return. The Indian left and opposition are on their side arguing that India is signing away sovereign rights. The argument is far from being settled. Even if the actual text is not finally agreed upon by either the US Congress or the Indian Lok Sabha, the major aim of the deal will have been achieved: India will have been internationally recognized as a responsible nuclear weapons state, and with it receives the global acknowledgement it has always sought.

In essence the nexus of energy, economic growth and global power status are now at the heart of India's foreign policy. This troika has changed foreign policy formulation, however maintaining the same goal Jawaharlal Nehru set out 60 years ago today.

Supporting US Foreign Policy in the Post-9/11 World

Policymakers' lives are dominated by their "in boxes" and the crises of the moment; rarely do they have time to contemplate far into the future. These are, of course, clichés. But clichés become cliché precisely because they contain an element of truth. As a policymaker, I confess that I often feel as though "long term" is later in the week. During the past year, my staff has been deeply involved in the formulation of our response to the attacks of September 11th, the planning for Afghanistan's post-conflict future, the Middle East peace process, exploring new ways to de-escalate the India-Pakistan conflict over Kashmir, keeping the Northern Ireland peace process on track, revising our approach to the instabilities shaking Latin America from Colombia to Argentina, and a host of other issues.

But to be more than the accumulation of responses to separate crises, a successful foreign policy depends upon bridging the intellectual gap between the imperatives of the present and the potential of the future. In turn, this often depends upon bridging the gap between policymakers and the Intelligence Community. After all, as Robert Bowie—a predecessor of mine as Director of the Policy Planning Staff who later served as a deputy director of the CIA—insightfully defines it, "intelligence" is "knowledge and analysis designed to assist action." Information and insights that do not "assist action" remain lifeless. Successful intelligence, therefore, requires a mutual understanding between policymakers and the Intelligence Community that is all too often lacking. Policymakers need to ensure that the Community is not working in a vacuum, that analysts know what is on our minds and what questions we need answered. At the same time, members of the Intelligence Community have a responsibility to seek out policymakers, understand their concerns, and tell them what they should be paying attention to. It is important to tell policymakers what they need to hear, not what they want to hear.

In the past year, the Intelligence Community has undergone soul-searching from within and intense scrutiny from without. As happened in the late 1940s and the mid-1970s, the Intelligence Community's mission and very structure are, in the aftermath of September 11th, being reconsidered and reoriented. I do not intend, however, to attempt to identify the "lessons" of the past year and suggest new mechanisms within the Intelligence Community to cope with the demands of our long-term campaign against terrorism. I will leave such matters for others. Instead, I want to step back from the current debates about the future organization of the Intelligence Community to consider basic matters of intellectual outlook and the practice of the intelligence craft that organizational restructuring alone will not touch.

This article is one intelligence consumer's attempt to help bridge the gaps between the present and the future on the one hand, and policymakers and the Intelligence Community on the other. To begin, I will sketch the main forces that this policymaker sees shaping international relations in what Secretary of State Colin Powell has called the "post-post-Cold War world." Then I will outline some important questions that will merit serious attention by the Intelligence Community in the years ahead.

The Five Fundamentals

Formulating a strategy for the global campaign against terrorism and implementing it have inevitably drawn the lion's share of policymakers' attention since September 11th. Likewise, the Intelligence Community has dramatically shifted resources to the fight against terror. As if these demands were not enough, at the same time, policymakers and the Intelligence Community have confronted a variety of crises and conflicts spanning from the Green Line to the Line of Control, from Colombia to the Caucasus. Our foreign policy, though, should be based upon an appreciation of the fundamental dynamics shaping the international environment—and not just the events of the past twelve months, no matter how significant they may be. Without such understanding, our foreign policy risks becoming merely tactical and temporary rather than strategic and sustainable.

A major challenge as we face pressing decisions of the day, therefore, is to identify the deeper forces at work transforming our strategic landscape. Thankfully, we have insightful analyses—many produced within the Intelligence Community—of the main forces defining our world at the dawn of the twenty-first century. While the specific lists may vary in minor respects, I believe there is a growing consensus that five fundamental factors are shaping the future of international relations: globalization, the fate of democratic governance, the changing nature of security, the evolution of our alliances and relations with other major powers, and the future of American power. Each in its own way is highlighted in the terrorist threat and our response to it. I want to discuss each in turn.

Globalization

Globalization is a basic reality shaping the nature of international relations at all levels. It should be viewed broadly, beyond merely economic exchange. Globalization is the totality and velocity of connections and interactions—be they economic, political, social, cultural—that are sometimes beyond the control or even knowledge of governments and other authorities. It is characterized by the compression of distance and the increasing permeability of traditional boundaries to the rapid flow of goods, services, people, information, and ideas. It is a multifaceted, transnational phenomenon.

Anyone reading *The Education of Henry Adams*—let alone recent academic analyses of the late nineteenth century—recognizes that globalization is not a new phenomenon. Just consider multinational corporations, transnational religious movements, substantial international capital flows, global pandemics, the emergence of global networks of commerce, and non-governmental organizations (NGOs) and private foundations working to better the lives of working men and women. All these elements of globalization predated not just the end of the Cold War, but the World Wars as well.

Nonetheless, since the end of the Cold War, globalization has unmistakably accelerated and extended its reach. Furthermore, although the nation-state remains the preeminent actor on the international stage, we have also witnessed how globalization has empowered a variety of non-state actors ranging from individual philanthropists and humanitarian NGOs to lone computer hackers and criminal cartels. Indeed, globalization has enabled the emergence of new kinds of global and virtual networks that, in turn, have accelerated further the pace of globalization.

Behind Globalization

The essential drivers behind this wave of globalization are economic, demographic, and technological. The global capitalist economy remains the most important transnational force in the world today. Global trade and investment, the diffusion of corporate "best practices," the freeing of labor markets, and the efficiencies achieved by global economies of scale are remaking the world every day. The benefits of the past decade's expansion of open economies and societies are unmistakable. Market economies promote growth that in turn sustains better education, health, social equality, and quality of life. At the same time, the market economy acts as a disruptive force, demanding institutional and intellectual innovation while unsettling the work patterns of everyday life. And it carries with it the risk of international economic contagion as we saw in the late 1990s and, again, this past year in Latin America. Economist Joseph Schumpeter was right to label capitalism's dynamic "creative destruction." Anyone who has invested in the NASDAQ over the past few years will undoubtedly agree.

Those nation-states that are unable or unwilling to integrate themselves into the global system risk isolation and stagnation. North Korea is only the most chilling example of a regime that has intentionally cut its people off from the world and forced them to suffer the horrendous consequences. Other governments are attempting a more subtle and difficult balancing act, hoping to insulate themselves from globalization more selectively through old-fashioned protectionism, targeted restrictions on the flow of information, or similar policies.

Disparities will increase between citizens living in the wealthiest countries that are the most integrated into the international system and those living in the poorest, least integrated ones. Strains within nation-states will also be felt as the effects of globalization spread differently across regions. Those who participate in the modern world will have radically different experiences, qualities of life, and perspectives than those who do not or cannot. Tensions between the two groups of people are inevitable—but how these tensions play out is not.

Demographic Factors

The most basic facts of life and death continue to matter to international relations. Almost all of the population increase in coming years—on the order of 95 percent—will take place in the developing world. The prospects for better jobs tied to the globalized economy will continue to draw people from rural areas; therefore, the developing world's citizenry will concentrate more and more in urban areas. Soon, for the first time in human history, the majority of the world's population will live in urban areas, straining state infrastructures and services sometimes to the breaking point. We see these dynamics already at work in megacities like Lagos, Karachi, and Jakarta and countless other cities around the globe. Furthermore, "youth bulges" will often result in widespread unemployment that simultaneously increases instability within the developing world and the pool of migrants eager to escape it. The disenchanted and disenfranchised members of these youth cohorts risk joining the ranks of terrorists, criminal organizations, and other groups that threaten to rend the fabric of societies around the world. At the same time, the developed world—especially Western Europe and Japan—will become grayer with each passing year as its population's average age creeps upward. Issues of immigration and national identity promise, therefore, to strain fault lines both within countries and between them. As people move, so do microbes. HIV/AIDS, tuberculosis, and malaria together cause 25 percent of all deaths worldwide. With an estimated 40 million people already infected, the national security threat posed by HIV/AIDS is no longer theoretical or prospective; it is clear and present today. It is, moreover, rapidly expanding its deadly reach beyond Sub-Saharan Africa. In the last 5 years, for instance, the HIV/AIDS infection rates in Eastern Europe increased 1300 percent. Even relatively low rates of infection will have enormous consequences for high population countries such as China and India. HIV/AIDS is particularly devastating because it often combines with other infectious diseases—notably tuberculosis—in lethal alliances. To make matters worse, drug-resistant strains of tuberculosis are becoming more prevalent. Such strains can defeat the most sophisticated antibiotics in modern medicine's arsenal.

The burden of infectious diseases can strain weak health systems to the breaking point and beyond, with pernicious effects on social, economic, and political stability of regions important to America's interests. The hardest-hit nations in Sub-Saharan Africa are experiencing precipitous declines in life expectancies, some falling over 30 years. Millions of orphans will need to be raised by the poorest societies on earth; many, forced to fend for themselves or exploited by others, will pose a clear source of instability in affected areas. The spread of HIV/AIDS and other infectious diseases, therefore, will not only pose a health risk, but threaten to destroy societies, devastate economies, and destabilize entire regions. Technological Breakthrough. The revolution in information and communications technologies has helped integrate the world and its economies as never before. While helping accelerate the economic dynamism of the past decade, these same technologies facilitate the coordination of transnational criminal and terrorist networks. Other technologies also have their own bright and dark sides. Developments in biotechnology, for instance, hold promise for medical and agricultural breakthroughs that will improve all our lives. However, the same trends allow new actors to inflict unprecedented disruption and destruction. At a time of anthrax attacks and terrorist threats to use nuclear, biological, chemical, and radiological weapons, the specter of weapons of mass destruction has perhaps never been more ominous.

The Dark Side of Globalization

Before September 11th, citizens of the United States tended to view globalization for the most part as a positive phenomenon. Every year more people than ever before benefited from speedy long-distance travel, e mail, cellular telephones, faxes, household satellite dishes, and the unprecedented flow of trade, investment, and information. But globalization always did have—and will continue to have—a dark side. The same networks that allow the free flow of commerce and communication can also carry from one continent to another drugs; refugees and illegal immigrants; diseases like HIV/AIDS; financial volatility and contagion; traffic in men, women, and children; and, as we now know all too well, terrorists. Indeed, international terrorism exemplifies this dark side of globalization as al-Qaida and its cousin terrorist networks twist the benefits and conveniences of our increasingly open, integrated, globalized world to serve their destructive agenda.

The al-Qaida threat does not reside in any one state. Instead, Usama bin Laden is (or was) a man without a country—his al-Qaida network is a multinational enterprise with franchises in 50 or more countries. Its global activities are coordinated by not only personal couriers but also the communication technologies emblematic of our age—cellular and satellite telephones, encrypted e-mail, internet chat rooms, videotapes, and laser disks. Like a skilled publicist, bin Laden has exploited the international media to project his image worldwide. Members of al-Qaida have travelled from continent to continent with the ease of a vacationer or business traveler. In an age marked by unprecedented mobility and immigration, they readily blend into communities wherever they move. They pay their way with funds raised through front businesses, drug trafficking, credit card fraud, extortion, money laundered from covert supporters, and possibly even the manipulation of stock markets. They use ostensibly charitable organizations for funding and recruitment. Money for their operations is transferred surreptitiously through numerous banks and money exchanges around the world—some legitimate and unwitting, others not. And in their hands the cars and airplanes that connect families and businesses become human guided missiles.

Globalization—including its darker potential—is a fact, not a policy option for the United States or anyone else. How we respond to it, though, is a matter of policy. Choices made will help determine whether people profit or find poverty, whether cleavages within and between societies will be ameliorated or exacerbated, and whether new opportunities will be seized or missed. The future of international relations will be shaped to a large extent by how the bright and dark sides of globalization interact and how nations and peoples respond.

Democracy's Future

In addition to globalization, the democratic wave that swept the world over the past thirty years is the second major factor shaping today's international environment. The twentieth century ended with the most democracies in history—119 of 192 countries. The spread of democratic institutions in turn has promoted fundamental democratic values such as freedom of the press and expression, the rule of law and equality before the law, respect for private property rights, and a dynamic civil society. Experience proves that individual liberty, free markets, good governance, and international peace are interconnected and mutually reinforcing. In many places, however, democracy has not yet grown deep roots. It remains vulnerable to disappointment and backlash if it does not steadily provide tangible material gains. Too often, we have seen that the precedent of one fair election can be easily overcome in countries lacking a robust democratic political culture and civil society. Tyranny, corruption, and intolerance, in turn, impoverish peoples, corrode civil society, and undermine the foundations for international stability. Furthermore, the very presence of democratic institutions and values can be seen as a threat by some established social and political orders. Democracy will continue to be opposed and besieged by those that it threatens. We saw this clearly in the intolerant, oppressive rule of the Taliban in Afghanistan and its alliance of aggression with the al-Qaida network.

Recasting Security

The changing nature of security and how we achieve it is the third basic factor defining the international context for our foreign policy. The terrorist attacks of September 11th and our ongoing campaign against terrorism highlight this reality. Our adversaries will not only be nation-states, but, as exemplified by the al-Qaida network, increasingly potent and ambitious non-state actors as well. They are also quick studies; they have undoubtedly learned from our operations in Afghanistan that the United States has both the will and the unmatched military wherewithal to destroy any conventional military threat to our security. But this overall conventional dominance will stimulate potential adversaries to develop so-called asymmetrical doctrines and capabilities tailored to deter or neutralize US intervention or inflict massive damage on the homefront. As part of this trend, countering the threats posed by cyber attacks and the proliferation and possible use of weapons of mass destruction will become increasingly important. These are threats of today, not some distant future: We have already suffered attacks with anthrax and foiled at least one "dirty bomb" plot. As new, expansive notions of "homeland security" attest, traditional conceptions of security are being reconsidered and the boundaries between "foreign" and "domestic" are increasingly blurred. The lines between intelligence, law enforcement, and military operations also promise to be less clear than in the past. The implications of these changes are testing the security structures—both domestic and international—inherited from the past century. One of the greatest challenges ahead, therefore, will be to devise and construct a security architecture appropriate for this age's transnational threats.

Relations with the Major Powers

This last observation leads naturally to the fourth factor shaping the international environment, namely the future development of our alliances and relations with the other major powers. Our core alliances will be critical to our future success just as they have been in the past. In the aftermath of the September 11th attacks, we have reaped the rewards of the investments made in our major alliances over the past 50 years. Witness NATO's unprecedented invocation of Article V of the NATO Treaty, Australia's invocation of Article IV of the ANZUS Treaty, and how both have matched words with deeds. Europeans and Australians have shed their blood alongside us during the Afghanistan campaign. There is also Japan's historic support for the campaign against terrorism. And consider our Western Hemispheric neighbours' invocation of the Rio Treaty and their commitment to combat terrorism in our backyard embodied in the Organization of American States' new Inter-American Convention Against Terrorism, adopted in June 2002. But these alliances cannot be taken for granted. The challenges of this new era are not those of the Cold War; the threat posed by bin Laden and his ilk is fundamentally different from that posed by Stalin and his. Our core alliances, therefore, must evolve to meet the demands of this new era or they risk falling into irrelevance.

At the same time, as we have seen dramatically since the horrific events of September 11th, we now have the opportunity to recast our relationships with many nations, including Russia, China, and India. The cooperation forged in the war against terrorism highlights how our future relations with these three major powers do not need to be shackled by the memories of past animosities or prickly relations. Indeed, it is not too much to say that we have never had better relations with all three countries at the same time. Today we do not see a serious danger of a war between any of the great powers. We should never forget what a remarkable change this is. The twentieth century was defined by struggles of power politics among the world's major nations. When the balance of power broke down, it gave us two world wars. When it held, it gave us a cold war. The true "peace dividend" of this era is our ability to turn our efforts from containment and confrontation to cooperation. Ensuring that this historic development becomes a lasting feature of our world will be a major challenge facing American policymakers.

A More Integrated World

Considering these five fundamentals together, we see that American foreign policy is at an historic turning point. As exemplified by the threat of international terrorism, in the post-9/11 world transnational challenges will be on a par with—and sometimes even more important than—traditional security considerations. American foreign policy is being reoriented to cope with the complexities of this era defined by the intersection of traditional and transnational security concerns. The best way to describe this new approach is as a process of integration in which the United States seeks to include other countries, organizations, and peoples into arrangements that will sustain a world consistent with interests and values embraced by the United States and many other governments and peoples, thereby promoting peace, prosperity, and justice as widely as possible. Integration of new partners into our efforts will help us with the traditional challenges of maintaining peace in divided regions as well as with transnational threats such as international terrorism, the proliferation of weapons of mass destruction, and the spread of infectious disease. It will also help us seize the opportunities of this era, including bringing into the globalized world those who have previously been left out.

We are doing this by persuading more and more governments and—on a broader level—people to sign on to certain key ideas as to how the world should operate for mutual benefit. Integration is about bringing nations together and then building frameworks for cooperation and, where feasible, institutions that reinforce and sustain such frameworks. We see this process of integration unfolding in the war against terrorism, where we are establishing both new norms and new frameworks for cooperation in the fight against a common foe. With American leadership, for instance, the United Nations Security Council unanimously adopted Resolution 1373 requiring all UN members to freeze terrorist financing, improve border security, clamp down on the recruitment of terrorists, share information, and deny terrorists any support or safe haven. Meanwhile, we have expanded our cooperation with countries and organizations around the world to make sure that these obligations are met. While much work remains, we have begun weaving a new international fabric that will help protect us from the worst elements of this era.

From Global to Local

While it is imperative to have an overarching policy framework that comprehends the fundamental factors shaping our world, in practice, foreign policy typically is local. In other words, foreign policy is not designed to deal with different forces separately or on a global scale, but rather with how they come together and interact to create concrete problems or opportunities in specific regions and countries. We see this in our global campaign against terrorism, where the campaign really comprises a series of coordinated but nonetheless distinct operations taking place simultaneously on many fronts—diplomatic, economic, intelligence, law enforcement, and military. Accordingly, I would like to suggest briefly, moving region by region, what basic questions US policymakers will need to have answered in the years ahead.

We should start with our neighborhood, the Western Hemisphere. With our two most important trading partners lying to our north and south, the Western Hemisphere's importance to our economic well-being is obvious. But our regional neighborhood's importance can be captured another way: imagine for a moment the impact on the United States and on US foreign policy if we confronted a hemisphere that was a cauldron of instability. Just remember how demanding the task of coping with instability in one small Caribbean country—Haiti—has been over the past decade. The health of our hemisphere is therefore both essential to our domestic well-being and a prerequisite for action abroad.

Here we have seen the promise of economic integration in NAFTA, along with the remarkable success of democracy as demonstrated by the recent elections in Mexico, Peru, and Nicaragua. But we are also witnessing in the northern Andes, as well as in parts of Central America and the Caribbean, how the dark side of globalization can threaten democratic rule, increase uncontrolled immigration, and multiply the spread of illegal drugs and terrorist-criminal syndicates. Argentina's and Brazil's economic woes might spread economic contagion and, equally important, undermine faith in economic openness—the so-called "Washington consensus"—as the best route to prosperity and freedom. Confidence in basic institutions seems to be faltering in the midst of the current economic slowdown throughout the region. What will come of an increasingly divided Venezuela? Will Colombia be the exception or the trendsetter for the region? Wither Argentina and the commitment to the "Washington consensus?" What will it take for us to complete negotiation of the Free Trade Area of the Americas agreement and solidify market economies from Chile to Canada? And what new security architecture will be needed to help preserve the peace in this hemisphere?

Looking to our traditional allies in Europe and Japan, we see a different set of challenges. On a daily basis we see evidence of both Europe and Japan acting more assertively in the international arena. On the other hand, both face significant institutional challenges that could preoccupy them—Europe in its deepening and expanding the European Union, and Japan in its need for basic political and economic reform. Europe and Japan also have to confront the aging of their populations with its wide-ranging implications. How will the interaction of these forces affect our alliance relations with Europe and Japan, and their ability to act on the world stage? Will they become content in their prosperity and look increasingly inward, as the Dutch did after the seventeenth century? Or will we be able to adapt existing institutions like NATO and forge new partnerships designed to look outward, and thereby face together both the transnational challenges and opportunities of this era and such traditional security challenges as working to bring peace and stability to the Middle East and the Korean Peninsula?

Russia has weathered the recent global economic slowdown better than most and it now has a measure of domestic stability. However, the economic, political, social, demographic, and environmental legacies of seventy years of communist rule risk shackling Russia to its past well into the twenty-first century. Since September 11th, we have made great strides in redefining our relationship, as evidenced by our cooperation in the war against terrorism, Russia's willingness to countenance a US military presence in the Caucasus and Central Asia, the Treaty of Moscow, and the creation of the NATO-Russia Council in May 2002. But can we capitalize on this momentum and make it self-sustaining? Will Russia be able to integrate itself successfully into the international order—for instance, by joining the World Trade Organization—and thereby fundamentally alter the trajectory of its development? Will Russia's demographic, economic, and geopolitical decline be reversed or is it systemic?

China and India count among their citizens one out of every three people on the face of the earth. They will, therefore, inevitably have much to say about the future of humanity. China and India face similar challenges. Both are vast multi-ethnic countries conscious of their own rich history; both are searching for international status commensurate with their size. They are rising powers, who have experienced remarkable economic growth as they have opened their economies. In both cases, the war against terrorism has offered new forms of cooperation with the United States and the international community. At the same time, their development has been uneven, with some regions falling significantly behind those better integrated into the globalized economic order. And both populations' shear size will continue to strain their environment as well as the capacities of state institutions. How will India and China manage their future development internally and internationally? Will they integrate themselves more fully into the globalized international system and expand cooperation with others to confront this era's distinctive transnational challenges? In answering this question, one must also take into account the basic differences in China's and India's situations, both internal and international. India is an established, vibrant, multiparty democracy whose openness promises to smooth its development. The Chinese leadership to date has attempted to promote development through economic freedom without corresponding political reform. Will the new generation of Chinese leaders continue to be able to square this circle or will they have to slow economic development to avoid real political reform? On the other hand, unlike China, India faces the immediate risk of military conflict with a neighbour, Pakistan. In the coming years, therefore, India is much more likely to be distracted from both internal development and a broader international agenda by the prospects of and preparations for war. So, while China's relationship with Taiwan must be managed, a more immediate question is how the conflict between nuclear-armed India and Pakistan can be stabilized and moved toward de-escalation, if not resolution.

Finally, in Africa, the Middle East, the Persian Gulf, and Central Asia, states often lack robust civil societies, democratic institutions, and integration into the global order. At the same time, they confront demographic shocks posed by urbanization, youth bulges, and, especially in the case of Sub-Saharan Africa, the devastating HIV/AIDS pandemic. Their economic development is often times limited by dependence upon the exploitation of natural resources. The continued importance of fossil fuels and other natural resources to the international economy ensures the strategic significance of these regions. Countries in these regions will remain the most vulnerable to collapse of central state authority, criminal and political violence, and recruitment for terrorist activities. How can the states of these regions withstand the challenges of globalization and integrate themselves into the international order? How can we, along with our partners, encourage them to move toward better governance, prosperity, and stability? What will be the implications of their possible failure?

Current Challenges of Assessment

We will not attempt to answer these questions. I will leave that to the members of the Intelligence Community. We want to highlight, however, that these questions share a common character. They do not centre upon predicting certain events, such as the onset of a financial crisis, a country's negotiating position, or a surprise attack. Nor do they centre upon identifying and detailing certain trends, like the rate of China's GNP growth or the epidemiology of HIV/AIDS. Answering such questions will continue to be critical, especially for the formulation of our foreign policy at the more tactical level of planning specific military operations, conducting negotiations, or preventing terrorist attacks. No one doubts, for example, that the preeminent concern of our Intelligence Community is helping to prevent another September 11th. Yet the broader, strategic questions of the sort outlined above tend to centre upon the complex dynamics of how different factors—traditional and transnational—interact. The Intelligence Community, therefore, must come to grips with these complexities, and communicate them in a way to "assist action," even as it continues to provide policymakers with the more tactical intelligence they demand.

The Intelligence Community will not fulfil its responsibilities if its efforts stop with simply the identification and analysis of these complex dynamics on a national, regional, and global scale. Policymakers need to comprehend not only these dynamics, but also how others will see—or not see—them, and how they may act in light of them. This demands a fine-tuned understanding of the relevant actors, their organizations, and their decisionmaking processes and capabilities. As Ernest May argues in his classic Knowing One's Enemies, this sort of assessment in the first half of the twentieth century focused on nation-states' military and material capabilities and the decisionmaking proclivities of their leadership. Assessment became more difficult between the two world wars in proportion to the growth in the size and complexity of the government apparatus of the major powers, the replacement of homogeneous ruling classes with more diverse leaders, and the increase in relevant information to analyse. Against this historical backdrop, we can easily see how the task confronting intelligence analysts at the dawn of the twenty-first century is more demanding than only a few decades ago. With the end of the Cold War, and the lack of a great power as a military adversary, we find ourselves needing to better understand not just possible opponents, but also the thinking and likely behaviour of friends, neutrals, and potential partners across a full spectrum of issues. Furthermore, assessments can no longer focus primarily upon governments, but must also include non-state actors of all stripes, whether Médecin Sans Frontières, CNN, IBM, or al-Qaida. The structure and leadership of these organizations can be even more difficult to analyse than national governments' decisionmaking processes. Finally, the volume and flow of potentially relevant information has increased seemingly at an exponential rate.

Producing Results

This brings me to my final point. Robert Bowie often said that the purpose of our work in government "is not merely to produce literature, but to produce results." The Intelligence Community produces good literature, but in order to produce results, analysts have to get much closer to the policymakers. This is not so much a matter of bureaucratic structure or organization as it is of practice and professional culture. We appreciate the tradition in the Intelligence Community that insists that analysis should be insulated from policymaking in order to prevent politicization. But, in my experience, an even greater danger to intelligence analysis is irrelevancy. The Intelligence Community's product can be less relevant than it should be because analysts do not understand what is really on the policymaker's mind, so they address the wrong questions— or, when they have the right questions, their intelligence fails to have the impact that it should because their answers do not reach the policymaker in a timely fashion or digestible form.

In order to help produce results in our foreign policy, therefore, intelligence analysts must overcome at least some of their scruples and organizational culture. Analysts must constantly, persistently, and, if need be, annoyingly press to get close to policymakers and peer over their shoulders to see what is on their agenda. And when they see that something critical is missing from that agenda—when policymakers are neglecting an issue that analysts know to be relevant and significant—then analysts must impress upon policymakers why they should pay attention to it. This is especially true with analyses having a long-term or over-the-horizon focus. Typically, policymakers have a hard time seeing how their current decisions relate to longer-term developments, so they tend to ignore or discount the long term. Analysts must help the policymaker avoid this mistake. To produce results, their analyses of the sort of complex, long-term questions suggested here must connect the dots, pointing out to the policymaker why and how long-term trends and their dynamics matter—and why and how what he or she does today can shape these developments.

Intelligence analysts should also resist allowing fears of losing influence with a policymaker lead them to check their analytic swing. If analysts do not use their access to give unvarnished assessments for fear of jeopardizing access, then what is the purpose of the access to begin with? Policymakers tend to appreciate timely candor because it is always better to confront an unpleasant development sooner rather than later, if only to have more time to formulate a response to it. Policymakers may vent at insightful messengers bearing unwelcome news, but they rarely kill them because they recognize their value. Finally, intelligence analysts must understand that policymakers usually will not call for them to deliver a message. Since they will not come looking, analysts must go in search of them. As my good friend Bob Blackwill, currently US ambassador to India, once said in this regard, "Take the initiative to establish ties. This is an essential obligation of intelligence managers, because policy officials will rarely seek them out." (This is especially true with transnational issues that do not easily fit into existing bureaucratic or intellectual cubbyholes.) Intelligence analysts must understand that to devote 99 percent of their effort to conducting and writing a study and only 1 percent to marketing it is both foolish and a disservice to policymakers. To produce results, they have to market their work relentlessly. If analysts have something to say, they should not only say it, but press to say it directly to the policymakers most involved in the issue.

There is no denying that this is a tall order. But it is not impossible. There are many successful examples of this sort of collaboration and exchange between intelligence analysts and policymakers. For example, the release of the NIC's report *The Global Infectious Disease Threat* in 2000 helped to transform policymakers' understanding of the issue, and also recast broader policy debates about the nature of national security in this globalized era. More recently, under the leadership of Assistant Secretary Carl Ford, the State Department's Intelligence and Research Bureau (INR) has begun implementing a series of changes in accord with what I am advocating. Borrowing military language, Ford has instituted a "J-2" approach where INR office directors and analysts participate in the daily meetings of the Secretary of State's "regional commanders"— the Department's functional and regional bureaus. INR is thus better able to tailor its analyses to policymakers' questions and judge what policymakers need by way of context and over-the-horizon assessments. INR has also taken the bold step of setting aside its traditional primary intelligence product, the Secretary's Morning Intelligence Summary, in favour of more detailed, in-depth analyses called INR Assessments. I for one can vouch that these new intelligence products constitute a considerable step forward. But more needs to be done throughout the Intelligence Community.

In closing, I want to suggest a rule of thumb that all intelligence analysts should try to follow. I call it the "Riedel Rule" after Bruce Riedel, a CIA analyst with whom I worked during the first Bush administration. Bruce once told me that he did not feel he was doing the job of marketing his analyses unless he got at least two parking tickets in downtown Washington a month. In this era, the Intelligence Community has to be earning more parking tickets. This may be bad for the wallet of individual analysts, but good for their relationship with policymakers in this post-9/11 world.

2

Principles and Objectives of India's Foreign Policy

The Making of Indian Foreign Policy: The Role of Scholarship and Public Opinion

In the older democracies the mechanisms for forging 'elite consensus' on foreign policy and the role of the mass media have come in for some trenchant criticism. It is not our purpose to join that debate on the alleged manipulative nature of elite consensus within a democracy. This chapter merely assumes that elite consensus is critical for the conduct of state business in democracies and informal mechanisms do exist in most of them to shape and reshape national consensus on a range of issues, including foreign policy. The chapter also believes that reformulating domestic consensus is especially important in periods of structural change at home or in the international system. There are some studies that help understand changing domestic consensus on foreign policy in the United States.

Given the absence of similar studies in India, this chapter relies, to a large extent, on the author's own last three decades of experience navigating between think tanks, the media and the academia that focused on studies of foreign policy, national security and international relations. The chapter concludes that it is difficult to discern the existence of such a 'permanent establishment' in India shaping the nation's foreign policy. What may exist instead is an informal network that is led by a small but shifting group of activists within and outside the government. In the following sections, the chapter lays out the reasons for the absence of a significant permanent establishment and the prospects for one emerging in the near future, especially in the context of India's increasing weight in the international system and its emerging self-perception as a great power.

The Elusive Domestic Foreign Policy Consensus

The very existence of a credible foreign policy establishment presupposes a degree of agreement within the elite on the core objectives of external engagement and a grand strategy to achieve them. I would argue that there never was such a consensus in modern India on the ends and means of its foreign policy. The author would suggest that this is one of the principal reasons for the absence of a permanent establishment that can mediate between decision makers, experts and the public at large. To be sure, there is the widespread belief within India and those outside who study its external relations that there was once a golden age of 'Nehruvian consensus' on foreign policy. That assertion might say something about the contemporary political contestations but reveals little about India's foreign policy history. As a charismatic and domineering political figure, Jawaharlal Nehru did have his way on defining the foreign policy of India in the early years of the Republic. That does not in any way imply there was a national consensus. During 1959-62, Nehru found himself utterly isolated when matters turned difficult with China, large sections of his own party and public opinion turned hostile, and bureaucratic structures came under stress.

A dispassionate look at India's foreign policy record might suggest that there was no national consensus either before or after independence. Throughout the 20th century, the Indian political elite was at odds with itself on characterising the nature of external environment, setting a list of priorities, understanding the shifting dynamic among the great powers, defining a hierarchy of external threats, and identifying friends and enemies. The differences on how to address the grievances of the Muslims in the subcontinent and their relationship with the larger Islamic community have always been profound and continue to hobble India. Some writers have argued that the worldview of the Indian National Congress and the Muslim League were fundamentally divergent. Indian attitudes to the developments in the Middle East at the turn of the 20th century and the wisdom of the *Khilafat* movement.

The massive expansion of the Indian armed forces to serve the British in the two world wars generated profound divisions within the Indian national movement about the appropriateness of their use abroad. So did the creation of the Indian National Army by Subhas Chandra Bose and his alignment with Japanese fascism in the Second World War. There were a range of other issues that were controversial, including the broader question of India's attitude to great power relations.

These are just a few illustrative differences. The absence of a consensus within the national movement on these issues had a huge impact on the nature of the post-Partition territorial arrangements, the dynamics of war and peace in the subcontinent, and India's relationship with the Great Powers.

In the post-independence period, many of India's diplomatic initiatives and ideas that were later seen as representing the very essence of India's foreign policy did not come through a pre-existing national consensus. They were products of the existence of a strong leader like Nehru and his very definitive world view. In the 1950s the Indian communists, who later became a great champion of 'Nehruvian' consensus, rejected the principle of 'nonalignment' as 'immoral' neutrality between 'good' and 'evil'.

For them, Nehru was a 'running dog' of imperialists. It would take them three full decades before recognising the 'anti-imperialist' content of India's nonalignment. The conservatives in the Congress Party, many socialists, and the Hindu nationalists, on the other hand, saw nonalignment as part of Nehru's appeasement of international communism.

Nehru's decisions to take the Kashmir question to the United Nations Security Council, join the British Commonwealth, reticence on the Soviet intervention in Hungary, and the emphasis on nuclear arms control rather than decolonisation at the first summit of the non-aligned movement were among the many controversies that led to deep national divisions on foreign policy during the Nehru years. Nothing, however, reveals the sharpness of those divisions and exposes the current myth that Nehru's policy was more 'anti-imperialist' than the controversies over his policy towards China.

The vigorous national contestations of Nehru's positions on the two core territorial issues of independent India – the Kashmir dispute with Pakistan and the boundary dispute with China – makes one wonder what the 'Nehruvian consensus' was all about. My objective here is not to go into the merits or demerits of Nehru's world view or his stewardship of India's foreign policy. It is to simply note the profound differences within India in the early years of its interaction with the world and its management of relations with its neighbours.

Nehru's successors too had to constantly innovate on the diplomatic front and risk domestic opposition; they did not have the luxury of a pre-existing national consensus on foreign policy to guide them at any of their many critical moments. Indira Gandhi's reluctance to criticise Moscow for snuffing out the Prague Spring in 1968 resulted in the resignation of a cabinet minister, Ashok Mehta. Her decision to sign a security treaty with the Soviet Union in 1971 was derided by many centrist scholars in India as a departure from a 'strict' interpretation of nonalignment.

The treaty was not the product of public discourse, scholarly input, and rigorous political scrutiny. It was a foreign policy coup, a brilliant one at that, presented to the nation as a *fait accompli* at a crucial moment in the effort to liberate East Pakistan. Until as late as the 1977 general elections, the Janata Party, which brought together the entire opposition to Indira Gandhi, was suspicious of the 'secret provisions' in the Indo-Soviet treaty and promised to restore what it called 'genuine nonalignment'.

Mrs Gandhi's decision to test a nuclear device in 1974, Foreign Minister Atal Bihari Vajpayee's outreach to Israel during 1977, his visit to China in 1978, Rajiv Gandhi's reversal of India's positions on the border dispute with China (1988), Inder Kumar Gujral's good neighbourly policy (1996-98), Prime Minister Vajpayee's nuclear tests in 1998, and Prime Minister Manmohan Singh's civil nuclear initiative with the United States in 2005 were all foreign policy issues that deeply divided the political classes in India. None of those decisions emerged out of debates within the foreign policy community or stayed within the boundaries of a presumed mainstream national discourse on foreign policy. In most of these cases, broad based support for these decisions emerged only over an extended period of time. As argued by K. Subrahmanyam, "Indian foreign policy was always a leadership function and more often than not did not command a consensus. Nonalignment as a strategy (to be distinguished from nonalignment as an ideology with which Nehru had hardly anything to do), development of close relations with the Union of Soviet Socialist Republics, nuclear tests, strategic weapons programme, economic liberalisation and globalization and the strategy of the balance of power were all initiatives of leaders – Nehru, Indira, Rajiv, Narashima Rao, Vajpayee and now Dr. Singh. Such initiatives, when they prove successful, become established national policies."

The International Relations Community's Conformist Trap

The absence of an enduring domestic consensus on independent India's foreign policy was not surprising given the extraordinary diversity of the nation and the multiple intellectual strands that went into the making of its national movement. India's consciousness of international affairs and the relevance for its own independence began to grow rapidly after the First World War. But the breadth and depth of the interest, however, would remain limited. Only a few among the leaders of the national movement took consistent interest in international affairs and reflected on how India should react or take advantage of them. This trend line inevitably extended itself into the post-independence period, when Nehru had virtually a free hand in shaping new India's foreign policy. During the early years of independence, there were enough towering personalities with strong views within and outside the government who would question and criticise Nehru's approach to the world. It was inevitable though that debates on foreign policy would eventually conform to the broader political fault lines within the nation. As communists, socialists, conservatives, and a variety of regional formations unveiled their own separate attacks on Nehru's foreign policy, the discourse resonated among their supporters and sympathisers among the intellectual classes, the media and the academia. These criticisms were not always consequential in political terms, given the Congress party's dominance of the political system. They nevertheless provided an intellectual atmosphere in the 1950s that was open and vibrant.

The 1950s saw the attempt to structure a loose but foreign policy establishment that sought to bring together public intellectuals, bureaucrats, professionals, businessmen, scholars and journalists under the rubric of the Indian Council of World Affairs in New Delhi. Nehru took an active interest in promoting what we might now call a civil society initiative. The Institute of Current World Affairs (ICWA) was soon complemented by the establishment of a School of International Studies across the road. The school that was eventually merged into the Jawaharlal Nehru University in New Delhi would become the main source of international scholarship over the next few decades.

In the mid-1960s, the Institute of Defence Studies and Analyses (IDSA), designed as an autonomous institution funded by the Ministry of Defence was co-located with the ICWA and the School of International Studies.

New Delhi's India International Centre and its 'Saturday Club' provided a forum for the movers and shakers of the 'system' to thrash out a range of issues, including national security and foreign policy. Together they offered a nucleus around which a strong and influential community of international relations professionals might have been built. The discourse on international affairs was not limited to Delhi, Calcutta, Bombay, Madras, Allahabad, Jaipur were all important centres of research and publication activity. The major national newspapers published across the nation took great interest in world affairs. The Indian elite was plugged into the international relations community around the world, published in international journals, and hosted research scholars from abroad. Given New Delhi's relative openness to both the East and West during the Nehru years, India became the biggest arena for competing ideological propaganda unleashed by Washington and Moscow. Whether it was effective or not, it added to the extraordinary dynamism of India's intellectual debate during the 1950s and 1960s.

India's public square began to lose some of its vitality and diversity from the late 1960s and down went the project of building a credible international relations community. As Indira Gandhi drifted towards left wing populism at home, moved closer towards the Soviet Union, and sharpened the rhetoric of third worldism, the domestic political discourse on foreign policy began to acquire a monochromatic hue. The biggest victim of this has been academia, especially its humanities divisions. The international relations community, given the close proximity of its subject to the conduct of national diplomacy, suffered even more. The hegemony of the pseudo-left radicalism over the media and the academia actively promoted by the Congress Party in the 1970s snuffed out much of intellectual dissent, both liberal and conservative. The centralisation of the academia in the 1970s disempowered the older centres of foreign policy discourse in the regions. Once 'politically correct' priorities were identified, resources from the central government flew to such approved destinations as Soviet studies, resulting in the utter neglect of American and Chinese studies. The deep suspicion of the United States that took root in the 1970s steadily strangulated the channels of discourse between the Indian international relations community and its counterparts in the West. As India turned its back on Asia in preference for the non-aligned stage, the academic and other contacts in Asia too dried up. The difficult relations with China and Pakistan also meant that the studies of India's neighbourhood got steadily eroded across the nation.

This sweeping damage to the community was compounded by a powerful new imperative of conformism that paralysed international studies and much of the humanities research across the nation. The only source of funding for research, conferences and travel were centralised government institutions, the University Grants Commission and the Indian Council of Social Science Research. Although there was space for independent research and critical studies of Indian foreign policy, there was no incentive in the academia or the media for such an approach. Criticism or original ideas largely came from political forces and journals on the margins rather than mainstream academic institutions. It is not that either Indira Gandhi or Rajiv Gandhi preferred a disempowered international relations community. In her second term, Mrs Gandhi was looking to break out of the ideological rigidities of the 1970s that were constraining Indian diplomacy. Rajiv Gandhi chose to depart from every presumed canon of the famed 'Nehruvian' consensus – on India's relations with the United States, China, Pakistan and Israel as well as on nuclear weapons policy, to name a few. Neither the contemporary media accounts nor the later academic analyses have fully explored the bold foreign policy innovations under Rajiv Gandhi. When the Congress governments in the 1980s were looking for new ideas on foreign policy in order to end India's growing marginalisation, the conformist academic and media communities were of no great help. They were good as cheerleaders for their preferred political leaders; but not as generators of new ideas or new stratagems for the conduct of foreign policy.

The one exception to the deadening conformism of the 1970s and the 1980s was the IDSA. (Disclosure: the author was on the IDSA staff from 1983-92) In one of the paradoxes of the Indian international relations story, the one bureaucrat who drifted into international relations research and stayed with it, Subrahmanyam was prepared to defy the presumed limits on the foreign policy discourse. As a consequence, the IDSA, under his leadership, was able to launch a national debate on nuclear policy at a time when the subject seemed so forbidding. For the next few decades, the IDSA would be at the forefront of the nuclear discourse in India.

Under the leadership of Subrahmanyam, the IDSA also focused the elite's attention onto the security politics of the Indian Ocean after the British withdrawal from the East of Suez, and made the case for an interest-based foreign policy, but also as a tool to mobilise pressure on the politicians and bureaucrats deciding foreign and national security affairs.

In the 1980s, the IDSA was home to feverish activity by a small group led by Subrahmanyam that tried to simulate the activity of a full-blown foreign policy establishment. Writing foreign policy speeches for political leaders from the government and the opposition, developing public advocacy, running open media campaigns against certain decisions of the government, sending policy briefs on emerging issues to the highest levels of government, rationalising the government's diplomatic decisions, explaining Indian policies to international audiences, drawing in serving bureaucrats and soldiers to spend time researching at the IDSA, deputing IDSA staff to the Foreign Office and the news agencies, and bombarding the media with articles and features were some of the IDSA's many activities. There was no way that the intensity and depth of this campaign could be sustained by any organisation. The IDSA under Subrahmanyam, however, demonstrated the possibilities of constructing a permanent foreign policy establishment that did not owe its loyalty to any particular party or leader, was not tied down to one particular department or ministry in the government, was neither pro-West nor pro-East, neither left nor right, could argue on the basis of national interest, develop policy options without having to access governmental information, bring together serving and retired bureaucrats, political leaders, senior editors, reporters and businessmen, and create facilities for any one to develop the skill for gathering open source intelligence.

The Changing Institutional Balance

When Subrahmanyam started writing for newspapers as the director of IDSA in the 1960s, there was barely concealed condescension from the traditional international relations community. The prevailing view was that 'serious scholars don't write in newspapers'. While the Indian academic attitudes towards media might not have changed significantly over the last four decades, the power of the public forum has dramatically increased in the intervening period. As the Indian democracy matured, the media began to acquire greater visibility if not influence on policy making. The area of foreign and national security policies was no longer immune to the impact of the media.

One of the unintended consequences of Indira Gandhi's short-lived Emergency Rule during 1975-77 was a palpable increase in the power of the print media and its new self-assurance. That the rulers of Delhi could be overthrown in elections helped generate a more equal two-way relationship between the print media and the government.

If the 1980s saw the steady accretion of the print media's power in the country, there has been a dramatic surge in the power of the private electronic media since the late 1990s. This in turn has had a significant impact on the national security and foreign policy discourse within India. That the Indian media could be treated as a hand maiden of the foreign office bureaucracy was a commonly held view within the South Block.

This perception might have been valid when a small but docile group of foreign office 'beat' correspondents would deferentially take dictation from mid-level bureaucrats in the foreign office. Those days, however, are long gone, as a number of factors have altered the equations between media and the officialdom. The class background, educational qualifications, and the pay of the media personnel has dramatically evolved during the 1990s, and they no longer have a reason to acknowledge the presumed superiority of the officer class, nor are the new generation of journalists dependent on a variety of favours dispensed by the state machinery. The media's access to political leaders within and outside the government has become closer over the years and many journalists themselves have effortlessly moved into political parties and the parliament. The tabloidisation of the media meant it is constantly on the lookout for juicy human interest stories about the foreign office and the rest of the bureaucratic system; it could make or break personal reputations of senior officers. From being a one-sided relationship, the media-foreign office relationship is a two-way street of mutual give and take. Even more significant was the weakening of New Delhi's power structures after 1989. The replacement of one party or one family rule by weak coalition governments meant the political classes were less domineering and more eager to please the media. Just as a host of other institutions, including the judiciary and the election commission to name a few, asserted themselves in the last two decades, the fragmentation of political power in the centre strengthened the media's clout. If the politicians needed good press, the bureaucrats were quick to adapt in the 1990s as they sought to leverage the press for their own individual advance or in winning policy battles within the government. The media scene in Delhi began to resemble that in Washington, where different sections of bureaucracy routinely leak information on a selective basis to shape public opinion.

Weak governments and strong media meant the press and television could whip up popular passion and utterly complicate the functioning of the government in such crisis situations as the hijacking of the Indian airliner IC814 at the end of 1999. Even more significant was the fact that focused arguments in a section of the Indian English media turned the Indian government from an active supporter of the international negotiations on the Comprehensive Test Ban Treaty (CTBT) during 1993-95 into a ferocious opponent during 1995-96. Central to this turnaround was the massive mobilisation of the nationalist sentiment against the CTBT in India in a short period of time.

Since the turn of the millennium, the media has become the principal theatre for intellectual and policy contestation on the direction of Indian foreign policy. This was most visible in the passionate discourse on the Indo-US civil nuclear initiative that saw the left parties withdraw support from the Singh government, which in turn had to go to the floor of the parliament to demonstrate majority support in July 2008 different sections of the media root for different directions of change, the media does not simply neutralise itself; it has become a potential brake on new initiatives as well as a facilitator of new moves by the government. This in turn has put a new premium on the political classes and the security establishment reaching out to the media and leveraging its influence.

The media is not the only new actor shaping India's foreign policy in the last two decades. As India moved towards a state-led socialist economic path, its business community too became marginal to the foreign policy of the nation. Although businessmen were occasionally employed for specific diplomatic purposes, Mrs. Gandhi used the Hindujas to reach out to the Shah's Iran in the 1970s. Similarly, Vajpayee tapped the Hindujas to reach out to the British Prime Minister Tony Blair in the wake of Pokharan nuclear tests of May 1998. The objective was to soften the reaction within the G-8 that Britain was chairing and facilitating meetings between the National Security Adviser Brajesh Mishra and top officials of the Western nations. Since the launch of the economic reforms, the business community has become an important influence in shaping relations with other nations as well as influencing the domestic public opinion and media on a range of political issues including those on foreign policy.

Large individual business houses like the Tatas and Ambanis, as well as business associations like the Confederation of Indian Industry (CII) and the Federation of Indian Chambers of Commerce and Industry (FICCI) have become recognisably important in diplomacy as well as national discourse on foreign policy. The British businessman, Laxmi Mittal was tapped by New Delhi in this decade to facilitate India's search for equity oil around the world, especially in Central Asia. During his visits abroad, it has become customary for the Prime Minister to take with him large business delegations. Joint forums of Chief Executive Officers have become an important vehicle for moving crucial bilateral relations forward and pressure points for internal bureaucratic change. Given the weakness of the universities and the think tanks, the CII and FICCI have also appropriated some of their functions, for example developing Track Two and Track One and a Half dialogues and often acting as think tanks on specific policy issues. Some of these initiatives did become rather consequential. Initiated in early 2002, the CII-Aspen Indo-US strategic Dialogue has met every six months, brought together influential voices in both countries and cleared the ground for major new bilateral initiatives. One of its rounds in Jaipur in early 2005 helped generate a mutually acceptable framework for resuming civil nuclear cooperation. The essence of this understanding was reflected a few months later in the Bush-Singh nuclear deal. While some see this as a positive development, others see it negatively.

The new forces shaping public opinion and influencing foreign policy are not limited to the national theatre. There is no doubt that different regions of India had always had some influence on the nation's foreign policy towards some of the neighbouring and ethnically kindred countries. The influence of Tamil Nadu politics on India's policy towards Sri Lanka is well known influences on the making of foreign policy, traditionally a 'national endeavour', have steadily increased during the last two years thanks to the emergence of coalition rule at the centre, in which regional parties have become critical components. This 'municipalisation' of foreign policy, interestingly, has not always led to the 'regional' prevailing over the 'national', as the local forces acquired high stakes in federal power structures. Nevertheless, the growing impact of local interests on India's foreign policy in recent years could be seen as the successful result of a campaign of the Sikkim government in New Delhi to open up trade with Tibet. Equally important has been the growing contact between the chief ministers of the two Punjabs across the Radcliffe line and the attempt to promote the shared cultural identity of 'Panjabiyat'.

Among the other forces that have emerged in recent years has been the military. After years of enduring the jack-boots of civilian control, the armed forces have begun to find their voice on national security. Organisations such as the United Services Institute have been revived, many retired members of the armed forces are now a regular fixture in the public discourse and have joined political parties. All three Indian services have now established their own think tanks that have begun to develop capabilities for research on foreign and national security issues and intervene in the public debates. Equally important has been the rise of what might be called the Track Three that has sought to mobilise activist groups across the nation on critical foreign policy issues. Unlike the Track Two process that involves experts and retired diplomats and soldiers, Track Three reaches out into the wider civil society and has been fairly effective in making points on war and peace issues in the region. Civil society leaders like Nirmala Deshpande, not generally known to take an interest in foreign affairs, played a key role in promoting Indo-Pak dialogue and reconciliation in the post Kargil phase.

Meanwhile, the strongest force in the making of Indian foreign policy, the bureaucracy, has had to adapt to the rising power and influence of the new institutions. In all those democracies that feature a permanent bureaucracy, universities and think tanks tended to be relatively less important in shaping foreign policy. In Britain and France, small collegial bureaucratic elites have dominated the making of foreign policy and selling it to the political classes as well as the public. The absence of such a bureaucracy in Washington and the ease of moving in and out of government have allowed the emergence of a wide and deep foreign policy establishment in the United States. It was but natural that the Indian model would look a lot similar to that of Britain and France in this respect. Given the extraordinary task of managing a large and diverse country, the weight of the permanent bureaucracy in making national security policies seemed to steadily increase. The Indian Foreign Service did inherit some of the finest traditions of its precursor, the Indian Political Service.

Many of the early civil servants retiring from the Foreign Service made their reputation as scholars and publicists profoundly influencing the national discourse on foreign policy. The writings of Sardar K. M. Panikkar and K. P. S. Menon Sr. readily come to mind. With his prolific writing after his retirement in the early 1990s, J. N. Dixit seemed to carry on that tradition until his death in 2005.

When it came to the making of foreign policy, however, the South Block was a closed shop. Thanks to Nehru's leadership of the Ministry of External Affairs in the first years of the Republic and the sustained interest in foreign affairs demonstrated by Indira and Rajiv, the Indian Foreign Service also enjoyed a measure of autonomy from the growing dominance of the Indian Administrative Service. While outside experts made inroads into the economic and technical ministries, the national security ministries remained thoroughly insulated from external 'penetration'. The Indian Foreign Service would not even make room for other services let alone outside experts, even on a temporary basis, into its fold. The monopoly on information on world affairs, and the development of sophisticated cadres in Russian and Chinese affairs reinforced the condescension in South Block that they have little to learn from outsiders. But nearly two decades of globalization, the emphasis on commercial diplomacy, the information revolution, an irreverent print and electronic media, the emergence of Track Two and Track Three formations, and above all the fragmented structure of power in New Delhi have meant the South Block had to cope with a very different template. If the imperative of adjustment has been relentless, not all in the Foreign Office and diplomatic corps have managed to adapt. Those who did have been far more effective in driving Indian foreign policy in new directions.

The Foreign Policy Vanguard

The marginalisation of the international relations scholarship and the underdeveloped potential of the foreign affairs think tanks did not in any way mean that history would stop for India's international relations. Ever since India embarked on the path of globalization nearly two decades ago, New Delhi has found many new opportunities for improving its standing in the regional and global stage. Nor can there be any doubt that Indian diplomacy had demonstrated significant strategic imagination in recent decades. Among the many achievements on the foreign policy front were the Look East policy that was launched in the early 1990s, the post-Pokharan diplomacy that limited the costs of the nation's nuclear defiance in 1998, the negotiation of the civil nuclear initiative with the United States and the mobilisation of international support for it during 2005-08, and the attempts, not entirely successful, to restructure relations with both China and Pakistan. With neither the benefit of distilled academic wisdom nor of an insightful policy road map, India has constantly surprised itself and the world with its capacity for thinking on the run and generating major unexpected breakthroughs. I would argue that this was possible because of the existence of tiny, informal and consequential networks spanning the full spectrum of the Indian elite opinion and acting as the vanguard of India's new foreign policy. Some of the examples below illustrate the impact of this vanguard.

One, a sustained campaign by a handful of columnists in alliance with a few decision-makers forced a significant turn-around in India's official position on the CTBT from a long-standing supporter to a vehement critic during 1994-96. A similar attempt to reverse the governmental position on the CTBT after the nuclear tests of 1998 in order to dampen the nuclear disputes with Washington, however, was unsuccessful. (The author was part of both the campaigns.) If the United States Supreme Court had ruled in favour of Al Gore at the end of 2000, the second campaign, in favour of the CTBT, might have had a longer life. Although the vanguard did not always win, its readiness to walk the roads not previously travelled challenged the conventional thinking and created space for those political leaders who were willing to take risks.

Two, as the foreign minister of India during 1996-97 and Prime Minister during 1997-98, Gujral invested what little political capital he had in redefining India's relations with her neighbours. While he acted out of conviction, his attempt faced fierce resistance within the bureaucracy, the political class and the media. Yet a small section of the foreign office leadership was prepared to flesh out Gujral's convictions into policy. This paid off in settling the Ganges water dispute with Bangladesh. While the criticism of Gujral was indeed vicious, he did get vocal support from a small but influential section of the media. The "Gujral Doctrine' was controversial when it was first unveiled but became the basis for neighbourhood policies of those who followed him – Atal Bihari Vajpayee and Dr. Singh. Realists in the Foreign Office did not take long to recognise the many good uses that the Gujral Doctrine could be put to. That New Delhi must act non-reciprocally towards its neighbours and create stakes for its neighbours in the success of India, in the name of promoting a 'peaceful periphery' has now become the reigning doctrine in the South Block. Foreign policy consensus could always be created in India if a credible new path could be cleared by the vanguard.

Three, on the three most important accounts of Indian foreign policy, Pakistan, China and the United States, the vanguard signalled not only intellectual boldness but also the capacity to persist with lines of action that few scholars either suggested or predicted. Much of the credit for this goes to the political leadership – in two widely different governments – which eagerly explored solutions to the Kashmir dispute with Pakistan, signed onto a new framework for the resolution of the boundary dispute with China, and defied all conventional wisdom in seeking a strategic partnership with the United States.

This could not have been done without the self-assurance of a handful of senior bureaucrats who had to throw out much of what they learnt during the long careers in the Foreign Office in grabbing the new opportunities to resolve India's long-standing strategic problems. The inevitable political risks involved in this policy enterprise could be insured only by a vigorous and credible intellectual defence in the public square – which brought in another element of the vanguard, the opinion-makers. A mere manipulation of the mass media was not possible because all sides of the debate had unlimited access to the public ear. The structuring of a new consensus also demanded an effective alignment of key constituencies like the corporate sector and the neutralisation of powerful voices in the opposition.

Four, the vanguard has also had some impact on the vocabulary and concepts of mainstream foreign policy discourse within the nation. A handful of bureaucrats, speech writers, and journalists have begun to inject concepts and notions that were not part of India's foreign articulation for decades. Although the Foreign Office had become the very repository of cynicism in external affairs, the speeches it wrote for the leaders tended to be full of high principles and normative rhetoric. While balancing was an important element of Indian diplomacy from the very beginning, the concept of 'balance of power' would never figure in the speeches except in its denunciation. During the last few years, we have seen senior officials increasingly referring to balance of power in positive terms, openly acknowledging India's interest in a "multipolar Asia". Similarly, Dr. Singh's speeches began to push 'democracy' as one of the major identities of India in world affairs. We have also seen increasing references to India's 'responsibilities' as a rising power as opposed to the traditional objections to the domination by the rich and powerful. We have seen the Indian emphasis in the nuclear debate shift from vehement denunciations of a discriminatory nonproliferation regime to claims of India's 'impeccable" nonproliferation credentials. Much of the new usage has been promoted by the columnists in the media and found its way into official speeches by ministers.

Beyond a 'Few Good Men'

That a small group of individuals have had extraordinary influence reshaping the national debate on India's new foreign policy in recent years is not in doubt. What is clearly in question is whether the reliance on a vanguard, however clever it might be, is good enough for India. An emerging great power with the potential to shape international relations in the 21 st century surely cannot afford to rely on a narrow and thin base of thinking and decision-making. Although the vanguard's triumph in engineering fundamental changes in India's nuclear policy and transforming its entrenched hostility towards the United States is impressive, the domestic debate on the civil nuclear initiative has also revealed its many limitations. As it seized an opportune moment in 2005 to fast forward Indo-US relations, it inevitably confronted an unprecedented resistance to a foreign policy initiative. The boldness of the political leadership, the creativity of its foreign policy aides, the muscular support from a section of the media, and the clear interest of the business community was not enough to stop the domestic debate on the civil nuclear initiative drifting into the biggest political crisis ever on a foreign policy issue in the nation's history. The murky parliamentary vote of confidence in the Singh government in mid-2008 marked the culmination of a debate that divided all major agencies involved in the formulation of national security policy and the political parties that had to eventually take sides.

Reflecting on how the nuclear initiative was negotiated and implemented, one wonders if a more vibrant international relations community, a better informed media, and a reformed security sector could have helped India avoid spending so much time examining a gift horse in its mouth. A good international relations infrastructure was never going to be enough to convince the Indian communists or persuade the Muslim community of the virtues of a strategic partnership with the United States. Not any amount of sophisticated reasoning would have made it easier for the Department of Atomic Energy to recognise that President Bush might be representing a very different political tendency in the United States to the offensive nonproliferation bureaucracy in Washington they had dealt with for decades. These were political and institutional realities that inevitably paralysed the Congress Party and the Singh government. It was also quite clear that a more widely based foreign policy establishment could not have stopped the Bharatiya Janata Party (BJP) from its absolutely opportunistic opposition to the nuclear deal with the United States that it had initiated. Consider the example of Brajesh Mishra, the powerful national security adviser to Vajpayee who played a key role in the decision to conduct the nuclear tests and in the post-Pokharan negotiations with the international community. His eventual support for the nuclear deal after expressing initial reservations revealed two important things. One, there is indeed a basis for a bipartisan foreign policy establishment built around the networks of the permanent bureaucracy. The other was that 'expert consensus' made no difference to political calculus as the BJP simply disowned Mishra in 2008.

The existence of a wide and deep foreign policy establishment cutting across party lines in itself could not have short circuited the tortuous political evolution of India's foreign policy. Nevertheless it would seem entirely reasonable to posit that the existence of such an establishment, with all its different elements in full flow, would make it a lot easier for India to put to rest the many demons in its worldview. The reformation of India's security sector, the upgrade of its international relations studies, the modernisation of its think tanks, and the globalization of its media are all urgent and worthwhile tasks in themselves. When done, they will all contribute to India's greater awareness and more effective engagement of the world. It is important, however, to note that such a reformation would be led by New Delhi. The Chinese Communist Party has the power to decree such reforms, create new institutions that could serve as adjuncts to its emerging status in the international arena, and articulate a coherent doctrine on its rise. It would be extravagantly unrealistic to expect India to do the same.

The expansion and modernisation of India's intellectual infrastructure on international relations studies is more likely to resemble the American experience in some important aspects. As in the United States, so in India, the building of foreign policy software is likely to follow rather than precede the nation's emergence as a great power. The private sector and civil society initiatives are likely to play a larger role in India in the eventual creation of a world class international relations infrastructure. The permanent bureaucracy of the security sector will not reform itself except under extreme political pressure. The university system, which is critical to the modernisation of international relations studies, has withered under the dominance of a Human Resources Development ministry mired in the statism of the 1970s. The changed environment in India, however, offers room to challenge many of the old governmental controls on the academia, skirts them by expanding the private sector research, and above all demands more openness within India and a rediscovery of India's fearless internationalism. When it does eventually acquire a tangible shape, India's permanent foreign policy establishment is bound to reflect the nation's historical inheritance, its internal diversity, cultural specificity and the unique regional context.

Multi-faceted Diplomacy in the Indian Foreign Policy

Indian foreign policy in the recent years resembles a very complex matrix which requires fine tuning in accordance with the changes in the international politics. It consists of India's aspirations for being the leading power in the region, its multi-dimensional security needs in a very unstable region and its requirements for a growing economy. Satisfying all of these factors requires a multi-faceted diplomacy that enables India to act in such a way that it can balance the interests of different states. This analysis will try to demonstrate the fundamental aspects of Indian diplomacy briefly perhaps not adequately.

India is in a region which is marked with instability. In the North East, it is neighbour with China who is the fastest growing country of the world, emerging to be a greater actor in the world politics in the 21st century. In the North West it's decades old rival, Pakistan. Same region also consists of Iran and Afghanistan in the west and an increasing US presence in Afghanistan and Central Asia where Russia also exerts power. Such a geography brings with itself a diplomatic game that balances different actors. India's aspirations to be a permanent member of the United Nations Security Council requires a more delicate diplomacy. It becomes a much more intricate issue due to its decades old conflict with Pakistan over Jammu and Kashmir and a powerful China in the East that boosts up its needs for military power. Finally, India is dependent on Persian Gulf for its energy needs in order to sustain a growing economy that is consist of 1,060, 000 billion people with about 26.1% poverty rate and great inequality within the society, makes it a difficult task to accomplish.

Therefore Indian foreign policy evolved from the leadership of Non-Aligned Movement during the Cold War into a more pragmatic multi-faceted diplomacy. Multi-faceted diplomacy denotes the establishment of cooperation with different states on different issues simultaneously. The states that are cooperated with may have conflicts with one and other however the state who pursues multi-faceted diplomacy are trying to disassociate issues in a way to avoid a conflict with any of the parties. Through such an act, the state is able to achieve its interests in two or more fronts. Emerging Indian-Israeli relation could be viewed as an outcome of this kind of an understanding. Meanwhile, India is also developing its cooperation with Iran while it tries to keep its relations with USA warm even try to upgrade it to a long-term strategic partnership. Furthermore India's relationship with Russia is managed in a good level. India's bidding for a permanent seat in the UN Security Council could also be interpreted as an effort to enhance its capacity to pursue multi-faceted diplomacy in its foreign policy.

India's Security Needs

India's security needs have always played a dominant role in the formation of its foreign policy. Its threat analysis was based on nuclear China in the North East and the everlasting conflict with Pakistan in the Jammu-Kashmir region. Nuclear China led India to go nuclear in 1974. Emergence of China as the fastest growing country in the world once again perceived as a competing power in the region. This is similar with USA's perception of China as a possible rival power in the 21st century. This competition is especially based on the needs for energy resources in order to sustain growing economy. These energy resources will be supplied from the Persian Gulf and the Caspian Sea region however the statistics demonstrates that although the Caspian Sea resources will be important at the margins, the Persian Gulf will continue to exist as the dominant supplier. Thus in this context, US can need India to balance China in the region in long term. Therefore US-Indian relations are interpreted as having a potential to be a strategic partnership. Another dimension of this cooperation is the mutual grievance from terrorism. After September 11, India is one of the first countries that declared its support to USA's war on terrorism. In the last decade, Islamic fundamentalist groups have attacked India more than a dozen times. Most of these groups are based in Pakistan and they are receiving moral or economic support from Pakistani institutions. The basis of the conflict is the conflict over Jammu and Kashmir which lasts since the Independence of India from Britain in August 1947. However, a major obstacle that prevents the development of Indian-American relations to a next level is the strategic position of Pakistan for US's war against Taliban and Al-Qaeda. Pakistan gave full permission to USA to operate in its borders against Al-Qaeda.

Although Indian officials interpret this relationship as shortsighted, in the short-term Pakistan is very important for US to achieve its goals in Afghanistan. Since January 2004, Pakistani-Indian relations are changing in a positive way. Since November 2003, there is ceasefire between the two states and in September 2004, leaders of the both states declared their intentions to achieve real results because of this dialogue. Improvement in Indian-Pakistani relations may enhance Indian-American relations into a next level.

Indian-Israeli Cooperation

India's security requirements led to the development of an interesting cooperation between India and Israel, which is based on the trade of military equipments. This relationship demonstrates the shift in Indian foreign policy since the end of the Cold War and the nature of it recently. India did not establish full diplomatic relationship with Israel until 1992 because India as one of the leading actors of the Non-Aligned Movement supported the Palestinians in their course of liberating the occupied territories. Ariel Sharon's visit to Indian in September 2003 reflected the change in the bilateral relations. However Indians try to keep this relationship away from the public scrutiny due to the sympathy towards Palestinian cause in the Indian society with 140 millions Muslims but still India tries to delink its policy towards Palestinians with its relationship with Israel since 1992. One of the factors of this relationship is the interpretation of Islamic fundamentalist organizations that attacks India and the Palestinian organizations such as Hamas, Islamic Jihad and Hezboullah as similar. Some of the Israeli officials claimed to extent that this has been an alliance against international terrorism. Although this shared view of combating international terrorism is an important factor in the development of the relationship between two countries, the bulk of the relationship is based on the defense collaboration between two states. India replaced Turkey as the largest arms market for Israeli arms exporters. Unlike other states that considers the balance of power in South Asia while selling weapons to India, Israel is much more pragmatic on that and it tries to increase its level of exports to India. Israel's high tech weapon industry supplies India with conventional armament. During Sharon's visit, India and

Israel talked on developing a anti-ballistic missile system in India. Such a development can tilt the balance of power in the region extensively. However the development of Indian-Iranian relationship adds another factor that should be taken into consideration while making an analysis. International community is eager to see the way India will manage to handle these contradictory relations.

Indian-Iranian Cooperation

The progress in Indian-Iranian bilateral relations is based on the mutual interest of parties in the expansion of trade between each other. Iran tries to break its isolation through developing partnerships in the East because of increasing US pressure while India tries to enter the Persian Gulf and Central Asia energy market through Iran. India is currently the fourth in the energy consumption ranking and its energy consumption rise will be highest after China in 2025. Hence, Iran is a very strategic country by being the second biggest oil producer in OPEC as well as preserving the second largest natural gas reserves. Therefore, access to these resources is quite important for India to satisfy its energy needs, same objectives are shared by China also. Thus there maybe a competition for these resources between China and India. However, recently an Indian official talked about extending a possible pipeline project to China that will carry Iranian oil through Pakistan to India. Realization of this project is quite doubtful since there is much risk. Due to the conflict between Pakistan and India, militants may threaten the security of the pipelines although Pakistani government declared that they ensure the protection of the pipeline. For the Iranian part, India is important to balance Pakistan. More importantly, Iran is developing its military capabilities through the cooperation with India. India is especially trading air and naval armament to Iran. These commercial military relations may be critical if the US pressure on Iran increases and the crisis about Iran's nuclear program escalates. The level of this military cooperation is also crucial for Israel who interprets Iran as a hostile state. Rand Corporation signifies this relationship, as one of the ten security developments that do not draw necessary attention and Indian officials tend to play down these bilateral relations. The current world conjecture can make the management of these bilateral relations extremely hard for India given the increasing pressure on Iran by US and Israel regarding Iran's nuclear program.

However, India is staying neutral by saying nothing regarding this issue hence separating these two relations from one and other in line with its policy of multi-faceted diplomacy. While this may be interpreted as a contradiction by US given the declarations that were made previously by Indian officials who were calling US to fight against nuclear proliferation. Also India's bid for the Security Council permanent membership may require a sacrifice on its relations with Iran to get a positive remark from US. On the other hand, if these relations stay under a certain level and the tension regarding Iranian nuclear program does not escalate then India can handle these conflicting relations without much problem.

India and the UN Security Council

One of the central objectives of Indian multi-faceted diplomacy is to obtain a permanent seat in the UN Security Council. In order to achieve this goal, India is trying to be a central actor not only in South Asia but also in Middle East. Hence, the development of relations with Iran and Israel can also be interpreted in this sense. India's major claims for being a permanent member are being the largest democracy in the world, major actor in its region, growing economy and being a nuclear power. Therefore, it claims to be a balancing power. It is also assuming a role of bridging the West and the East while fighting international terrorism. However, alongside these roles, its major setback is not being able to solve the conflict with Pakistan hence not being able to maintain security within its borders. India is acting together with Germany, Brazil and Japan. Up to now, France, Britain and Russia declared their support for India's bid for membership while the positions of China and US are not clear.

Multi-faceted Diplomacy in Turkish Foreign Policy

The analysis of India's multifaceted diplomacy poses the question of whether or not Turkey is capable of conducting such a policy. Turkey also have some basic similarities with India in terms of being a central actor in its region as well as cooperating with different actors that have conflicting interests such as the USA, the EU, Arab states and Israel. However, Turkey has two major differences from India that constrains Turkey in the engagement of a similar policy that easily. Primarily geographic proximity is a prominent factor in Turkey's relations with the Arab States, Israel and the EU while India has a considerable distance with Iran and Israel. Therefore delinking the interests of different actors is a very challenging task for Turkey and most of the time not possible. Secondly, the nature of the relationships that Turkey is conducting is quite different from India. India's relation with both Iran and Israel is based on trade, which enables India to separate the two relations from one and other more easily under the guiding principle of economic rationale. When one considers the nature of Turkey's relations, the degree of political penetration is very high. This can be seen in its strategic partnership with the USA, in the integration process with the EU or its military cooperation with Israel. Looking at India's performance in delinking Pakistani issue from its relations with the USA, one can observe that India is not performing as well as its relations that are conducted under economic rationale. Turkey's new policy to intensify its relations with Africa and South East Asia may be similar to India's policy towards Iran and Israel, through which Turkey can engage into multifaceted diplomacy since economic rationale will be an achievable objective

The Growing Influence of Business and Media on Indian Foreign Policy

Dr. Manmohan Singh was perhaps the first Indian Prime Minister to so clearly articulate the rising influence of civil society and business in the making of Indian foreign policy. Turning a 19th Century aphorism on its head, the Prime Minister seemed to suggest that it is no longer trade that 'follows the flag', but 'the flag' that follows trade. It is of course clear that this view of international relations is intimately related to the nature of society we are talking about. It is only in democratic societies that civil society has any significant influence on the foreign policy. Business interests could still influence foreign policy in non-democratic societies, if the regime in question has commercial, business and wider economic interests to pursue through its foreign policy. However, public opinion can shape foreign policy only by influencing domestic politics. Needless to add, business and media have for long been instruments of diplomacy. However, this paper is not about diplomacy. Its purpose is to examine the influence of business and media on foreign policy the Nobel Prize economist and the guru of strategic economics, T. C. Schelling claimed, "Aside from war and preparations for war, and occasionally aside from migration, trade is the most important relationship that most countries have with each other."

In an Influential Essay Entitled 'Trade Policy is Foreign Policy'

Indian foreign policy in the post-independence period was shaped essentially by geopolitical considerations and the priorities of nation-building. The requirements of economic development did have a direct bearing on foreign policy, as India's first Prime Minister Jawaharlal Nehru clarified in his very first speech on foreign policy in the Constituent Assen.bly in December 1947. Richard Cooper took the view that while traditionally trade policy had dominated 'high foreign policy', the Cold War had brought political issues to the fore and reduced the salience of business interests in shaping foreign policy. The end of the Cold War, the economic transformation of China and the processes of globalization, accelerated by the Uruguay Round of multilateral trade negotiations and the spread of regional trade blocs, have raised the profile of business and economic factors in the foreign and strategic policy considerations of most nations. The past decade has also witnessed increased global migration and the globalization of media, with new satellite technologies and the internet making McLuhan's 'global village' truly global. These trends have impacted on the choices available to governments in dealing with national and international issues and bilateral, regional and multilateral relations. This has had its inevitable impact on India, which has been transformed this past decade by its increased economic openness. This in turn has shaped India's relations with the world economy and global communities.

The Influence of Business on Foreign Policy

The liberalisation of economic policy in 1991 opened in government-business interaction in India. Not only did business leaders accompany the Prime Minister, External Affairs Minister and Union Finance and Commerce Ministers on their visits abroad, but their views began to be better articulated through the two principle chambers of business, the Federation of Indian Chambers of Commerce and Industry (FICCI) and the Confederation of Indian Industry (CII). The CII's Partnership Summit, in fact, became a major diplomatic event with foreign leaders invited to it. FICCI's initiatives through the South Asian Business However, the Nehruvian era in economic policy was one of central planning and the public sector occupying the 'commanding heights' of the Indian economy. Hence, business-to-business relations willy-nilly became state-to-state relations. It was only in the 1980s that Indian business, especially the private corporate sector, came into its own and began to influence political thinking on foreign policy issues. Prime Minister Rajiv Gandhi was the first Indian Prime Minister to invite business leaders to join him on official visits abroad. This practice received further boost during the tenure of Prime Minister Narashima Rao.

Forum were another such effort in the South Asian Association for Regional Cooperation (SAARC) region. In the immediate post-independence period, Indian business had little influence in shaping political thinking on foreign policy issues. Nehru's dominating personality, India's immediate concerns with its geopolitical neighbourhood and the larger dynamics of decolonisation, post-colonial development and cold war shaped India's foreign policy options. To be sure, national economic interests did play an important role in shaping foreign policy, as already mentioned. Contrary to more recent thinking, Nehru did not adopt a hostile view either towards the West or towards western business. On his first visit to the United States as Prime Minister in 1955, Nehru sought out United States business and sought greater United States economic engagement with India. It was the United States that spurned Nehru largely because the United States was focused on postwar reconstruction in East Asia and Western Europe and also because it was not enthusiastic about Nehru's plan for public sector-led industrialisation in India. In subsequent years, India's inward-oriented industrialisation strategy meant that even Indian business was more focused on the domestic market and was satisfied with protectionist policies. This ensured that the normal synergy one expects between the interests of business and foreign policy choices democratic governments make was weak. India's nonalignment policy did not yield any significant economic benefits for Indian business, perhaps also because Indian business was not outward-oriented and did not seek markets and investment opportunities in developing countries. India's friendship with the Soviet Union had spin-offs in defence and strategic industries which were all in the public sector. The only important private sector beneficiaries of India's relations with the Soviet Union were tobacco growers in Andhra Pradesh (many of whom liberally funded the local communist parties!) and a few traders who dipped into the rupee based trading opportunities. It was only in the 1980s, when Indian business began to look at market opportunities abroad, especially during the term of Prime Minister Rajiv Gandhi, that the external economic and business interests of Indian business began to shape official thinking on foreign policy. The CII became actively involved in projecting Indian interests abroad and in pursuing Track-II Diplomacy at home and abroad.

i) First, the economic crisis of 1990-91 and the end of the Cold War; The real turning point, however, was 1991. Several factors contributed to increased business engagement in Indian diplomacy:
ii) Second, the change in India's negotiating stance at the World Trade Organization (WTO);
iii) Third, though only towards the end of the 90s, the outward orientation of large Indian companies; and
iv) Fourth, India's success in software and the globalization of Indian information technology (IT) and software business.

The Economic Crisis of 1990-91 and the End of the Cold War

The timing of India's external payments crisis in 1990-91 was significant. It occurred almost in parallel with the collapse of the

Soviet Union. Facing for the first time the prospect of external debt rescheduling, the Indian government tried hard to secure multilateral and bilateral support. It found great difficulty in securing such support without adopting policies that would open up the Indian economy to greater play of market forces. It also found it had very few friends in G-7 capitals. Hence, the policy of economic liberalisation was launched in part to address the problem of India's economic isolation in the context of the post-Cold War world.

The factors driving external economic liberalisation were independent of the felt and expressed need of domestic enterprise. Domestic enterprise was keen on internal liberalisation but was not very enthusiastic about external liberalisation. In fact, as tariffs came down and quantitative restrictions on imports were removed, domestic business enterprise became restive. While the Chambers of Commerce officially welcomed these initiatives, some leading business groups mobilised themselves to campaign against what they called the wrong sequencing of reform. The 'Bombay Club', a group of businessmen who met in Bombay to draw a charter of demands laced with protest against the government's external liberalisation policies, argued that the latter should wait till internal liberalisation had been completed and Indian business had secured 'a level playing field' vis-à-vis global multinationals. The negative middle class reaction to such 'trade unionism of business elites' forced Indian business to rethink its strategy and encouraged it to back off. Such middle class reaction was increasingly shaped in the 1990s by the global success of Indian professionals, especially in the field of information technology.

In fact, CII embraced enthusiastically India's new 'Look East' policy, inviting Singapore's Prime Minister Goh Chok Tong as the Chief Guest to its Centenary Celebrations in Calcutta in January 1995. India's 'Look East' policy, of engaging the Association of Southeast Asian Nations' (ASEAN) economies and also Japan and South Korea was a direct outcome of the end of the Cold War and India's outward-economic orientation. As the key architect of the reforms of 1991, the then Finance Minister Dr. Manmohan Singh openly acknowledged the experience of South Korea and ASEAN in re-orienting Indian economic policies. This gained Consequently, the three Chambers of Commerce – CII, FICCI and the Associated Chambers of Commerce – began to offer compromise formulas that would combine the interests of domestic business with the imperatives of economic liberalisation. They understood the imperatives of balance of payments management, where mollified by a liberalised exchange rate mechanism, easing of foreign exchange controls, greater access to external finance and the trade-offs secured on internal economic policies. They also understood the imperatives of the post-Cold War world and India's need to seek new external relationships for India new access to Asian capitals. India got on to the fast-track in being invited to be a partner country of ASEAN by the late 1990s.

The investment CII and FICCI made in trade diplomacy was of great use for Indian business and for the Indian government. Indian business also emerged as an important participant in 'Track-II' diplomacy on the trade front. CII set up an office in Geneva and representatives of Indian business accompanied the Indian commerce minister on important travels abroad

Change in India's Negotiating Stance at the World Trade Organization

Almost on a parallel track with these policy changes was the change in India's negotiating stance at the WTO. Till 1990 India firmly opposed a new round of multilateral trade negotiations under the General Agreement on Trade and Tariffs. Even after the Uruguay Round was launched, India opposed new areas like trade in services and trade-related intellectual property rights from being brought into trade negotiations. Indian industry played an important role in campaigning against the new agenda being promoted by the developed economies. Sector specific lobby groups were set up by Indian businessmen to campaign against trade liberalisation through the multilateral route.

After 1991, India changed course. Interestingly, Indian industry changed course too! Rather than block the Uruguay Round, both the Indian government and industry opted to negotiate and secure an outcome favourable to India. This marked a new phase in Indian business's diplomatic engagement. CII and FICCI actively canvassed support for the Indian point of view in various world capitals. They invited foreign dignitaries to well-organised and well-attended gala events of Indian business organisations in New Delhi and Bombay and sought to win them over to their point of view. The message was clear – don't destroy the Indian private sector, we can be your allies in the spread of market capitalism in this part of the world. By projecting private Indian business as an ally in the onward march of market economies in the post-Cold War world, Indian business established new relationships for India in developed industrial economies.

India was not wholly satisfied with the outcome of the Uruguay Round, but the process marked a fundamental shift in India's trade diplomacy. Not only did India emerge as an active participant in the WTO process, it was also able to establish itself simultaneously as a champion of the interests of developing economies and as a willing negotiator with developed economies. This 'bridge power' status in multilateral negotiations was new for India, having been a long time leader of the nonaligned and on the wrong side of the Cold War divide. Indian industry played a crucial role in facilitating this transition. The experience gathered in the Uruguay Round negotiations helped Indian business to take a more pro-active role in the Doha Development Round process. Indian business chambers took the initiative, for the first time, and played a pro-active role in trade diplomacy. Rather than wait for the government to take the lead, business chambers began crafting their own strategy for the Doha Round. FICCI constituted a trade policy group in 1999, drafting the services of an officer of the Indian Administrative Services (on secondment from the government to FICCI), that outlined broad parameters for the Doha Round negotiating strategy related to trade diplomacy.

Abandoning the 'protectionist' rhetoric of the 'Bombay Club' of the early 1990s, both CII and FICCI adopted a pro-active negotiating stance. Trade liberalisation in the 1990s and the increased exposure of Indian business to external competition forced Indian business to adopt a pro-active role in Indian trade diplomacy. This then became an important route through which business associations began to influence Indian foreign policy options. Since 'trade policy is foreign policy', and since in the era of globalization trade policy has strategic consequences, the growing involvement of Indian business in crafting Indian trade policy options gave them a new profile in influencing foreign policy outcomes. Another important factor that contributed to a greater engagement of business with foreign policy was the rise of China, as a business rival. China's entry into the WTO opened in India-China trade relations. By year 2000, Indian business became worried about dumping of cheaper Chinese goods.

A third factor, a more recent one, that has contributed to the increased involvement of business in foreign policy, has been the growing interest of Indian business groups in overseas investment. Major Indian business groups began investing abroad in the 1980s. However, it is only in the past five years that there has been a quantum increase in foreign investment.

While China has emerged as India's biggest bilateral trade partner overtaking the United States (though still lagging behind the European Union), fear of China grips Indian business. It has begun to shape business thinking on relations with other Asian economies, including the strategic importance of the India-ASEAN Free Trade Agreement. Like in so many other countries, business pro-activism in foreign policy has been greatly influenced by the rise of China as a trading power.

The Outward Orientation of Large Indian Companies

The main stimulus for this was the policy of the National Democratic Alliance government to increase capital outflows as part of its strategy to manage a surge in capital inflows since the early 2000s. Outward investment by Indian entities increased sharply from around US$2 billion in 2003-04 to US$14.4 billion in 2006-07.

The rising interest of Indian firms, both in the services and manufacturing sector, in foreign trade and foreign investment has increased their interest in shaping India's diplomatic Outward investment by Indian firms has a wide geographical spread, including the United Kingdom (where Indian investors top the charts on inward investment into United Kingdom), the United States, China, Russia, Southeast Asia, South Asia and Africa. In each of these bilateral equations, the role of prominent business leaders, in particular, and of business interests, in general, has increased considerably. Business leaders increasingly 'facilitate' meetings between officials and politicians of countries, they influence the bilateral agenda, and they contribute funds to political parties or leaders when asked to initiatives with respect to various regional forums and specific countries. Indian business delegations now routinely accompany the Prime Minister when he travels abroad. The Prime Minister meets accompanying business leaders before he goes in for a bilateral meeting with the host head of government to understand their concerns with respect to the country being visited. Regional forums like SAARC, the Bay of Bengal Initiative for Multi-Sectoral Technical and Economic Cooperation, ASEAN and the European Union invite Indian business leaders to participate in parallel meetings along with the Prime Minister. It would be incorrect to dismiss such travel as mere diplomatic and business tourism. The views of business leaders are discussed even within closed door meetings between high officials, and issues like market access, investment opportunities, visa regimes, are increasingly focused on business perspectives. High profile global acquisitions by business tycoons like Lakshmi Mittal (steel) and Ratan Tata (steel and auto), high profile global contracting out by major Indian companies like Reliance and India's energy diplomacy have given such business leaders great influence in bilateral relations. Perhaps one must make a distinction between the diplomatic influence and interest of non-resident and largely globalised business leaders of Indian origin, like the Hindujas and Mittals, and the more nascent business diplomacy of increasingly globalising Indian business leaders like the Tatas and the Ambani Brothers.

The Hinduja Brothers, for example, have been known to be influential in various capitals of the world for many years. The legendary 'continuity' in their influence in Iran, from the days of the Shah to those of the Ayatollahs, has earned them a special place in the business lobbyists hall of fame. However, they are no longer unique. Several other businessmen have emerged with similar 'bipartisan' influence in the corridors of power in various capitals. They lubricate the system and help Indian diplomats and politicians secure access and strike deals. The Hindujas have been 'diplomatically active' in a wide range of countries including the United States and the United Kingdom. They played a helpful role in the political lobbying associated with India's civil nuclear cooperation agreement with various member countries of the Nuclear Suppliers Group.

Similarly, Lakshmi Mittal has been diplomatically active in Central Asia and Europe. The lower profile of business leaders of Indian origin in South-east Asia, as compared to their Chinese-origin counterparts, may have meant that Indian business played a less important role in shaping India's relations with the region, though even here wider business interests have without doubt shaped India's strategic relations.

'Track-II' Diplomacy An important consequence of this is the willingness of Indian business groups to invest in 'Track-II' diplomacy and in shaping foreign policy perspectives. One of India's largest business houses has funded a think tank focused on strategic policy and foreign affairs, with several former diplomats hired as faculty. This is the Observer Research Foundation, funded by Mukesh Ambani's Reliance Industries. While Mukesh Ambani has directly funded a foreign policy research institute, other Indian companies have funded 'Track-II' diplomatic initiatives through CII and FICCI.

CII runs several 'Track-II' dialogues funded by various member companies. The countries covered so far include the United States, Japan, Singapore and Malaysia. Business leaders with country specific interests invest in these dialogues and also participate in them. Thus, Ratan Tata has consistently funded, and often participated in, the CII-Aspen Strategy Group dialogue on India-United States relations. Launched in 1999, partly to contain the diplomatic damage of the Pokhran II nuclear tests and build bridges between Indian and United States opinion makers, business leaders and legislators, the India-United States Dialogue has been sustained over eight years, with two meetings every year, one in the United States and another in India.

Other business leaders like Sunil Mittal, Sunil Munjal, Harpal Singh and Gautam Thapar have invested and participated in these and other such dialogues. FICCI has also initiated a similar effort with the Woodrow Wilcon Centre and the Heritage Foundation. An important initiative of FICCI has been the Forum of Parliamentarians set up to engage elected representatives from

India and their counterparts in the United States, the United Kingdom, Germany, the European Union, Singapore, Japan and Pakistan.

According to FICCI's Secretary-General, Dr. Amit Mitra, "The IUFP (India-United States Forum of Parliamentarians), constituted six years ago along the lines of the 'India Caucus' and 'Senate Friends of India' Group in the United States Congress, provides an important platform to the Indian Parliamentarians to develop and strengthen India-United States relations through Track-II initiatives. Encompassing all aspects of bilateral relations, the forum makes an earnest effort to facilitate wider exchange of views, dialogue and discussions on bilateral and global issues between Indian parliamentarians and their counterparts in the United States, senior Administration officials, business leaders, opinion-makers and the Indian-American community, thereby adding an important parliamentary dimension to bilateral ties."

The Forums of Parliamentarians is a multiparty body of seven Forums with 130 members belonging to various political shades of India with many of its members serving on important parliamentary committees. The forums with the United States, the United Kingdom Germany, the European Union, Singapore, Japan and Pakistan launched consecutively since the formation of the IUFP in March 2002, have played a significant role in promoting inter-parliamentary exchange and dialogue with its counterparts in these countries. The Forums have gone beyond and facilitated dialogue with senior government officials, leading think tanks experts, business leaders and civil society at large, in these countries on several issues of bilateral and global concerns. FICCI has also recently launched similar forums with Commonwealth of Independent States, Russia, China and Italy. The India-United States Forum played an important role in shaping the thinking of young Parliamentarians on the issue of India-United States civil nuclear cooperation agreement, and in providing a forum for newly elected Parliamentarians from Pakistan to interact with their Indian counterparts.

In 2007, FICCI's India-United States Forum of Parliamentarians took the initiative to launch 'The India-Yale Parliamentary Leadership Programme', a first of its kind for Indian parliamentarians. This programme gives parliamentarians an opportunity to spend time at Yale University to reflect on a wide range of issue they deal with as members of parliament. The Second India-Yale Parliamentary Leadership Programme, conducted in June 2008, covered topics like 'The Economics of Mitigating Climate Change and Sustainable Development'; 'Global Economic Risks and the New Financial Order'; 'Three Decades of Reform, Rule of Law and Governance Challenges in China'; 'Poverty and Economic Development'; 'Religion and Politics'; 'Reform of Higher Education in India'; '2008 US Presidential Election – Predictions and Realities'; 'India and Globalization'; 'Effective and Strategic Political Communications'; and so on.

There has always also been a 'below the radar' role for business in diplomacy. This is normally confined to a few influential business leaders who may provide 'facilitation' for unofficial contacts between diplomats and political leaders. A business leader could act as a 'conduit' for 'backroom' and unofficial discussion and pre-meeting negotiation between heads of government. As Indian businessmen globalise and become part of the global 'cocktail and golf circuits', and fund politicians and political parties in other countries they are also able to shape relations between India and other countries. This 'below the radar' role of business leaders is on the rise and can be seen in South Asia, in rest of Asia, in Africa, in large parts of Europe and in India's relations with major powers like the United States, Russia and China. Another form of 'below the radar' influence for business is their funding of politicians, lobbies and interest groups in foreign countries. While some of this activity would normally be regarded as 'illegal gratification' of policy makers, some countries permit public funding of lobbying efforts, ranging from payment to advertisements in the media to sponsoring interest and focus groups, supporting 'Track-II' diplomacy and other public diplomacy efforts, including support for university chairs and research centres.

Globalization of Indian

IT and Software Business

The Indian IT, software and business process outsourcing industry has without doubt changed India's global profile. Its impact on Brand India is well known. Visiting Heads of State and Government now routinely add Bangalore and Hyderabad to their itinerary. A visit to the Infosys or Wipro campus or to Cyberabad is a high profile part of India's economic diplomacy. India's success in these areas, as well as in the entertainment sector, has contributed to enhancing India's 'soft power'. Indian IT and software capabilities now open doors for Indian diplomats abroad in the corridors of power. This has given business leaders in these sectors high level access both within India and in other world capitals. More importantly, the economic importance of software business and business processing outsource for the Indian economy has ensured that such business interests can no longer be ignored by Indian foreign policymakers. In fact, the promotion of Indian capabilities and business interests in these areas is intrinsic to the projection of Indian 'soft power', both in developed and developing countries.

All this cannot be dismissed as mere diplomacy. It is having a palpable influence on foreign policy as well. Today India can not ignore the business interests of its burgeoning IT, knowledge and data processing sectors in crafting its foreign policy options. Indeed, India's relations with the United States, in particular, and with the 'English-speaking' world, in general, has increasingly been influenced by the enormous pull of business and professional interests involved in this sector. Billions of dollars are now at stake for Indian software, data and business processing companies in western markets. The sharp decline in India-Russia economic relations in the 1990s, as compared to a similarly dramatic increase in India-China trade and the importance of United States and Asian markets for Indian business have become important determinants of India's foreign policy options.

The Influence of Media on Foreign Policy

The media has an obvious role in shaping public opinion on foreign policy issues in a democracy. However, the influence of media on foreign policy is shaped by two important factors, first, the extent of domestic political disagreement or consensus on foreign policy issues; and second, the relationship between the government of the day and the media. Indian foreign policy was marked by a high degree of domestic political consensus in the initial years after Independence. Few in the national press questioned Jawaharlal Nehru's overall foreign policy orientation. During the Cold War there was a weakening of this consensus in the press, with some favouring a closer relationship with the West and the others favouring a stronger 'anti-imperialist' stance. The mainstream public and political opinion in India favoured Nehru's path of 'nonalignment' in the Cold War. Contrary to popular western, especially United States, view of 'nonalignment' as an 'ideological anti-West and pro-Soviet' stance, Nehru's nonalignment was essentially a pragmatic and nationalist assertion of India's independent and autonomous stance in international affairs. Nehru was in favour of good relations with the West as well as with Soviet Union, but sought for India an 'independent' voice in world affairs. This stance had broad national support and the media of the time went along with this stance.

Given the political dominance of the Congress Party and a high degree of consensus among mainstream political parties the media had at best a marginal role to play. There is no doubt, however, that the Cold War played itself out through the columns of the Indian media but the moot point is that this did not influence official thinking in any significant way.

The Indian Ministry of External Affairs has traditionally maintained a close connection with influential editors and columnists to ensure, what a high ranking Indian diplomat has dubbed, a 'cozy relationship'.

Given the high degree of freedom that Indian media enjoys, foreign governments have, from time to time, tried to win friends and influence opinion in the media. The Indian government also seeks to do this. However, its approach is to 'win' over the media to its point of view, rather then be influenced by any independent thinking within the media. The media is viewed as an instrument for promoting the government's view point, not as the 'Fourth Estate' whose 'independent' voice must be heard. During the Cold War period, the governments of the day were fairly successful in securing broad media support for their foreign policy.

While some journalists view this with deep suspicion and may even refuse to accept the government's hospitality as a way of defending media freedom, one must not exaggerate the success that the governments have in winning over the media to their viewpoint.

Ironically, a substantial part of the work of the External Publicity Division of the Ministry of External Affairs has in fact been in dealing with domestic media rather than international media. The Division is more often engaged in seeking internal publicity for external policy rather than external publicity for internal policy. In India's increasingly fractious political environment and given rising budgets of private media organisations, government freebies and junkets have declining influence in shaping media thinking on major policy issues.

The electronic media, like Parliament, has become an arena in which party political differences on foreign policy do get articulated more forcefully because of the nature of the medium. In fact, television news channels may have contributed to increased public discord on foreign policy by deliberately strait-jacketing all 'discussions' into binary, conflictual 'for-and-against' debates. Rather than facilitate a consensus such 'argumentative' debates foster divergence. While television resorts to this practice to increase viewer attention and make news more 'entertaining', this has increased the role of the media in shaping political thinking on foreign policy issues.

It is difficult to point to any important example where the Indian government shaped thinking on Indian policies in any significant way in any foreign media. Equally, it is difficult to offer any example where the government of the day has altered its policy in foreign affairs or bilateral relations due to pressure from the media. In fact, Indian diplomats often take pride in claiming that they can 'get the media they want'. This is, without doubt, changing with the breakdown of the domestic political consensus on foreign policy issues, and the pervasive influence of 24x7 television news channels. The last decade, therefore, marks a turning point in the role of the media in shaping foreign policy. This is on account of three very different factors:

i) the gradual erosion of the domestic political consensus on foreign policy, giving the media the role of an arbiter and an independent analyst of contending political views;

ii) The media revolution and expansion, with the rise of television and business journalism and the growing importance of private corporate advertisement revenues, as opposed to government support for media, in influencing media economics; and

iii) Finally, the increasing influence of the middle class and the business class in the media has also influenced media thinking on foreign policy.

An early example of the media playing an important role in shaping public opinion and government policy with respect to a foreign and strategic policy issue, in the context of domestic political discord, was the role played by the English daily *The Times of India* in 1996 on the issue of India signing up on the Comprehensive Test Ban Treaty (CTBT) agreement.

Some critics of the media may dismiss its role as peripheral given the limited reach of media in an educationally backward society. To be sure, foreign policy always engages the elite much more than the masses. Hence, it is rarely a subject for mass politics, except perhaps in the case of India-Pakistan relations, and that too in northern India. Indian political parties were divided on the issue of India's stance on the CTBT since India had for a long time advocated such a test ban and had, in fact, sponsored the CTBT. However, when CTBT got linked to Nuclear Proliferation Treaty renewal and India felt it was being discriminated against on the question of its nuclear status, the view gained ground that India should not sign CTBT. A major debate took place in the columns of Indian newspapers in which the *Times of India* editorially called for India rejecting CTBT in the form in which it was then being proposed. India can be a signatory only as an acknowledged nuclear weapons power and not as a non-weapon state. This finally became the official Indian position. The entire mainstream media has been a strong and consistent supporter of the India-United States agreement on cooperation in civil nuclear energy. Overwhelming media support for the civil nuclear agreement, with the exception of *The Hindu*, under the pro-Communist Party of India editorship of N. Ram, and *The Asian Age*, during the editorship of M. J. Akbar, strengthened the government's hand in politically defending its case at home, against political criticism from Left and Right opposition. More than print, television played an extremely influential role in generating public support for the nuclear accord. No major television news channel campaigned against the agreement, while many of them took a strong supportive stance.

However, the fact remains that with the decline of large pan-Indian national political parties and the emergence of fractured coalitions, difference between political parties on national policy issues, including foreign policy, is bound to grow. With such diversity of opinion in the political arena, the national media can secure for itself an influential autonomous role provided it is able to articulate a national policy that will find wide public acceptability and will stand the test of professional scrutiny.

The objective basis for such independent and informed view on foreign policy options within the media exists, even if in actual fact nothing is done to tap into that potential. Large media groups no longer look to the government alone for their survival. The phenomenal growth in the advertisement budgets of private corporates has increased the autonomy of the media with respect to the government, even if this has resulted in growing corporate influence on the media. In the context of our discussion what this means is that media can adopt a stance independent of the government, perhaps reflecting the interests of business and the professional classes, on foreign policy issues. News coverage of countries in the Indian media is increasingly influenced by revenue considerations.

Finally, we do believe that Indian media does not as yet view itself as an active player in foreign policy, even if some newspapers give more coverage to foreign affairs than others. One important reason for this is that Indian media has not found a business plan to justify greater foreign coverage and the posting of foreign correspondents. Among the world's 'major powers' Indian media has the least number of foreign correspondents. Only a handful of print and television organisations have correspondents posted in major world capitals and However, this, in turn, does not have any significant impact on government policy, as yet.

This increased relevance of business and middle class preferences for media policy implies that their world view will count for more in shaping media thinking on foreign policy. This is demonstrated by the near-unanimous support for the India-United States nuclear agreement in the business and English-language media. The policy preferences of these two segments of the media in the foreign policy arena do tend to influence Indian language media also. However, perceptions on foreign policy in Indian language media vary, due to local political, social and cultural factors. For example, the national media is less interested in India's policy towards Sri Lanka than the Tamil language media. Similarly, there is much less coverage on developments in the Islamic world in the national media as compared to the Urdu language media, that caters largely to a Muslim readership.

The thinking of these categories of readers, who may be politically influential in specific regions and constituencies, do not always get reflected in the national media, including television. It is the views of the more articulate middle classes that gets a greater play in national and mass media.

What this means, of course, is that any news about the United States or Pakistan is almost always front page and headline stuff, while news about most other developing countries makes no waves. The visit of the United States President, for example, secures saturation coverage in the Indian media, but the India-Africa Summit meeting in 2008 was not even reported on the front pages of most newspapers.

Such preferential bias in the media's treatment of different regions, countries and international issues may influence public opinion and even the thinking of politicians. However, in the corridors of decision-making, especially when it comes to the permanent civil service, contrarian thinking in the media and disagreeable media coverage is at best a nuisance to be tolerated, not a viewpoint to be taken account of in formulating policy. in neighbouring countries. There has, in fact, been a scaling down of foreign correspondents, with most Indian media drawing on news put out by foreign news agencies and foreign media partners. While China has emerged as India's largest trade partner and is India's biggest neighbour, only three media organisations (one subsidised by the government) have correspondents stationed in China.

Assessing the influence that religious nationalism has on foreign policy in the context of coalition governments, as both Israel since its creation and India, since 1996, have had, is not easy. In Israel the overlapping agendas of secular and religious Zionists, especially in relation to issues such as the Jewish settlements in the Occupied Territories, complicates analysis. In India the continuity between the foreign policies pursued by the BJP-led National Democratic Alliance (NDA) government and the Congress-led United Progressive Alliance one suggests a broad consensus regarding perceptions of national interest and foreign policy objectives that tends to cloud the notion of a distinct Hindu nationalist foreign policy vision.

Religious Nationalism and Foreign Policy

A recent survey of the role of religion in international relations enumerated a number of factors that made the continuing influence of religious movements and parties on Israeli policymaking likely (Haynes 2007; 344-5). Perhaps most important among these is the convergence between national security concerns and religious interests, something clearly apparent in the handling of the issue of Jewish settlements in the Occupied Territories over the past thirty years. One critical observer suggests that 'Since 1967, the cutting edge of imperial Israel has been provided by Jewish fundamentalism' (Masalha 2000: 105). Yet there has been little attempt to systematically analyse the role of religion in shaping foreign policy outcomes. A study of religion and public policy in Israel published in 1996 concluded, after having chosen to totally disregard foreign policy, that issues of peace and war would test the viability of its analysis (Sharkansky 1996: 156)!

Central to the religious nationalist perspective on foreign policy, whether in India or Israel, is the sanctity of the land. In Hindutva, Who is a Hindu (1923) the chief ideologist of Hindu nationalism, Veer Damodar Savarkar, defined a Hindu as a person who "looks upon the land that extends... from the Indus to the Seas... as his Fatherland (Pitribhu)... as his Holyland (Punyabhu), as the land of his prophets and seers, of his godmen and gurus, the land of piety and pilgrimage' (quoted in Gottlob 2003: 154-155). For over a century Zionists, whether secular or religious, have based their claim to Palestine on God's biblical promise to Abraham: 'To your descendants I give this land, from the river of Egypt to the great river, the river Euphrates' (Genesis 15:18), although interpretations of what this should mean in practise in setting the borders of Israel have varied considerably (Shindler 2001/02).

Menachem Begin, the incurably romantic first Likud prime minister of Israel and disciple of Jabotinsky, wrote, "faith itself creates reality" (Begin 1951: 11). A defining feature of the New Zionism that brought together most followers of Likud with the Jewish settlers and the National Religious Party was the emphasis on the Land of Israel (Eretz Israel) over the State of Israel (Ram 2003: 28). Begin wrote in 1951, "this wandering people had returned to its Homeland. The secular tour was ended." (Begin 1951: 372). Forty years later, his successor, Yitzhak Shamir, addressing the Middle East Peace Conference in Madrid, declared: 'No nation has expressed its bond with its land with as much intensity and consistency as we have... Only Eretz Israel, the Land of Israel, is our true homeland.' (Shamir 1994: 238). Even more than for the Revisionist Zionists, it is attachment to Eretz Israel that frames the attitude of the ultra-Orthodox parties to Israel as a state. Following the Six-Day War this, together with the fact that that their followers tended to be more hawkish, inclined them towards pursuing a harder line in foreign policy (Dowty 1998: 181). However, the attitudes of the different ultra-Orthodox parties towards the Occupied Territories are not uniform (Reiser 1991: 79-83). Shas in particular seemed inclined to pursue an ambivalent or pragmatic line over territorial compromise, trading Shas votes in the Ehud Barak government (1999-2000) on agreements with the Palestine National Authority and the dismantling of unofficial settlements for funding concessions (Weissbrod 2003: 86). Together with its electoral strength, this helped the party replace the National Religious Party as the central religious player in government.

For the spiritual leader of the National Religious Party, Rabbi Tzvi Yehuda Kook, the son of Israel's first Ashkenazi Chief Rabbi, there were no Occupied Territories, only redeemed land. After the Six-Day War he demanded their complete annexation and Jewish settlement in line with the halakhah (Masalha 2000: 113; Dowty

1998: 228). His followers responded by establishing Gush Emunim in 1974 and with the new Defence Minister, Shimon Peres, readily responding to pressure, were able to begin significant settlement activity in 1975-76 (Shahak 1999: 55-6). In 1977, Menachem Begin knelt before Kook after becoming Prime Minister (Lustick 1993: 110) and in the decade that followed the transformation of large chunks of the Occupied Territories into Eretz Israel proceeded apace. Begin's successor, Yitzhak Shamir, even compared the settlers to Israel's founding fathers, 'creating the historical facts for which future generations of Israelis will bless them' (Shamir 1994: 151). When settlers engaged in anti-Arab terrorism in the early 1980s it took five years for the security forces to arrest the perpetrators and all the convicted were soon pardoned (Maoz 2006: 257).

The rise of Gush Emunim drew together the secular and religious right in Israel with a tacit alliance taking shape between religious nationalists, secular Zionist extremists and annexationist elements in Labor as well as Likud (Maoz 2006: 489). The effect on the discourse and practise of politics were apparent. It was not just religious nationalists who denounced the 1993 Oslo Accord with the Palestine Liberation Organisation as a violation of the holiness of Eretz Israel but Yitzhak Shamir, who likened to it to a golden calf, a reference to how the people of Israel had turned to idol worship while waiting for Moses to come down from Mt. Sinai (Exodus 32:1-6). Yigal Amir, the religious Zionist who in 1995 assassinated Prime Minister Yitzhak Rabin, who had signed the Accord, voted in the 1992 elections not for any of the religious parties but for the secular Zionist extremist Moledet (transfer) Party that advocated the transfer of Palestinian Arabs out of Occupied Territories.

Religious extremists in Israel have become more nationalist while religious nationalists have become more extremist (Hazan 1999: 126). The ultra-Orthodox are also affected by this symbiosis of nationalism and religiosity with the marked growth in "nationalist-Haredi" (Dowty 1998: 183) being reflected in the changing attitudes towards military service on the part of young Haredi males (Stadler 2003). Eleven per cent of Israeli men are ultra-Orthodox and excused from military service to engage in religious study (this translates into an annual number of about 30,000) (McGirk 2007: 29; Stadler 2003: 18). Religious Zionists by contrast combined military service with Talmudic study (Sandler 1993: 152-3) with the NRP's yeshivot hesder programme being used by the settler movement to infiltrate and influence the Israel Defence Force (Shahak 1999: 91-3). This has given rise to concerns about reconciling a growing reliance on religious Zionist soldiers, often regarded as being especially committed and ruthless fighters, with the need to maintain army discipline if action needs to be taken against Jewish settlers (McGirk 2007: 28-9).

The centrality of the future of the Occupied Territories for Israel's security has made the role of religious nationalism in foreign policy of great import. In the case of India no such issue of transcendent significance exists. Although the 60-year dispute with Pakistan over Kashmir has always been a focus for Hindu nationalism, the problem for the idea of Hindu nationalism has been how to come to terms with the fact that Indian religious tradition has been quintessentially plural rather than singular. By bequeathing what was, from the viewpoint of modern Hindu nationalists, a messy civilisational unity to the subcontinent, the bewilderingly overlapping peculiarities of the multiplicity of Indian religions and cultures (Indian variants of Islam, Christianity, Zoroastrianism and Judaism, as well as the traditions rooted in the subcontinent – Hindu, Buddhist, Jain, Sikh) have served to deny Hindutva the kind of coherent corpus of tradition that Jewish religious nationalists are able to draw upon. Though, like Israel's Arab foes for Zionists, religious or not, the existence of Pakistan and India's large Muslim minority provide an 'Other' for Hindu nationalists, the sense of the 'We' remains less than convincing for the majority of Indians.

This was part of the reason why when the BJP found itself leading a coalition government in Delhi in April 1998, it was in the foreign rather than the domestic arena that they took their most dramatic initiative, within weeks making public India's military nuclear programme by carrying out a series of tests in the Rajasthan desert. Faced with overwhelming pressure to sign the Comprehensive Test Ban Treaty (CTBT) and abandon India's forty-year-old policy of maintaining nuclear ambiguity, a policy also pursued by Israel, a Congress government would probably also have reflected the preponderant view in the Indian security community and acted likewise. Yet that the decision was eventually made by India's first Hindu nationalist prime minister so soon after taking office gave it particular resonance. It seemed the most striking manifestation of the assertive militaristic nationalism of the votaries of Hindutva; the realisation of a long held aim of the BJP and its precursor, the Jana Sangh, that India should produce nuclear weapons. (It was not just Indians who noted that the tests were codenamed Shakti, after the Hindu goddess of strength and energy, just as India's medium-range missiles had been called Agni, after the god of fire. So did Strobe Talbott, the US Deputy Secretary of State deputed by President Bill Clinton to conduct talks with India on the nuclear issue (Talbott 2004: 21,50).)

India's adoption of nuclear weapons was not the product of an aberrant Hindu nationalist obsession. However, AB Vajpayee, unlike his immediate predecessors, and despite heading an unstable new coalition government, had few qualms about taking the final decisive step. Having been a leading member of the Hindu nationalist movement that had for four decades favoured India's adoption of nuclear weapons, he did not share the moral scruples that had arguably inhibited Congress leaders since Nehru. Moreover, unlike other cherished Hindu nationalist fetishes, most notably the construction of a temple to the god Ram on the site of the Babri mosque destroyed in 1992, national security was relatively uncontroversial as far as the coalition the BJP led was concerned. Vajpayee could afford to act decisively without risking the survival of his government. It was the conjuncture of the shift in the distribution of power in the post-Cold War world and the advent in government of Hindu nationalists with a predilection to follow realist perspectives in making foreign policy that caused India's abandonment of four decades of nuclear ambiguity.

Apart from Vajpayee, other politicians privy to the nuclear test decision also harboured few misgivings on the subject. Former Home Minister LK Advani, who in the 1980s played an important role in committing the BJP to the Ram Janmabhoomi campaign, had favoured the development of nuclear weapons as president of the Jana Sangh in 1974, and of the BJP in 1987. More abrasive than the emollient Vajpayee, he unnerved US envoy Strobe Talbott at a meeting in July 1998 by musing about the happy day when the entire South Asian subcontinent, as well as Myanmar (Burma), would be 'reunited' in a single 'confederation' (Talbott 2004: 101). Set against the RSS' conception of Bharat Mata (Mother India) extending from Iran in the west to Singapore in the east 'with Sri Lanka (Ceylon) as a lotus petal offered at her sacred feet' (Golwalkar 1980: 111), and the history of Hindu nationalist hostility to Pakistan, it was not a reassuring vision. Yet, while relations were often tense, the policy of the BJP-led government towards Pakistan proved not strikingly different from earlier periods. Vajpayee, after appearing to lead the country to the brink of war after cross-border incursions by Pakistani-backed Muslim militants in 1999, 2001 and 2002, ended his premiership by initiating a peace process, since continued by his Congress successor.

Religious nationalism, security interests and Indo-Israeli military cooperation It is only in recent years that the nexus between religion and nationalism in India and Israel has attracted attention as a factor in leading to a convergence of foreign policies in the face of the Muslim foes they each confront (Prashad 2003; Pant 2004; Blarel 2006). Having itself just suffered the trauma of religious partition, and mindful of the sensitivities of the large Muslim population that remained, India was the only non-Muslim country to vote (unsuccessfully) in the United Nations against both the partition of Palestine (in 1947) and the admission of Israel to membership of the organisation (in 1949).

Despite extending recognition to Israel in 1950 and the emigration of some 20,000 Indian Jews to Israel in subsequent decades, for more than forty years the two countries did not even have diplomatic relations and contacts were generally low level, spasmodic or indirect.

However, since the establishment of full diplomatic ties fifteen years ago, a substantial relationship has developed in areas such as defence (under the BJP-led government Israel became India's biggest arms supplier and India Israel's chief client) (Koshy 2006: 155), civil trade (especially involving the diamond industry) – India became Israel's second biggest trading partner in Asia in 200-and tourism (India has become a favoured destination of

Israeli tourists). The coincidence of the advent in 1977 of Begin's Likud-led government in Israel and the Janata coalition in India (with Vajpayee as Minister for External Affairs) led to an inconclusive secret visit by Israeli Foreign Minister Moshe Dayan. A decade later a triangular dynamic that became an important feature of Indo-Israeli relations first appeared with the formidable Zionist and emerging pro-India lobbies in the United States overlapping to apply pressure on Rajiv Gandhi's Congress government to move faster towards developing relations with Israel (Chiriyankandath 1989). However, it was only in the wake of the end of the Cold War that in January 1992 the Congress government of PV Narashima Rao finally established full-diplomatic relations with Israel, a course long advocated by the BJP and its precursor, the Jana Sangh (Baxter 1969: 200-01).

Indo-Israeli cooperation intensified after the BJP-led government took office in Delhi in 1998 with frequent exchanges of visits by cabinet ministers culminating in Ariel Sharon becoming the first Israeli premier to visit India in September 2003. The Indo-US rapprochement marked by US President Bill Clinton's successful visit to India in 2000 and the threats from militant Muslim violence faced by all three states (India, Israel and the US) provided a further fillip to this cooperation, especially after the September 11th, 2001, al-Qaeda terrorist attacks on New York and Washington.

Addressing the American Jewish Congress in May 2003 India's National Security Advisor Brajesh Mishra, noting the presence of many members of the US Congress who were friends of Israel and also of India, spoke of the 'shared values of our peoples' and of how the US, India and Israel faced 'the same ugly face of modern day terrorism'. At the end of Sharon's visit to India Israeli Deputy Prime Minister Yosef Lapid echoed these sentiments when he spoke of American support for such an unwritten axis to combat international terrorism.

The non-partisan basis for Indo-Israeli military cooperation became apparent by its maintenance after the Congress-led government came to power in 2004. Defence Minister Pranab Mukherji noted the 'convergence when it comes to securing the country' (Koshy 2006: 253). His successor, AK Antony, informed parliament in May 2007 that Indian defence purchases from Israel amounted to over US$5 billion and two months later a cabinet commission chaired by Prime Minister Manmohan Singh approved a US$2.5 billion on a new joint venture with Israel to build missiles to strike aerial targets (Kumaraswamy 2007). Whatever mutual admiration there may be-calling for the construction of a grand temple in Ayodhya in January 2006, BJP President Rajnath Singh referred to how Jews had kept their national aspirations alive by venerating the Wailing Wall in Jerusalem—the burgeoning ties between India and Israel owe much more to perceptions of mutually advantageous security cooperation than religious nationalist sentiment.

India and Israel : The Limitations of Religious Nationalism

The Zionist founders of Israel expected it to resolve the issue of Jewish identity in the modern world (Ravitzky 2005: 159). Instead it simply provided a focus for continued controversy, both over what kind of state for the Jews Israel should be and its place in the world. Domestically, by essentially recognising Orthodox Judaism as the de facto official state religion, the compromise arrived at between Ben-Gurion and the ultra-Orthodox at Israel's creation proved an obstacle to a fully-fledged debate on the relationship of religion to the state (Ben-Zadok 2001: 143). Formulations such as the definition of Israel as 'a Jewish and democratic state' in the Basic Law on Human Dignity and Liberty enacted in 1992, elided the two central contradictions of the Zionist state – the Orthodox Halakhic religious interpretation of the word 'Jewish' (Neuberger 1999: 81-2) and the way in which the state's democratic character is permanently limited by defining it as 'Jewish'. As one of the most outspoken critics of the Israeli state put it, for Israeli Jews unprepared to accept fundamentalist strictures, all varieties of Jewish fundamentalism are dangerous while for the Palestinian Arabs and Israel's neighbours, the messianic variant of the religious nationalist camp represent the greatest danger (Shahak 1999: 148-9).

Baruch Kimmerling defined the opposing visions of Israel in the following terms: an Eretz Israel based on primordial Jewish kinship, borders based on Jewish history and laws on Jewish tradition, and a State of Israel based, however ambiguously, on the Western civic tradition, negotiated borders and secular law (Kimmerling 1984). A clear parallel can be drawn between this Israeli dichotomy and the Nehruvian and majoritarian 'Hindu' visions of India (Chiriyankandath 2000: 21). The crucial difference was that in a state not established on religious identity it was possible to devise a constitutional framework and develop a polity that transcended the limitations of a nationalism circumscribed by the cultural parameters of a religious group.

The circumstances of the genesis of the modern state of Israel have left it locked into an existential conflict, one in which the strategy of the 'Iron Wall' has remained, literally and metaphorically, the overarching template for foreign policymaking. A decade after the Oslo Accord, Israel was engaged in building an actual wall through the Occupied Territories to keep out potential Palestinian attackers as Israeli analysts warned of how the strategy of the wall needed 'to be rebuilt around a Jewish state, not a bi-national inferno' (Navon 2004: 37). Yet this will not solve Israel's dilemma that as long as it remains a Jewish state ruling over politically marginalised and resentful Palestinian Arabs, both in the Occupied Territories and its pre-1967 borders, this 'domestic' political fact will trammel its foreign policy and preclude it securing its position internationally.

In post-Independence India too what Indian secularism should mean in practice has remained a live issue, especially with the political salience of Hindutva in the last two decades, and owing to the state legacy (Pakistan and Bangladesh on its borders) of the religious partition of the subcontinent. These linked factors have helped inspire an influential, albeit somewhat crudely realist, strand in Indian strategic thinking.

Bharat Karnad exemplifies this. Criticising Indian leaders for being responsible for a 'soft state' and lacking the will to power, he rhetorically concludes his polemic for India to become a nuclear superpower by arguing that 'the bulk of the people, attuned to the vagaries of machtpolitik depicted in the ancient Hindu texts and conditioned by life-long deprivation, are hard as nails, crave respect for India in the world and are willing to make whatever sacrifices' (Karnad 2002: 701).

Yet the reality is that India owes much of the greater stature she has gained on the world stage since the end of the Cold War not to the formal acquisition of military nuclear capability but its rapidly expanding economy and 'soft power' attributes such its democratic record, cultural exports (film, food, music etc.), the benign aura shed by the legacy of Gandhi and Nehru and the wealth and skills of the global Indian diaspora. These were the elements of power emphasised by the outgoing BJP Minister for External Affairs, Yashwant Sinha, in his last major speech, one in which he also described national unity and social harmony as a '*sine qua non* for India's progress in the international arena'. He declared: 'India's biggest strength is its secular and multi-cultural ethos... To damage our heritage of tolerance and pluralism or to waver in upholding these principles is the biggest setback that can occur to our great power ambitions' (Sinha 2004).

Pakistan's Talibanization : No Strategic Threat to India

Introductory Observations

Pakistan's Talibanization is inevitable and should not have come as a strategic surprise to discerning strategic analysts. Pakistan's Talibanization has been inevitable due to acts of complicity and commission by the Pakistan Army military hierarchy and the permissive toleration by the United States of Pakistan Army's strategic delinquencies in this direction for over a decade now. The Pakistan Army created, nurtured and continues to sustain the Taliban along with Al Qaeda as a "strategic asset" to be used both against the United States and Afghanistan on its Western flanks and against India on its Eastern flanks with more specific reference to Kashmir. These entities were the instruments of proxy war in the Pakistan Army's armory against India along with other Jehadist organizations like the Laskar-e-Toiba created by the Pakistan Army.

India more specifically has from 1989 till today has been incessantly battling Pakistan Army's instruments of proxy war to begin with in the Kashmir Valley and now extending to the whole expanse of India in terms of terrorism, suicide bombings and sabotage. India over such a long period of time successfully contained Pakistani proxy war laced with Islamic Jehadi contours and did not succumb to this Pakistani menace. This despite the regrettable strategic meekness and timidity of successive Indian governments of different political dispensations in India's counter-terrorism responses. This also despite the susceptibility of each Indian Government to succumb to external pressures advising restraint against Pakistan.

The Indian Armed Forces have stood their ground all along against Pakistan's state-sponsored proxy wars and there is no reason to doubt that the Indian Armed Forces would be inadequate in dealing with any renewed or reinvigorated military threats from a "Talibanized Pakistan" in the form of nuclear, conventional or asymmetric warfare. A Talibanized Pakistan should be considered of no more "strategic concern" than an adversarial Pakistan which in the last sixty two years initiated four major wars against India and incessant irregular warfare without any results.

The Indian media has gone beserk in sensationalizing and raising the bogey of Pakistan's Talibanization as some sort of insurmountable military threat to India. Some project it as "Barbarians at the Gates" and while others project the "Unstoppable Taliban" as being only an hours drive or so from Indian borders. At times one gets a sneaking feeling that this Indian media hysteria on the Talibanization of Pakistan is externally inspired to induce in the Indian policy establishment and in Indian public opinion, pressures for an Indian policy orientation that would incorporate a fixation that India at any cost must contribute to stemming the tide of Pakistan's Talibanization.

The point already stands made that the creation of Taliban was fathered by the Pakistan Army and its delivery midwifed by the United States. If the Taliban in its contemporary manifestations today poses a strategic threat to Pakistan and the United States, then the Taliban threat has to be met strategically and militarily by Pakistan and the United States. India never ever figured anywhere in the process of the emergence of the Taliban and nor has India assisted in the Talibanization of Pakistan India therefore has no moral or strategic compulsions to stem the Taliban tide.

Having made the statement of the case, this chapter now attempts to marshal facts and perspectives as follows to dispel the hysterical proportions imparted by the Indian media and some policy analysts on the creeping Talibanization of Pakistan under way:

- Pakistan and the Taliban: A Brief Reality Check.
- Pakistan's Talibanization Facilitated by Pakistan Army Ceding Strategic Space by its Withdrawals from Frontier Regions.
- Impeding Talibanization of Pakistan: Factors That Can Come Into Play.
- Talibanized Pakistan: Strategic and Military Contours.
- Talibanized Pakistan: A Strategic Window of Opportunity for India.

Pakistan and the Taliban: A Brief Reality Check

Innumerable books and analyses by Western and noted Pakistani analysts exist on the Taliban and their disruptive roles in Afghanistan and Pakistan. This chapter sets out a reality check incorporating salient facets which reinforce the statement of case made in this chapter and those which assist in the understanding of the perspectives offered. Essentially therefore, this reality check would incorporate the following:

- The Taliban was a Pakistan Army creation executed under the orders of Benazir Bhutto Prime Minister of Pakistan in mid 1990s.
- Pakistan Army used the Taliban as an instrument of military subjugation of Afghanistan. Pakistan Army Officers, ISI officers and Pakistan Army regulars were used to stiffen Taliban cadres for operational purposes.
- Talibanized Afghanistan was used by the Pakistan Army and ISI to set up "Islamic Jehadi factories" to tram cadres for global Islamic Jehad. Both the Taliban and the Al Qaeda were co-opted and exploited for this purpose. The horrific 9/11 assaults on USA homeland were the end results.
- Post 9/11, the United States launched its military intervention to displace the Taliban regime in Afghanistan and destroy terrorist infrastructure. Pakistan Army played no part to assist the United States.

- Pakistan Army regime undo General Musharraf overnight switched sides and agreed to assist US global war on terrorism.
- Surprisingly and regrettably for reasons undefined the United States assisted the Pakistan Army to withdraw nearly 12,000 Pakistan Army personnel and Taliban cadres from Konduz in Afghanistan by a US airlift.
- Following the establishment of the US sponsored democratic regime in Kabul, Pakistan Army has "double-timed" the United States by continued de-stabilization of Southern Afghanistan through a revived Taliban enjoyed safe havens in Pakistan's border regions.

Notably, the United States and NATO Forces have not been able to neutralize the revived Taliban threat due to Pakistan's Army's complicity with the Taliban in providing safe havens for them in Pakistan. Since the Pakistan Army is a "blind spot" of United States policy establishment and strategic community, the United States has even under the new US Administration, unable to come to grips with the simple strategic reality that for stabilization of both Afghanistan and Pakistan the United States needs to "discipline" Pakistan Army's strategic delinquencies and its continuing dancing in cohorts with the Taliban in direct detriment of US national security interests.

Pakistan's Talibanization Facilitated by Pakistan Army Ceding Strategic Space

Pakistan's creeping Talibanization raises one very significant question and that is as to how the Taliban have made headway in Pakistan when the Pakistan Army has had no strategic distractions on its Eastern borders for the last four to five years. In 2004 under US pressure the Pakistan Army had a ceasefire agreement in operation with India along the LOC. This ceasefire was unilaterally broken in mid-2008 by the Pakistan Army under its present Chief of Army Staff, General Kayani. This after firing strategic broadsides at the United States that he would neither train nor regroup the Pakistan Army for operations on the Pak-Afghan frontier and that the Pakistan Army would concentrate on its primary mission against its main threat i.e. India. Vacating the western frontiers by the Pakistan Army on the plea of an Indian threat was only a fig-leaf cover for Pakistan Army's real design of allowing the resulting vacuum to be filled in by various Taliban militias to the detriment of US national security interests.

Pakistan's creeping Talibanization has occurred as the Pakistan Army started withdrawing from the frontier regions of South Waziristan, North Waziristan and now lately from the Swat Valley. The military vacuum so caused by the Pakistan Army in these areas were speedily put under the effective control of the various Taliban warlords. Pakistan's state sovereignty ceased in those areas consequently. Pakistan Army's military withdrawal from these critical areas bordering on Afghanistan raises two questions (1) Pakistan Army withdrew from these regions after their military failures in regaining control of the Taliban ensconced in these regions, or/and (2) Pakistan Army withdrew from these regions as part of a well calculated plan to cede these regions to Taliban control so that the Pakistan Army could plead a plausible deniability exit that the heightened Taliban operations against the US and NATO Forces in Afghanistan were being launched from areas not under control of the Pakistan Army.

On both counts the United States should realize the strategic dilemma and dead-end that it has been forced into in Afghanistan by the Pakistan Army. If it is militarily ineffective against the Taliban, then the Pakistan Army cannot be expected to control and prevail the creeping Talibanization of Pakistan. The second count seems more likely and that the Pakistan Army is complicit in the creeping Taliban spread over Pakistan's heartland, secure in the belief that ultimately the end game of such a process would be the forcing of the United States exit from Afghanistan, thereby leaving Afghanistan once again to be retrieved under Pak control through the Taliban.

The last contention above gets reinforced in that the Pakistan Army is alternately and selectively preventing Taliban reclaiming Pakistan territory, as it did earlier in Bajaur. It also defeats the argument that the Taliban is unstoppable by the Pakistan Army. It also follows that the current bogey of Talibanization of Pakistan is a myth and bogey deliberately cultivated by the Pakistan Army to pressurize the United States on the following counts

(1) United States would pressurize India to yield and compromise on the Kashmir issue to accommodate US strategic sensitivities (2) Make the United States to increase military aid to Pakistan Army (3) Force the United States for massive developmental aid to Pakistan's Taliban prone areas but actually would once again be diverted to the Pak Army.

Impeding Talibanization of Pakistan

Pakistan's creeping Talibanization is a product of the Pakistan Army's well crafted blueprint. It seems to be a well calibrated process with the Pakistan Army secure in the belief that it can control the calibrated Taliban escalation. Should for whatever reason, if the Taliban breaks out from the Pakistan Army calibrated blueprint, then three main actors come into play to impede and stop Pakistan's Talibanization.

The three main actors that can impede Pakistan's Talibanization are (1) The Pakistan Army (2) The United States (3) The Pakistani Public especially in Punjab. The Pakistan Army can be forced to impede Pakistan's Talibanization by strong coercive pressure by the United States or by the self-preservation instincts of the Pakistan Army to refurbish its strong domestic image.

The United States has two options to impede Pakistan's Talibanization. The first has already been stated above. Should the Pakistan Army be not inclined to submit to United States demands for impeding the Talibanization of Pakistan, then the United States needs to be strategically prepared for a United States military intervention in Pakistan with the following aims (1) Elimination of Taliban and Al Qaeda from the Pakistani firmament (2) Gain control over Pakistan Army's nuclear arsenal and (3) Pakistan Army be disciplined and purged of its Islamist ideology.

The third actor to impede Pakistan's Talibanization, and the most significant of all is the Pakistani public and more especially the Punjabis of Pakistan's heartland and the core of the Pakistan Army. Lately in the Op-Eds and features in the Pakistani English newspapers there is evidence that the Pakistani Punjabis are not going to willingly accept the Talibanization of Punjab.

There are also indications that should the Pakistan Army be unwilling to rein-in the Taliban, then the peoples power would came into play both against the Pakistan Army and the Taliban and Al Qaeda. This could spell civil war in Pakistan and its possible disintegration.

It would be interesting to watch how China and Saudi Arabia react to a civil war ensuing in Pakistan enmeshed as they are in Pakistan both by bolstering the Pakistan Army and moreso, the Taliban and Al Qaeda. Colossal amounts of Saudi money has gone into financing the Taliban and China has been involved significantly in the arming of the Taliban.

Talibanized Pakistan: Strategic and Military Contours

Remotely probable, but not a distinct possibility currently, should an entire Pakistan fully. Talibanized emerges, then its strategic and military contours need to be examined and the nature of threat that it poses to India, more specifically. It is ones strong belief that a fully Talibanized Pakistan cannot emerge without a fully Talibanized Pakistan Army. The most notable casualties in the emergence of a fully Talibanized Pakistan Army would be the disintegration of its military hierarchy, command and control structures, professional integration and professional military competence.

In terms of strategic and military contours, a fully Talibanized Pakistan could hardly pose an integrated military threat to any of its neighbours except for irregular warfare. The major deduction here that one would like to offer is that a Talibanized Pakistan would be dominated by warring Taliban warlords more engrossed in infighting amongst themselves and possibly embroiled in a civil war or battling the major actors intent on impeding Pakistan's Talibanization.

Surely, a Talibanized Pakistan is likely to give a spurt to terrorism and proxy war against India. An India fully expectant and prepared for such an eventually can certainly defeat such military adventurism as it has been done in the last 62 years against Pakistan Army adventurism. In terms of sustaining a Talibanized Pakistan militarily, only China and Saudi-Arabia can come into play. China had a propensity of sustaining "rogue regimes" the world over. China would however in sustaining a Talibanized Pakistan militarily would have to contend with US and Western sanctions, displeasure and development of counter-strategic pressure points against China in Tibet and Xinjiang.

A Tragic Indian Parable Vs China's Strategy

There is an ancient Indian story that applies to the future of the country and its idiot leaders.

A man had one son and a donkey. After loading the donkey with goods for sale, the father and son went from their village to the market in the city. On the way, the father told the son to ride the donkey. In the first village they passed on their way, a number of passers-by commented how inconsiderate the young son was in riding the donkey while the elderly father walked. The shamed son dismounted and let his father ride the donkey. In the next village people criticized the father for riding while his young small son walked. The father and son having no convictions, thoughts or policy of their own, then decided that both would ride the donkey. In the third village on the way, people cried shame on these fellows both riding a donkey already laden with goods. One wisecracked, "these two hefty fellows are sturdy enough to carry the donkey instead of the donkey carrying them". The foolish father and son like India's politicians of all parties then began carrying the donkey. They came to a narrow bridge without rails and lost their balance. All three fell into the river and drowned in the torrential current.

Nehru turned a blind eye at Chinese encroachment on India's borders in 1962. He neglected defence and military procurement and had to beg President Kennedy for American planes and arms and appeal to the Soviet Union to restrain China. At that time, the Soviets were having differences with Mao and America had fought China in Korea earlier and had skirmishes over Quemoy and Matsu islands in the Straits of Taiwan. China occupied Aksai Chin and kept it but withdrew from the Northeast of India. Pakistan ceded parts of Kashmir it occupies and the Chinese constructed the Karakoram highway, an all weather road link between China and Pakistan. About a decade earlier China had occupied and annexed Tibet obtaining control over the water supply of Pakistan, Indian north Burma, Vietnam. The Indus, Mekong, Brahmaputra, Salween, Yangtze and Yellow rivers all arise from Tibet. Unlike

Nehru's idiocy of a future plebiscite and Article 370 prohibiting India's citizens from settling or buying land in Kashmir, China flooded Tibet and Sinkiang with Han Chinese to make the Tibetans and Uighurs a minority in their own land.

China exploited America and Nixon's foolishness to come to terms with it without the humiliating subjugation that Manmohan Singh agreed to in the civil nuclear deal. At the just finished G8 meeting America introduced a backdoor clause barring any transfer or sale of nuclear enrichment technology to India. The US reneged on the earlier deal just as it had done before about supply of enriched uranium to the Tarapur power plants. Manmohan Singh performed a humiliating bow as he had done to Musharaf at the NAM meeting in Havana. He is so happy that he gets invited to the G8 meetings even if it is to keep pulling the string of the *Punkah* like in the days of the British Raj. China used the forum to threaten to dethrone the dollar as a reserve currency. Please note the difference in behaviour.

During the 1965 war with Pakistan, India had to stop fighting, agree to a ceasefire and Lal Bahadur Shastri was summoned to Tashkent and agreed to the imposed peace terms as India was dependent on Russia for ammunition. Shastri suffered a heart attack and died. Indira Gandhi smartly toured many western capitals to prepare India's case for the Bangladesh War, signed a friendship treaty with the Soviets to assure munitions supply and the use of the Soviet veto in the UN Security Council till Pakistan was routed and Dacca captured. Times have changed.

Manmohan Singh is a mere puppet of Sonia and knows nothing of world history and even less of economics besides the brainwashing he received about the prevalent economic fads of his times in the Socialist phase of the London School of Economics. America despite its nuclear arsenal and high tech military is a waning power. Its glory based on insurmountable debt and its military power has failed in Iraq and Afghanistan currently and it failed in Korea in the fifties and Vietnam in the sixties and seventies. The Soviet Union collapsed but ignorant Manmohan Singh has no clue as to America's current status when he hitched India's wagon to America at the cost of alienating Russia as the dispute and extortion that Russia demanded for the Gorshkov shows. China once again threatens India by claiming Arunachal and warning India, that it is foolish and destined for disaster if it competes with or stands up to China militarily. These statements were made in reference to India re-opening airbases in Ladakh, Assam and Arunachal and posting squadrons of the advanced Sukhoi aircraft. India should not be deterred by Chinese threats but it should be adequately prepared. China has airbases on the Tibetan and Arunachal border and has stationed medium range nuclear and conventional missiles there, just like it has done on the opposite coast of Taiwan. In addition, it has built rail lines all the way to the Indian border in Tibet and Arunachal. India has no decent rail or adequate road links to Arunachal and Ladakh even after 60+years.

China's Missile Power

China has perfected cruise missiles to neutralize US aircraft carriers in the Pacific and is rapidly increasing its surface and submarine (including nuclear) fleets. It has demonstrated anti-satellite weapons capability to convince the US that it can neutralize its satellite and network centric war capabilities. I would not be surprised if the recent hacker attack on US and South Korean government sites allegedly attributed to North Korea was launched with tacit blessing and encouragement from China, as a trial balloon and implicit threat. It has concluded border agreements with all its neighbours except India, is supplying Pakistan with planes, cruise missiles and nuclear weapon technology. Its string of pearls strategy has given it port facilities in Myanmar (Bay Of Bengal), Sri Lanka (off India's southern tip), Gwadar, Baluchistan (at the mouth of the Persian Gulf). It supplies arms to Myanmar, Sri Lanka and Bangladesh. It is the leading trading partner of Russia, America, EU, Korea, Japan and Brazil. It is giving aid to African countries and is the largest creditor of America which dare not assist India against any Chinese attack, for fear of China dumping dollars to collapse the US economy.

Our idiot leaders don't understand that no one will side with India this time in a war with China. I am not implying that we should kowtow to China. We should be fully prepared to stalemate it and inflict severe damage. We can't do that when we don't have enough howitzers, ammunition, aircraft or logistic facilities to supply our armed forces at the borders with China. For years Indian governments have been delaying and postponing the purchase of medium range multi-role combat aircraft, attack helicopters, howitzers, most likely hoping to get bigger and better bribes for officials, ministers and political parties. We need to build rapid and robust rail and road links and redundant military airports at our borders, put geo-stationary orbit reconnaissance satellites with high resolution cameras in the skies over our borders with Pakistan and China and move substantial troops with armor, artillery and attack helicopters to bases close to our borders but not close enough to be perceived as an offensive threat. Much of our borders with the two major adversaries are mountainous and thus roads and rails are difficult to build and easy to destroy by aerial bombing, that is why we need state of the art attack helicopters available from Russia, Italy, South Africa, Britain and America. As long as America keeps arming Pakistan with weapons meant to attack India, we should only buy from America if there is no alternative supplier or if their arms are markedly superior and pricing is affordable, without restrictions in use.

3

India and Non-Alignment

India played an important role in the multilateral movements of colonies and newly independent countries that developed into the Non-Aligned Movement.

Origin of Nonalignment Movement

Nonalignment had its origins in India's colonial experience and the nonviolent Indian independence struggle led by the Congress, which left India determined to be the master of its fate in an international system dominated politically by Cold War alliances and economically by Western capitalism and Soviet communism.

The principles of nonalignment, as articulated by Nehru and his successors, were preservation of India's freedom of action internationally through refusal to align India with any bloc or alliance, particularly those led by the United States or the Soviet Union; nonviolence and international cooperation as a means of settling international disputes. Nonalignment was a consistent feature of Indian foreign policy by the late 1940s and enjoyed strong, almost unquestioning support among the Indian elite.

The term "Non-Alignment" itself was coined by Indian Prime Minister Jawaharlal Nehru during his speech in 1954 in Colombo, Sri Lanka. In this speech, Nehru described the five pillars to be used as a guide for Sino-Indian relations, which were first put forth by Chinese Premier Zhou Enlai. Called Panchsheel (five restraints), these principles would later serve as the basis of the Non-Aligned Movement. The five principles were:

1. Mutual respect for each other's territorial integrity and sovereignty
2. Mutual non-aggression
3. Mutual non-interference in domestic affairs
4. Equality and mutual benefit
5. Peaceful co-existence

Jawaharlal Nehru's concept of nonalignment brought India considerable international prestige among newly independent states that shared India's concerns about the military confrontation between the superpowers and the influence of the former colonial powers. New Delhi used nonalignment to establish a significant role for itself as a leader of the Third World in such multilateral organizations as the United Nations (UN) and the Nonaligned Movement. The signing of the Treaty of Peace, Friendship, and Cooperation between India and the Soviet Union in 1971 and India's involvement in the internal affairs of its smaller neighbours in the 1970s and 1980s tarnished New Delhi's image as a nonaligned nation and led some observers to note that in practice, nonalignment applied only to India's relations with countries outside South Asia.

Early Developments

The movement had its origins in the 1947 Asian Relations Meeting in New Delhi and the 1955 Asian-African Conference in Bandung, Indonesia. India also participated in the 1961 Belgrade Conference that officially established the Nonaligned Movement, but Jawaharlal Nehru's declining prestige limited his influence. In the 1960s and 1970s, New Delhi concentrated on internal problems and bilateral relations, yet retained membership in an increasingly factionalized and radicalized movement. During the contentious 1979 Havana summit, India worked with moderate nations to reject Cuban president Fidel Castro's proposition that "socialism" (that is, the Soviet Union) was the "natural ally" of nonalignment.

In 1980s

Under Indira Gandhi in the early 1980s, India attempted to reassert its prominent role in the Nonaligned Movement by focusing on the relationship between disarmament and economic development. By appealing to the economic grievances of developing countries, Indira Gandhi and her successors exercised a moderating influence on the Nonaligned Movement, diverting it from some of the Cold War issues that marred the controversial 1979 Havana meeting. Although hosting the 1983 summit boosted Indian prestige within the movement, its close relations with the Soviet Union and its pro-Soviet positions on Afghanistan and Cambodia limited its influence.

The end of the Cold War left the Non-aligned Movement without its original raison d'être, and its membership became deeply divided over international disputes, strategy, and organization. During the 1992 Jakarta summit, India took a middle position between countries favouring confrontation with developed nations on international economic issues, such as Malaysia, and those that favoured a more cooperative approach, such as Indonesia. Although New Delhi played a minor role compared with Kuala Lumpur and Jakarta on most issues facing the summit, India formulated the Nonaligned Movement position opposing developed countries' linkage of foreign aid to human rights criteria.

Consequences

The early 1990s demise of the bipolar world system, which had existed since the end of World War II, shook the underpinnings of India's foreign policy. The Cold War system of alliances had been rendered meaningless by the collapse of the East European communist states, the dissolution of the Warsaw Treaty Organization (Warsaw Pact), and the demise of the Soviet Union. In the early 1990s, most colonies had become independent, and apartheid in South Africa was being dismantled, diminishing the value of anticolonialism and making it impossible for antiracism to serve as a rallying point for international political action (India and South Africa restored full diplomatic relations in 1993 after a thirty nine year lapse). The Panchsheel (Panch Shila), peaceful resolution of international disputes, and international cooperation to spur economic development which was being enhanced by domestic economic reforms were broad objectives in a changing world. Thus, the 1990s saw India redefining nonalignment and the view of India's place in the world. India also is a founding member of the Group of fifteen, a group of developing nations established at the ninth Nonaligned Movement summit in Belgrade in 1989 to facilitate dialogue with the industrialized countries. India played host to the fourth Group of Fifteen summit in March 1994. At the summit, Prime Minister Narsimha Rao and other leaders expressed concern over new trade barriers being raised by the industrialized countries despite the conclusion of a new world trade agreement.

India's Non-Alignment Doctrine

India's Nonalignment Doctrine as a foreign policy precept was formulated by India's first Prime Minister Jawaharlal Nehru. He continued as India's Prime Minister from its independence in 1947 until his death in 1964, a long spell of seventeen long years. He dominated India's political scene as the indisputable leader of the ruling Congress Party and in the process established India's ruling political dynasty which extends till today. The aura which he acquired as the more visible face of the Congress freedom struggle led to the endowment of a political charisma on him as the Prime Minister of the Congress Party which began governing India in 1947. As a consequence his political decisions became unquestionable including those in the foreign policy field. Foreign policy formulation became personalized in the person of the Prime Minister, Jawaharlal Nehru and continued as such even in the tenures of his dynastic successors, namely his daughter Indira Gandhi and his grandson, Rajiv Gandhi.

India's Nonalignment Doctrine was formulated by Nehru as the touchstone of new India's foreign policy and Nehru steered India in the international community accordingly. Nehru's passionate obsession to nonalignment led him to establish the Non-Alignment Movement (NAM) which he did in the company of leaders like President Tito of Yugoslavia, President Nasser of Egypt, President Sukarno of Indonesia and President Nkrumah of Ghana. They all were leaders of newly independent countries that emerged in the wake of the end of the Second World War and the shake-off of colonial rule of the European powers. But this did not deflect the first major criticism of international observers, and especially Western leaders that Nehru as a highly professed democrat had to rely on the dubious company of military dictators and civil autocrats as founding fathers of the NAM. This criticism grew over the years as NAM expanded and most of the members that were added to ultimately reach a figure of over seventy had similar backgrounds, more or less. It also included countries that were openly allied with the Soviet bloc like Cuba.

Nehru, it seems was attempting to craft a Third World Bloc in the bipolar structure of the Cold War era with idealistic hopes that the newly independent underdeveloped countries as a bloc could emerge as a ginger group in international affairs and extract maximum concessions from the Big Powers. Also, it was hoped that NAM and India in particular, would be able to stay clear of Cold War entanglement and conflicts. In the process, Nehru revealed in occupying the centre-stage of global politics with his high flown idealistic moral posturing. India gradually started losing international relevance in USA and the Western group of advanced industrialized countries as India's moral hectoring grew and India began adopting double standards in the Cold War standards.

The end of the Cold War and the new international realities that emerged forced India to recognize that nonalignment without political, economic and military muscle was not a workable concept and that if India was to actualize its latent great power potential, it had to shed its ideological obsession with nonalignment and join the international power game in the spirit of the REALISM school of political thought.

This was a total turnaround from the Nehruvian Doctrine of Non-Alignment and obviously had to be taken by a Prime Minister from outside the fold of the Nehru-Gandhi political dynasty. The man of the moment for this bold reversal of Indian foreign policy was P V Narashima Rao. Subsequently, the BJP Govt. under Vajpayee enlarged and added new horizons to India's foreign policy including the defining moment of the 1998 nuclear weapons tests. This has catapulted India into the Big Power league and has made Indian foreign policy trends so initiated as irreversible. So much so that the current Congress Government despite the Nehruvian Foreign Minister (since sacked over the Volcker Report) and Leftists pressure has found it prudent to stay the course set by the BJP Govt. India today is being widely accepted as an emerging key global player and figuring in the strategic calculus of USA, Russia, China and the EU as a force to reckon with It has achieved this only after discarding the archaic concept of Non-Alignment that it obsessively followed for four decades. Indians of the current generation who would be moving India to its rightful future would naturally question India's losses as a result of the Non-Alignment Doctrine of India's foreign policy?

The answers in brief of India's losses are as follows:

- National Security: It suffered as threat perceptions were de-emphasized and defence preparedness was ignored. It led to India's military debacle against China in 1962. It also severely impeded the evolution of independent India's appropriate strategic culture with the obsessive commitment to Pacifism and peace even at the cost of national security interests.
- Political Influence: It stood confined to NAM countries as political penetration into global political groupings and strategic partnerships was a taboo as per nonalignment precepts and these partnerships were not open to India bound down by such precepts.
- Economic Losses: India was self-prevented from integrating itself into a globalized economy and reaping the benefits of FDI, income generation and jobs generation. Socialistic pattern of economies was the hallmark of NAM countries. The result was poor rates of economic growth and stagnant economies which India could ill-afford for poverty-alleviation for its large population.
- Nuclear Weapons as Currency of Power: BJP Foreign Minister was right in pointing out that a moralistic nuclear policy (which again was a spin-off from nonalignment moralism) paid no dividends to India. India's defining moment to catapult into the Big League was delayed for a quarter of a century with all the attendant losses.

India's Non-Alignment Doctrine as a foreign policy precept, therefore, has been a monumental failure. It was more idealistic than visionary and lacked the vital content of any foreign policy, namely, realism and realpolitik to secure India's national security interests. It was a poignant failure for Nehru that at the most critical moment of his political career as Prime Minister, the 1962 Sino-Indian Conflict his NAM colleagues failed to come out in his favour the Chinese line; a factor that hastened his death in 1964. So much for nonalignment.

India Nonalignment

Nonalignment had its origins in India's colonial experience and the nonviolent independence struggle led by the Congress, which left India determined to be the master of its fate in an international system dominated politically by Cold War alliances and economically by Western capitalism. The principles of nonalignment, as articulated by Nehru and his successors, were preservation of India's freedom of action internationally through refusal to align India with any bloc or alliance, particularly those led by the United States or the Soviet Union; nonviolence and international cooperation as a means of settling international disputes; the Panch Shila, or the five principles of peaceful coexistence, as the basis for relations between states; opposition to colonialism and racism; and international cooperation to alleviate poverty and promote economic development. Nonalignment was a consistent feature of Indian foreign policy by the late 1940s and enjoyed strong, almost unquestioning support among the Indian elite.

In the 1950s and 1960s, Nehru's concept of nonalignment brought India considerable international prestige among newly independent states that shared India's concerns about the military confrontation between the superpowers and the influence of the former colonial powers. New Delhi used nonalignment to establish a significant role for itself as a leader of the Third World in such multilateral organizations as the United Nations (UN) and the Nonaligned Movement. The signing of the Treaty of Peace, Friendship, and Cooperation between India and the Soviet Union in 1971 and India's involvement in the internal affairs of its smaller neighbours in the 1970s and 1980s tarnished New Delhi's image as a nonaligned nation and led some observers to note that in practice, nonalignment applied only to India's relations with countries outside South Asia. The early 1990s demise of the bipolar world system, which had existed since the end of World War II, shook the underpinnings of India's foreign policy. The Cold War system of alliances had been rendered meaningless by the collapse of the East European communist states, the dissolution of the Warsaw Treaty Organization (Warsaw Pact), and the demise of the Soviet Union. In the early 1990s, most colonies had become independent, and apartheid in South Africa was being dismantled, diminishing the value of anticolonialism and making it impossible for antiracism to serve as a rallying point for international political action (India and South Africa restored full diplomatic relations in 1993 after a thirty-nine-year lapse). The Panch Shila, peaceful resolution of international disputes, and international cooperation to spur economic development—which was being enhanced by domestic economic reforms—were broad objectives in a changing world. Thus, the 1990s saw India redefining nonalignment and the view of India's place in the world.

India to Play Moderating Role at 116-nation NAM

Prime Minister Manmohan Singh travels to Cuba this month to attend the Non-Aligned Movement (NAM) summit with India hoping to play a moderating role in the 116-nation disparate body whose agenda is in danger of being hijacked by the likes of Venezuela, Iran, Syria and the hosts themselves. The 14th NAM Summit is being held in Havana for a second time-the first was in 1979-under the leadership of Cuban President Fidel Castro, convalescing after a major surgery. Whether Castro is able to chair the summit Sep 15-16 or lets his brother and acting president Raul Castro preside over it remains to be seen.

This will be Manmohan Singh's first meeting with Castro (he goes to Havana after a two-day trip to Brazil Sep 12-13), a global titan who came to New Delhi to attend the NAM Summit in March 1983 and is remembered in freeze-frame images for his bear-hug of a visibly embarrassed prime minister Indira Gandhi, as he handed over the chairman's gavel to her for India to assume leadership of the movement. Despite carping voices about the irrelevance of NAM in a unipolar world, the movement that began with the coming together of 25 countries at Belgrade in

1961, the present summit will have 116 countries, reflecting a steadily growing membership and accounting for nearly two-thirds of the 192-nation UN.

"A grouping as large as that, and the largest outside the UN, cannot be ignored," said a senior Indian official who is accompanying the prime minister to Havana. And India's role, say officials and foreign policy experts, will be to provide the voice of moderation in a movement of which it is one of its founding fathers and which sought to chart an often Left-leaning course contested by the US by not getting 'aligned' in the East-West ideological confrontation of the Cold War.

Since the end of the Cold War and the breakup of the Soviet Union, many felt that the movement had lost its raison d'etre. But the movement has shown no signs of dissipating and instead has added newer members-and more and more nations are seeking its leadership role. Egypt has already begun lobbying to host the next NAM Summit three years from now. For India, the summit comes at a piquant phase in its foreign policy, when it is seen as having moved too close to the US. The summit will take place just days before the US Senate is expected to pass the landmark nuclear deal that will put a seal on the unfolding "strategic partnership" between the two countries.

India's effort would be to get NAM to focus more on economic rather than political issues so that developing and underdeveloped countries are able to speak in one voice against protectionism, disparity in world trade, UN reforms and globalization as well as issues like environment and HIV/AIDS. "We are certainly moving beyond NAM. To the extent, NAM was time-specific, it responded to the situation of the Cold War. Now with the collapse of communism, the focus has shifted. The focus is very much on economic development. What various peoples of Asia and Africa need to do is to benefit from globalization," Ghana Foreign Minister Nana Addo Dankwa Akuffo-Addo told India Abroad News Service (IANS) recently, while endorsing India's stand.

Many countries are looking to India to provide the movement the direction and the leadership it badly needs. "We look to stronger countries like India to provide the leadership to NAM. It is not in the interest of nonalignment to see India float away from it. Nor is it in India's interest," says South Africa's high commissioner to India, Francis Moloi.

What India would be wary of are targeting of countries or groups of countries and the movement being made a forum or a lobby for countries-or their 'loose cannon' leaders from pursuing their own radical agenda. With Presidents Hugo Chavez of Venezuela, Mahmoud Ahmadinejad of Iran and Basher Assad of Syria forging strategic ties, diplomatic observers would closely watch their moves at forming an anti-US, anti-West front, and India, particularly, will seek to resist any moves seeking to "hijack" the charted agenda of the NAM.

These countries and, in some ways, Malaysia, which sees itself as a leader of Islamic countries, are seen by some as 'loose cannons' that may manipulate the agenda of such a large body to subserve their own diplomatic and strategic goals.

Non-Aligned Movement

The Non-Aligned Movement (NAM) is an international organisation of states considering themselves not formally aligned with or against any major power bloc. The movement is largely the brainchild of India's first Prime Minister Jawaharlal Nehru, former president of Egypt Gamal Abdul Nasser and Yugoslav president Josip Broz Tito. It was founded in April 1955; as of 2006, it has 118 members. The purpose of the organisation as stated in the *Havana Declaration of 1979* is to ensure "the national independence, sovereignty, territorial integrity and security of nonaligned countries" in their "struggle against imperialism, colonialism, neo-colonialism, racism, and all forms of foreign aggression, occupation, domination, interference or hegemony as well as against great power and bloc politics." They represent nearly two-thirds of the United Nations's members and comprise 55% of the world population, particularly countries considered to be developing or part of the third world.

Members have, at various times, included: Yugoslavia, India, Ghana, Pakistan, Algeria, Bangladesh, Libya, Sri Lanka, Egypt, Indonesia, Cuba, Colombia, Venezuela, post-1994 South Africa, Iran, Malaysia, and, for a time, the People's Republic of China. Brazil has never been a formal member of the movement, but shares many of the aims of NAM and frequently sends observers to the Non-Aligned Movement's summits. While the organisation was intended to be as close an alliance as NATO or the Warsaw Pact, it has little cohesion and many of its members were actually quite closely aligned with one or another of the great powers. Additionally, some members were involved in serious conflicts with other members (e.g. India and Pakistan, Iran and Iraq). The movement fractured from its own internal contradictions when the Soviet Union invaded Afghanistan in 1979. While the Soviet allies supported the invasion, other members (particularly Islamic nations) of the movement did not.

Because the Non-Aligned Movement was formed as an attempt to thwart the Cold War, it has struggled to find relevance since the Cold War ended. After the breakup of Yugoslavia, a founding member, its membership was suspended in 1992 at the regular Ministerial Meeting of the Movement, held in New York during the regular yearly session of the General Assembly of the United Nations. At the Summit of the Movement in Jakarta, Indonesia (September 1, 1992-September 6, 1992) Yugoslavia was suspended or expelled from the Movement The successor states of the SFR Yugoslavia have expressed little interest in membership, though some have observer status. In 2004, Malta and Cyprus ceased to be members and joined the European Union. Belarus remains the sole member of the Movement in Europe. Turkmenistan, Belarus and Dominican Republic are the most recent entrants. The application of Bosnia-Herzegovina and Costa Rica were rejected in 1995 and 1998.

Origins

Independent countries, who chose not to join any of the Cold War blocs, were also known as non aligned nations.

The term "nonalignment" itself was coined by Indian Prime Minister Nehru during his speech in 1954 in Colombo, Sri Lanka. In this speech, Nehru described the five pillars to be used as a guide for Sino-Indian relations, which were first put forth by Chinese Premier Zhou Enlai. Called Panchsheel (five restraints), these principles would later serve as the basis of the Non-Aligned Movement. The five principles were:

- Mutual respect for each other's territorial integrity and sovereignty
- Mutual non-aggression
- Mutual non-interference in domestic affairs
- Equality and mutual benefit
- Peaceful co-existence.

A significant milestone in the development of the Nonaligned movement was the 1955 Bandung Conference, a conference of Asian and African states hosted by Indonesian president Sukarno. The attending nations declared their desire not to become involved in the Cold War and adopted a "declaration on promotion of world peace and cooperation", which included Nehru's five principles. Six years after Bandung, an initiative of Yugoslav president Tito led to the first official Non-Aligned Movement Summit, which was held in September 1961 in Belgrade.

At the Lusaka Conference in September 1970, the member nations added as aims of the movement the peaceful resolution of disputes and the abstention from the big power military alliances and pacts. Another added aim was opposition to stationing of military bases in foreign countries. The founding fathers of the Non-aligned movement were: Nehru of India, Sukarno of Indonesia and Josip Broz Tito of Yugoslavia, Gamal Abdul Nasser of Egypt and Kwame Nkrumah of Ghana. Their actions were known as 'The Initiative of Five'.

Organisational Structure and Membership

Requirements of the NAM with the key beliefs of the United Nations. The latest requirements are now that the candidate country has displayed practices in accordance with:

- Respect for fundamental human rights and for the purposes and principles of the Charter of the United Nations.
- Respect for the sovereignty and territorial integrity of all nations.
- Recognition of the equality of all races and of the equality of all nations, large and small.
- Abstention from intervention or interference in the internal affairs of another country.

- Respect for the right of each nation to defend itself singly or collectively, in conformity with the Charter of the United Nations.
- Refraining from acts or threats of aggression or the use of force against the territorial integrity or political independence of any country.
- Settlement of all international disputes by peaceful means, in conformity with the Charter of the United Nations.
- Promotion of mutual interests and cooperation.
- Respect for justice and international obligations.

Policies and Ideology

Secretaries General of the NAM had included such diversified figures as Suharto, an authoritarian anti-communist, and Nelson Mandela, a democratic socialist and famous anti-apartheid activist. Consisting of many governments with vastly different ideologies, the NAM is unified by its commitment in world peace and security. At the seventh summit held in New Delhi in March 1983, the movement described itself as the "history's biggest peace movement". The movement places equal emphasis on disarmament. NAM's commitment to peace pre-dates its formal institutionalisation in 1961. The Brioni meeting between heads of governments of India, Egypt and Yugoslavia in 1956 recognised that there exists a vital link between struggle for peace and endeavours for disarmament.

The Non-aligned movement believes in policies and practices of cooperation, especially those that are multilateral and provide mutual benefit to all those involved. Many of the members of the NAM are also members of the United Nations and both organisations have a stated policy of peaceful cooperation, yet successes that the NAM has had in multilateral agreements tends to be ignored by the larger, western and developed nation dominated UN. African concerns about apartheid were linked with Arab-Asian concerns about Palestine and success of multilateral cooperation in these areas has been a stamp of moderate success for the NAM. The NAM has played a major role in various ideological conflicts throughout its existence, including extreme opposition to apartheid regimes and support of liberation movements in various locations including Zimbabwe and South Africa. The support of these sorts of movements stems from a belief that every state has the right to base policies and practices with national interests in mind and not as a result of relations to a particular power bloc. The Non-aligned movement has become a voice of support for issues facing developing nations and is still contains ideals that are legitimate within this context.

Contemporary Relevance

Since the end of the Cold War and the formal end of colonialism, the Nonaligned movement has been forced to redefine itself and reinvent its purpose in the current world system. A major question has been whether many of its foundational ideologies, principally national independence, territorial integrity, and the struggle against colonialism and imperialism, can be applied to contemporary issues. The movement has emphasised its principles of multilateralism, equality, and mutual non-aggression in attempting to become a stronger voice for the global South, and an instrument that can be utilised to promote the needs of member nations at the international level and strengthen their political leverage when negotiating with developed nations. In its efforts to advance Southern interests, the movement has stressed the importance of cooperation and unity amongst member states, but as in the past, cohesion remains a problem since the size of the organisation and the divergence of agendas and allegiances present the ongoing potential for fragmentation. While agreement on basic principles has been smooth, taking definitive action vis-à-vis particular international issues has been rare, with the movement preferring to assert its criticism or support rather than pass hard-line resolutions. The movement continues to see a role for itself, as in its view, the world's poorest nations remain exploited and marginalised, no longer by opposing superpowers, but rather in a uni-polar world, and it is Western hegemony and neo-colonialism that the movement has really re-aligned itself against. It opposes foreign occupation, interference in internal affairs, and aggressive unilateral measures, but it has also shifted to focus on the socio-economic challenges facing member states, especially the inequalities manifested by globalization and the implications of neo-liberal policies. The non-aligned movement has identified economic underdevelopment, poverty, and social injustices as growing threats to peace and security.

Current Activities and Positions

Criticism of US Policy

In recent years the US has become a target of the organisation. The US invasion of Iraq and the War on Terrorism, its attempts to stifle Iran and North Korea's nuclear plans, and its other actions have been denounced as human rights violations and attempts to run roughshod over the sovereignty of smaller nations. The movement's leaders have also criticised the American control over the United Nations and other international structures. While the organisation has rejected terrorism, it condemns the association of terrorism with a particular religion, nationality, or ethnicity, and recognises the rights of those struggling against colonialism and foreign occupation.

Self-determination of Puerto Rico

Since 1961, the group have supported the discussion of the case of Puerto Rico's self-determination before the United Nations. A resolution on the matter will be proposed on the XV Summit by the Hostosian National Independence Movement.

Anti-Zionism

NAM's Havana Declaration of 1979 adopted anti-Zionism as part of the movement's agenda. The movement has denounced Israel's occupation of the West Bank and Gaza Strip. It has called upon Israel to halt its settlement activities, open up border crossings, and cease the use of force and violence against civilians. The UN has also been asked to pressure Israel and to do more to prevent human rights abuses.

Sustainable Development

The movement is publicly committed to the tenets of sustainable development and the attainment of the Millennium Development Goals, but it believes that the international community has not created conditions conducive to development and has infringed upon the right to sovereign development by each member state. Issues such as globalization, the debt burden, unfair trade practices, the decline in foreign aid, donor conditionalities, and the lack of democracy in international financial decision-making are cited as factors inhibiting development.

Cultural Diversity and Human Rights

The movement accepts the universality of human rights and social justice, but fiercely resists cultural homogenisation. In line with its views on sovereignty, the organisation appeals for the protection of cultural diversity, and the tolerance of the religious, sociocultural, and historical particularities that define human rights in a specific region.

Working groups, task forces, committees

- High-Level Working Group for the Restructuring of the United Nations
- Working Group on Human Rights
- Working Group on Peace-Keeping Operations
- Working Group on Disarmament
- Committee on Palestine
- Task Force on Somalia
- Non-Aligned Security Caucus
- Standing Ministerial Committee for Economic Cooperation
- Joint Coordinating Committee (chaired by Chairman of G-77 and Chairman of NAM).

4

India and its Neighbours with Special Reference to Pakistan and China

Significance of Flora With Special Reference to Pakistan

The principal object of a Flora is to afford the means of determining any plant growing in the area circumscribed. This is usually achieved by a combination of keys and descriptions. As the information available about plants of different parts of the world is extremely variable, hence a vast range of floras are available ranging from concise or Field Floras to Research Floras. A reasonably good Flora is expected to provide a work, which can be used for proper identification of all our plant-wealth so that its utilization could be taken up on a scientific and systematic basis. As stated by van Steenis (1957) the correct identification of every plant is of utmost importance, for a plant's name is the key to its literature – in other words, the key to what we know about it. Generally people do not realize how important it is to know the plant wealth that God has given us, particularly in a country where we do not even have a Department of Botanical Survey.

Unfortunately, at the time of the creation of Pakistan in 1947, there was not a single comprehensive book available, which could deal with all the plants of the country. The only account available was J. D. Hooker's "Flora of British India" (1872-1897), which was about 75 years old at that time. Moreover, it did not include entire Pakistan. Some of the important areas like Balochistan and most of the North West Frontier Province were not included in this account. However, a number of lists and regional floras dealing with some limited areas were available. However, some regional floras and lists of plants of various regions were available. Reference may be made to Ali (1978) for these publications.

The plant collection in our region was started as early as 1820-1822 by W. Moorcroft who had collected in Ladakh and Kashmir, followed by V. Jacquemont in 1828-1832 in Punjab and Kashmir. J. F. Royle (1832-1834) also collected in Kashmir. N. Vicary was the first to collect in Sind in 1838; he also collected in Salt Range, Punjab and the Frontier region. William Griffith (1847) was the first collector in Baluchistan and Khyber Pass area in 1838. It is beyond the scope of the present chapter to give an account of the history of plant exploration, for which references may be made to *History and Exploration of Plants in Pakistan and Adjoining Areas* by R. R. Stewart (1982). One must pay rich tributes to R. R. Stewart (1890-1993) who had collected plants from all over Pakistan.

During the recent past, some outside groups viz., K.H. Rechinger, J.D.A. Stainton, S. Kitamura, J. Lammond and S.A. Bowes Lyon have been active in our country. Some local botanists such as Sultan Ahmed, E. Nasir, N.A. Qizilbash, A.H. Khan and Jan Muhammad are among the first to have collected the plants. Later, a number of enthusiastic botanists joined the band, such as Amin Siddiqui, S.M. H. Jafri, A. R. Beg, S.M.A. Kazmi, S.I. Ali, Y. Nasir, M. Qaiser, S. Qureshi, K. Aziz, Sultanul Abedin, A. Ghafoor, A. Hussain, S. Omer, K.A. Malik, S. Nazimuddin, Z. Ali, T. Ali, R. Rafiq, M. Shah and others (Ali, Omer & Qaiser, 2001). There are a number of areas, which are yet to be explored thoroughly, such as between Khyber Pass and Kurram Valley, mountain areas between Khyber Pass to Dir, Koh-i-Suleman Range between Zhob and D. I. Khan, Kirther Mountain range and Pabbi hills between Sindh and Balochistan, North and South Waziristans, Deosai Plain, Hunza, Baltistan, Chitral etc. New plants may turn up from other regions as well.

From 1947 to early 1960, 3-4 herbaria were present in the country with few thousand specimens, with the exception of the herbarium of Gordon College, Rawalpindi, due to Stewart who had collected extensively even before the creation of Pakistan. He continued collecting plants for about 50 years, till 1960, and left a rich heritage of about 60,000 specimens at Gordon College

Herbarium, Rawalpindi. During the last 25 years some new herbaria have also been established. Presently 9 herbaria are present in Pakistan with only about 530,000 herbarium specimens (Holmgren, K., Holmgren, N. H. & Barnet, 1990). Since most of the pioneer workers were British and few from other European countries therefore our historical and important collections were deposited in various European herbaria: Kew, British Museum (Natural History), London and Edinburgh or in India: Calcutta, Dehra Dun or Bombay, except some odd duplicates present either in Rawalpindi (RAW) or in the herbarium of the Punjab University, Lahore. Therefore writing a *Flora of Pakistan* by a Pakistan, based team was an uphill task due to lack of herbarium and library facilities. The work was only possible due to the publication of the monumental work, *"An Annotated Catalogue of the Vascular Plants of Pakistan and Kashmir"* by R. R. Stewart (1972).

It is pertinent to add here that the Floras of our neighbouring countries are being written by foreign teams such as *Flora Iranica* by K. H. Rechinger (Austria), *Flora of Afghanistan* by S. Kitamura (Japan), *Flora of Ceylon* (Sri Lanka) by Smithsonian group, *Flora of Iraq* by Guest & Townsend (U.K.), *Flora of Bhutan* by D. Long & H.J. Noltie (Edinburgh). It is encouraging to note that a revised approach has now been adopted for the production of 32 volumes Flora of India. Six volumes (vols. 1-3, 5 and vols. 12-13) have already been published (1993-2000). Hopefully, others are in the pipeline. Flora of [West] Pakistan project: Proposals for writing a Flora of West Pakistan were submitted in 1966-67 through the Agricultural Research Council, Government of Pakistan to the United States Department of Agriculture, under PL-480. The earlier 131 fascicles were published under the title of "Flora of West Pakistan". However, after the separation of East Pakistan as Bangladesh, the title of the Flora has been changed to "Flora of Pakistan". These projects were separately awarded to Gordon College, Rawalpindi and Department of Botany, University of Karachi under the supervision of Late Prof E. Nasir and Prof. Dr. S. I. Ali respectively with an understanding that the two groups work in close collaboration with each other. E. Nasir & S. I. Ali jointly edited the accounts of 190 families for *Flora of Pakistan* from 1970 to 1989. In 1989, Prof. Nasir migrated to Canada at the age of 81. His son Y. J. Nasir along with S. I. Ali edited the accounts of three families (No. 191-193). Y. J. Nasir in 1992 also followed the footsteps of his father and settled in Canada. S. I. Ali and M. Qaiser are now editing the *Flora of Pakistan* (1993 onwards).

The editors have frequently visited European herbaria in the course of editing the manuscripts. In addition, draft copies of the manuscripts were sent to various experts all over the world for vetting. Many authorities and friends have responded to our requests and pointed out short-comings and offered suggestions for improvements. It is a matter of pleasure to express our gratitude to all of them. To date 47 botanists have contributed to *Flora of Pakistan* including 16 contributors from abroad. Likewise 14 artists have contributed the illustrations.

The first fascicle of Flora of Pakistan was published in 1970. Todate the accounts of 215 families have been published involving 1389 genera and 4758 species spread over 6815 printed pages and accompanied by 1277 plates depicting 2879 illustrated taxa. Accounts of 5 families, involving c. 183 genera and c. 763 species are yet to be published. During the course of these investigations 125 new taxa were described, consisting of 6 new genera, 78 new species, 21 new subspecies and 22 new varieties. Endemism: Endemic plants are restricted to a particular region and not found anywhere else in the world. These endemic plants have a special significance and give unique individuality to a region. Pakistan is also reasonably rich in endemic plants though the flora of Pakistan does not include a single endemic family but todate 5 monotypic genera (*Douepia, Sulaimania, Kurramiana, Wendelboa* and *Spiroseris*) and c. 400 species (7.8%)) belonging to c. 169 genera and 45 families are endemic in Pakistan. About 80% of endemic flowering plants are confined to the northern and western mountains of Pakistan and Kashmir. Families with more than 20 recorded endemics are Leguminoseae (57), Asteraceae (50), Apiaceae (34), Poaceae (32) and Brassicaceae (21). The genus *Astragalus* contains 37, the largest number of endemics (Ali, 1978; Ali & Qaiser, 1986). Only recently some critical studies have been conducted on 9 endemic flowering plants of Gilgit and Baltistan. According to IUCN Red List Categories and Criteria (Anon., 2001) *Astragalus clarkeanus, Asperula oppositifolia* subsp. *baltistanica, Berberis pseudoumbellata* subsp. *gilgitica*, *Haplophyllum gilesii* and *Tenacetum baltistanicum* are found critically endangered (CR), *Aconitum violaceum* var. *weileri* and *Rhodiola saxifragoides* are vulnerable (VU). We do not have enough critical data about other endemic taxa. Hence it is obvious that remedial measures must be adopted for each taxon according to their nature of threats in order to protect them from extinction (Jan Alam & Ali, unpublished).

Economic importance: Pakistan is quite rich in economically important plants. These include plants that are important for food, fodder, medicine, timber etc., from the point of view of the germplasm resources of the cultivated plants of Pakistan, due attention should be given to the fact that northern Pakistan is an integral part of the Central Asian Centre of Diversity (Vavilov, 1950). The ancient trade route from China to Western Asia passed through this region resulting in the introduction of many crop and fruit species, which have been cultivated for thousands of years.

Thus the location of Pakistan in the proximity of major centres of diversity has also been a source of genetic enrichment of this area. Further, as the history of Pakistan goes back to the Stone Age, followed by Indus valley civilization (2600 B.C.-1700 B.C.) with well-developed agriculture, which further supports rich biological heritage.

The introduction of advanced cultivars (Mexi Pak wheat, IRRI rice etc.), the primitive cultivars that had evolved in response to the earlier prevailing environmental conditions and methods of cultivation are gradually disappearing. There is reason to believe that a number of such resistant genes get accumulated in these primitive cultivars which could provide protection against drought, diseases, extreme heat or cold etc. Wild plants, particularly those, which are related to cultivated plants, are also very important, for all cultivated plants have arisen from wild plants. Wild relatives of cultivated plants are hardy, capable of surviving under stress conditions and generally disease resistant. Hence these plants are extremely important from the point of view of overall germ plasm resources. Likewise those wild plants, which are directly utilized for various purposes, deserve our attention. Even those plants, which apparently are not economically important, may be of considerable ecological significance as soil binders etc. or hitherto some unexplored plant(s) may even prove to be of considerable medicinal value.

Suggestions for the next phase: As stated earlier, many critical areas, particularly mountain valleys require continuous efforts so far as plant exploration is concerned, so that more new taxa could be discovered. This will also lead to better understanding of the variation pattern facilitating evaluation of delimited taxa. Since the publication of the first issue of *Flora of Pakistan* in 1970 (Nasir & Ali 1970), about 38 years ago, a number of new taxa have been described and the fresh plant material is also available for study, hence evaluation of available resources is called for. The natural flora continues to change with time due to immigration of species, extinctions and evolution, more so with the current rapidly changing environmental conditions. It is therefore obvious that *Flora of Pakistan* will have to be revised and enlarged.

Consequent to the wide scale conversion of the natural ecosystems to agriculture, extensive unplanned urbanization and expansion of roads and highways, deforestation etc., in spite of the existence of 10 national parks, 82 sanctuaries, 83 game reserves the natural vegetation is being lost at a very high rate. Unfortunately we do not have any publication on Red List Categories of Pakistan as per recommendation of IUCN. This matter should be given top priority. In view of the Global Warming, Pakistan is going to face very difficult situation in not very distant future. Some of our coastal low lying areas are likely to be submerged. The glaciers in our mountains are already melting. If this trend continues, they may disappear by 2050 resulting in lesser amount of water in our rivers. The effect of concurrent higher temperatures is likely to lead to desertification. This may lead to very different environmental regimes resulting in the disappearance to many of our plants and the synthesis (through mutation, hybridization and selection) of many new types of plants. Hence, it seems desirable to strengthen and reorganize the institutions concerned with the study of our plant wealth.

India and Pakistan: On the Nuclear Threshold

This briefing book contains material from the National Security Archive's project on U.S. policy toward South Asia, which is documenting nuclear developments in India and Pakistan from the 1950s to the present. The archive is collecting U.S. government records that illustrate American policies and perspectives. Information is being collected from the National Archives and the presidential libraries, and through Freedom of Information Act (FOIA) and Mandatory Review requests, used to obtain the declassification of now-secret materials. A selective and focused collection of documents will be made available to researchers.

The project is creating a comprehensive history of nuclear developments in South Asia, including weapons programs in India and Pakistan, as well as international efforts to curtail proliferation in the region. Information about factors that influenced nuclear issues, such as the unresolved enmity between India and Pakistan, and India's perception of China as a security threat, will also be incorporated. The U.S. has generally opposed nuclear proliferation in South Asia, while seeking to preserve good relations with both India and Pakistan. At times, however, its commitment has been questioned, because it has seemed to subordinate nonproliferation policy to other concerns. During the Soviet occupation of Afghanistan, for instance, the U.S. provided massive levels of economic and military aid to its ally, Pakistan. The assistance was widely criticized, because Pakistan was demonstrably importing nuclear-related material, from China and other nations. Few doubted that it was engaged in an active nuclear weapons development program.

China's role as a leading provider of sensitive technology to Pakistan has repeatedly strained U.S.-China relations, and has complicated efforts to expand U.S.-China trade. The Archive's South Asia project is using the FOIA to seek the declassification of documents discussing this issue, and other contemporary and controversial topics. Materials collected for this project will, of course, reflect a U.S. perspective. As noted, nonproliferation policy is influenced by other concerns, including competition among the major powers. The Archive's efforts are directed toward enhancing understanding of U.S. decisions and the issues that influenced policy formulation. The analyst for the South Asia nuclear project is Joyce Battle, who prepared this briefing book. She is also the analyst for the Archive's documentation projects on the Persian

Gulf and U.S. policy toward Iraq. Materials collected for the latter project were published in a document set, Iraqgate: Saddam Hussein, U.S. Policy and the Prelude to the Persian Gulf War, 1980-1994 (Chadwyck-Healey, 1994). She has an MA in Middle East Studies from Harvard and an MS in Library Science from Columbia.

Briefing Book Documents

The documents in the briefing book date from 1961 to 1983. In 1961, India had an advanced civilian nuclear program, while Pakistan's was in its early stages. In 1983, nine years had elapsed since India's explosion of a nuclear device, and Pakistan's nuclear weapons program was well under way. During the early 1960s, India under Prime Minister Jawaharlal Nehru strongly advocated global disarmament, but was apprehensive about China's nuclear weapons program. India's concern increased following its October 1962 territorial war with China. The stakes were raised by China's first nuclear weapons test in October 1964. Many observers thought it increasingly likely that India would respond to China's actions by seeking its own weapons capability. War with Pakistan in 1965 further alarmed India: it was angered by China's outspoken support for Pakistan during the conflict, and disappointed by what it viewed as insufficient Western attention to its security needs. The U.S. considered various options that might dissuade India from developing nuclear weapons, including scientific cooperation aimed at enhancing India's national prestige. It also joined in cooperative arrangements with both India and Pakistan to monitor nuclear and missile developments in China and the Soviet Union. India, for its part, launched a campaign seeking security guarantees to shield it from Chinese nuclear attack, arguing that such assurances might make a nuclear weapons program of its own unnecessary. Various options were proposed: U.S. guarantees, joint U.S.-Soviet guarantees, guarantees from all the nuclear states, British guarantees, or guarantees in conjunction with the nuclear nonproliferation treaty, then being negotiated. U.S. policy makers seriously considered these proposals, although some doubted that they would deter India from developing a bomb.

The Embassy in New Delhi viewed India's overtures sympathetically, while the Defence Department opposed any commitment to India that would alienate Pakistan, a U.S. military ally. In 1967, both President Lyndon Johnson and Defence Secretary Robert McNamara supported the concept of guarantees during meetings with a visiting Indian representative. Later that year, U.S. and Soviet officials were still discussing security guarantees, hoping to induce India to sign the nuclear nonproliferation treaty. No agreement was ever reached, however, in part because India itself concluded that such commitments would not guarantee its security in the event of actual nuclear conflict. In May 1974, India tested a nuclear device, although it called the event a "peaceful nuclear explosion."

Its terminology did not forestall censure, both within the international community and from domestic critics. The test had serious consequences: India lost much of the foreign technical assistance that had till then sustained its civilian nuclear program. A Pakistani reaction to India's test of a nuclear explosive was predicted, and confirmed within a few years. By the mid-1970s, intelligence reports indicated that Pakistan had an active nuclear weapons program, and in 1983 the State Department noted that it had "unambiguous evidence" of this fact. Documents in this briefing book illuminate aspects of the internal debate among U.S. officials, as they attempted to formulate effective policies toward nuclear proliferation in South Asia while protecting sometimes conflicting interests and objectives.

Nuclear Threat Reduction in India and Pakistan

The Carnegie Endowment for International Peace (CEIP) published a draft report, 'Universal Compliance: A Strategy for Nuclear Security', in June 2004. The report proposes a strategic blueprint for US leadership to rethink international nuclear nonproliferation and global nuclear security. In this report, the recommended measures for nuclear risk reduction between India and Pakistan include:

- o Establishment of national risk reduction centres in both countries to administer agreed upon confidence-building measures.

- o Acommitment not to develop, produce, and use 'tactical' nuclear weapons.
- o Agreement not to flight-test missiles in the direction of the other country.
- o Agreement to flight-test missiles only from designated test ranges.
- o Provision of advance notification of the movement of missiles for training purposes.

The Henry L. Stimson Center's report, 'Reducing Nuclear Dangers in South Asia', argues that: "The stability-instability paradox that was formulated in the West to characterise the dangers of nuclear deterrence is alive and well in South Asia. This paradox holds that, while offsetting nuclear capabilities might indeed prevent a full-blown conventional or nuclear war, the presence of these fearsome weapons could also encourage the use of violence at lower levels in the expectation that escalation would be contained by a mutual desire to avoid the nuclear threshold." And that, "Kashmir has been inflamed since the advent of covert nuclear capabilities on the subcontinent, and tensions have grown even more pronounced with the demonstration of overt nuclear capabilities in 1998. The region is now experiencing crises with greater frequency and severity."

The report includes extensive deliberations during two workshops, November 14-18, 2002, and May 20-23, 2003, with participants from the US, India and Pakistan, convened by the Stimson Centre to discuss escalation control and scenarios that could lead to crossing of the nuclear threshold. It provides the following 'doable' steps in the near term:

- o Establishment of national risk reduction centresto serve as focal points for the administration of confidence-building measures.
- o Missile-related measures to formalise and properly implement the agreement concerning prior notification of missile launches; to formalise and extend the time-line for such notifications; to forego missile flight tests in the direction of the other country; to flight test missiles only from designated test ranges; and to provide advance

notification of the movement of missiles for training purposes.

- o Clarifying terminology or developing common terminology on nuclear-related programmes, deployment, and doctrine could reduce misunderstanding and increase crisis stability.
- o Leadership declarations affirming responsible nuclear stewardshipcould help defuse nuclear dangers and facilitate an improvement in bilateral relations.
- o Increased awareness of nuclear dangers, particularly with regard to the possible acquisition of nuclear materials by terrorist groups, would be advisable.

In the Stimson Center's report, the proposals collected in the workshops on escalation control are grouped in five categories: improving bilateral relations; nuclear risk reduction and strategic restraint; safety and security measures; and, improving intelligence through communication.

Both the reports, by CEIP and the Stimson Centre, have this presumption that 'deterrence' may not work between India and Pakistan as similar to the Cold War experience. Such assumptions are not completely invalid for the two countries did resort to nuclear rhetoric during the 1999 Kargil conflict and indulged in 'nuclear signalling' during the period of crisis in 2001-2. In addition, the absence of a doctrine without no-first-use policy and repeated calls from the Pakistani side to lower the threshold could have a certain bearing on the thinking of Western analysts. Already, the strategic debate had reached a slightly higher level than was normally prevalent in the subcontinent when the Indian Army Chief stated that a limited war with Pakistan is possible. Thereon, escalation control came into the purview of discussion in a more focused way.

For any future war in the subcontinent, the two most likely scenarios discussed in the Cooperative Monitoring Centre Occasional Paper of Sandia National Laboratories, are: a breakdown along the common border in Kashmir, and failure of nuclear policy. The authors propose an alternative approach through which India and Pakistan can begin to cooperate in managing their common border to prevent a breakdown. The ultimate concern in the report about the existence of nuclear weapons is the possibility of their use in a time of conflict. The following are the enumerations in the Cooperative Monitoring Centre Occasional Paper that focuses on the monitoring of nuclear safety, security, and stability:

- o The ability to assess the current operational and deployment status of nuclear weapons is perhaps the most critical factor in near-term crisis prevention.
- o Developing measures to prevent escalation.
- o National decisions to include both technical and procedural mechanisms to restrict use of weapons and delivery systems will permit more time to attempt diplomatic solutions to conflict before initiating weapons use.
- o Another element of nuclear stability is determining the readiness of launch systems. There may be a number of indicators associated with launcher alert status. These include: Flight parameters loaded, other software updates (if appropriate); Vehicle fuelled (missile or aircraft); Crews readied; Delivery vehicle in launch location (moved to launch point); Transporter system in ready position (e.g., transporter erector launcher [TEL] in raised launch position); Weapon armed. While most of these indicators of launch preparation are difficult to monitor, some, such as missile fuelling and launcher movements, might be monitored through electronic sensors.
- o There is the possibility of use through miscalculation or misinterpretation.
- o Sharing information on any of the concerns for safety, security or accident will require an infrastructure of capabilities and procedures. These include methods for providing timely, reliable, secure, accurate, and authenticated communications.
- o Ensuring safety of nuclear weapons and materials will primarily be a state responsibility because of the highly classified nature of most safety issues. These issues involve detailed design, as well as material and handling details. An expanded mission for hotlines between the Directors-

General of Military Operations and between the Heads of State might be established to address this critical issue.

Acknowledging the fact that only the Indian and Pakistani governments can decide whether and on what basis, to establish new risk reduction measures, the 'Working Group Report of the Centre for Strategic and International Studies (CSIS)' recommends the following steps for nuclear risk reduction:

- o A new communications mechanism-nuclear risk reduction centres (NRRCs) in India and Pakistan-should be established to complement existing bilateral channels.
- o The main functions of the NRRCs would be to provide each party a dedicated, secure means of: (a) notifying the other side about activities or events on its territory that might be wrongly perceived or misinterpreted that could lead to conflict, (b) sharing information that the two countries are obliged to exchange under existing security agreements, and (c) seeking and receiving clarifications about ambiguous events on the other' sterritory. Other functions could include the conduct of joint exercises of certain NRRC notification procedures, technical back-up during crises, and support for consultations on the implementation of existing confidence-building measures (CBMs).
- o Adequate infrastructure already exists in South Asia to support a wide range of secure communication options, including data, voice, video, or a combination of these.

  The approximate cost for a dedicated cable permitting teletype and voice communication would be US$10,000-50,000 annually. For a dedicated satellite channel permitting teletype, voice, and video, the annual cost would be roughly US$560,000.
- o The centres would operate on a continuous, round-the-clock basis. Written messages using agreed formats would be the norm, although voice and video capability would also be desirable. It would be the prerogative of each government to decide where it would institutionally house its NRRC and to determine how its NRRC would relate to other government organisations. The Indian and

Pakistani solutions to these questions need not be symmetrical.

The Working Group Report concluded, that "the circumstances in South Asia today are very different from the circumstances surrounding the current US-Russian relationship and the relationship that existed when the US-Soviet Centres were brought into being. To tailor a new communications mechanism to the needs of South Asia, the mechanism could appropriately take on a wider range of functions than the US and Russian Centres."

Rodney W.Jones assumes that there lies intense political conflict over Kashmir and that the escalation in South Asia has the potential of becoming a nuclear war. In one of the papers presented during the fourth nuclear stability roundtable during March 12-13, 2002, in Washington on 'Military Asymmetry and Instability in Emerging Nuclear States: India and Pakistan,' he suggests the following conditions of nuclear stability in the region:

- o High nuclear threshold (strong conventional defence)
- o Secure second strike capabilities (robust C4I)
- o Rough parity in size and defence space
- o Neither falling behind the other's first strike edge (good early warning?) Supposing that "nuclear deterrence might provide the security that allows a general improvement in security relations" in South Asia, the UNIDR (United Nations Institute for Disarmament Research) research paper depicts various aspects of nuclear confidence-building measures between India and Pakistan. Commenting on the current conflict situation between the two countries, the authors of the paper subscribe to developing CBMs in connection with the 'central issue-Kashmir'. An interim suggestion is made to work on the possibilities of addressing the 'central sore-cross-border terror raids' from Pakistan.

With regard to nuclear CBMs, according to the UNIDR paper, India and Pakistan should share the development of respective nuclear doctrines and security concepts to have clarity over 'red lines'; develop mechanisms on notification of ballistic and cruise missile tests; create nuclear risk reduction centres with robust safety systems to deal with the issues of accidental or unauthorised use; and install a secure and dedicated line of communication including safe command and control systems between the national authorities (the nature or constitution of national authority remains undefined). The paper categorically puts the 'Kashmir issue' to be discussed as in the final stages of CBMs between the two countries.

The UNIDR study concludes that the two countries should seize the ripe moment (that has begun since the two countries agreed to peace talks during the sidelines of the SAARC summit in January 2004) in the context of possibility of conflict. "Any future terrorist incident might provoke India into punitive action, which in the worst case might lead to uncontrolled or accidental responses, all the way to a nuclear exchange. This suggests that, although the nuclear aspects will have to be part of the general discussions on security, it might also be worth considering whether they can be made separable, in case the moment passes too quickly."

The aspect of geographical proximity of the two countries is also discussed in one of the reports dealing with nuclear threat reduction measures. Based on some hypothetical South Asian launch point-target combinations, the missile travel time between India and Pakistan is estimated between 8 to 13 minutes.

Taking account of the danger of false alarms and miscalculations, the Pugwash Discussion Paper of 2002 suggests that a posture of De-alert (most basic measures would be to keep the weapons de-mated from delivery systems; use of locking devices), and installation of best available safety measures into the weapons, like use of Insensitive High Explosive (IHE) and fire-resistant pits would significantly reduce the risk of inadvertent or unauthorised use of weapons.

From the above discussed strategic policy recommendations, there emerge two sets of proposals that could draw attention of the diplomats and strategic planners of India and Pakistan. In the first set, one can identify mechanisms for escalation control and nuclear force management within each state. The second set includes possible measures of nuclear CBMs by the two countries to work towards long lasting stability in the region.

Issues Related to Escalation Control and Nuclear Force Management

- o Leadership declarations affirming responsible nuclear stewardship (avoidance of shrill rhetoric).
- o Developing strategies to avoid escalation of conventional confrontation to nuclear exchange level.
- o Avoiding sensitive targets in the event of a conventional war.
- o Raising the level of nuclear threshold (strong conventional defences).
- o Securing second strike capabilities.
- o Review of decision-making to develop, produce, and use 'tactical' nuclear weapons.
- o Regular assessment of each other's current operational and deployment status of nuclear weapons (missile fuelling and launcher movements might be monitored through electronic sensors).
- o Determining the readiness of launch systems.
- o Improvements in intelligence to avoid miscalculation or misinterpretation.
- o Acquisition of technology to help provide prompt and accurate information concerning missile launches and nuclear detonations.
- o Advancement in respective command and control mechanisms including establishment of effective early warning systems.
- o Refraining from giving pre-delegation of authority to use nuclear weapons.
- o Effective physical safety of nuclear materials and installations.
- o Ensuring safety and security of nuclear weapons and materials.

Steps Required for Nuclear CBMs

- o Improving bilateral relationship.
- o Sharing knowledge of decision-making processes.

- o Agreement on advance notification of missile testing and movements.
- o Flight test missiles only from designated test ranges.
- o Provision of advance notification of the movement of missiles for training purposes.
- o Review of policy decisions related to tactical nuclear weapons (including development, production, or use).
- o Establishment of multi-layered, reliable, secure, accurate, and authenticated communication mechanisms.
- o Establishment of Nuclear Risk Reduction Centres (NRRCs).

Most of the above-mentioned studies on South Asia suggest that problems related to Kashmir may be the spark to trigger a nuclear exchange between India and Pakistan. Linking of the Kashmir issue with Indo-Pak nuclear strategy is quite complex. In fact, such an assumption indirectly endorses (and is born out of) Pakistan's nuclear blackmailing. In reality, it is the Pakistani military that has crossed the Line of Control (LoC) in the past to provoke Indian defence. Pakistan does not adhere to no-first-use (NFU) and keeps making frequent calls to lower the nuclear threshold in the apprehension of India taking reprisal measures to stop Pakistan-sponsored terrorism in Indian territory.

Pakistan insists on Kashmir being the 'core' issue of stability/ instability between India and Pakistan. India maintains that the scourge of 'terrorism' in South Asia has adverse implications for both regional and international security. In between the two exclusive views, remains a pertinent question unanswered-who is to guarantee that if the issues related to Kashmir remains resolved, towards which India has already been making significant efforts, Pakistan's military-ISI sponsored terrorist activities in other parts of India would end? In such a complex security environment, bilateral confidence-building measures alone would keep the escalation under manageable limits.

Pakistan's Nuclear Posture

Pakistan is considered to have as many as 50 nuclear weapons and enough highly enriched uranium (HEU) stock for 50 more, including the additional capacity to produce five to ten bombs a year. According to a more recent estimate, Pakistan is said to possess 55-90 weapons of highly enriched uranium and 20-60 plutonium bombs. No definitive information at official levels is available on such speculative assessments. The possible delivery systems for weapons are aircraft and missiles.

Pakistan President Pervez Musharraf has gone on record to say that the weapons are in a "disassembled state." Few other terms have also been used to project the deployment status of Pakistan's nuclear weapons such as "operationally deployed" or "in the component form." While the term component form has not been spelt out, it seems that "the situation in Pakistan may be murky and may in fact best be described as partial deployment."

Replying to the question of an interviewer, "Can you say, are the nuclear weapons ready to go as they are, or are they, as I have heard, in different parts, have to be assembled first?" Musharraf said: "Yes, you are right. They are not mated (inaudible). And there is geographical-they are geographically apart. They cannot be-they are not ready to be fired. So really, it's not the concept that NATO has been having (inaudible) United States system, where your finger has to be on a button and then finally can be pushed. That's not the condition there."

As far as the doctrinal aspect is concerned, Pakistan has not announced any comprehensive doctrine document. However, two basic elements that emerge from statements by the country's leaders are: "a rejection of the NFU policy, and the role of nuclear weapons as minimum credible deterrent."

Realising the gap between the military strength in conventional terms, there is a view prevalent in Pakistan that an NFU posture of Pakistan could provide India the leverage of conventional attack. In the backdrop of such military planning, by asking for a 'no-aggression-pact' Pakistan seems to preclude even an Indian reprisal for its misadventures like the one in Kargil in 1999 and support to cross-border terrorism against India. Also, another factor of security complications for India vis-à-vis Pakistan is that "country's chief patrons, principally the US and China, are bound to try and [set] right the inherent imbalance in power by assisting it in ways inimical to Indian interests." The implication for Pakistan being designated a 'major non-NATO ally' of the United States is being seen in India as more American military assistance to Pakistan. Pakistan's Ambassador to United Nations has argued: "We have to rely on our own means to deter Indian aggression. Wehave that means and we will not neutralize it by any doctrine of no first use." Pakistan's doctrinal declaratory policy is kept deliberately ambiguous. And, in terms of ability to ensure survival, Pakistan wants to have sufficient number and types of assets to create 'reasonable doubt'.

Relevant to the current discussion is the bottom line for use of nuclear weapons by Pakistan. This has been spelt out by Gen. Khalid Kidwai, Head of Strategic Planning Division (SPD) under the National Command Authority (NCA), to a delegation of Italian Scientists. Toquote him: "Nuclear weapons are aimed solely at India. In case that deterrence fails, they will be used if India attacks Pakistan and conquers a large part of its territory (space threshold); India destroys a large part either of its land or air force (military threshold); India proceeds to the economic strangling of Pakistan (economic strangling); or India pushes Pakistan into political destabilization or creates a large scale internal subversion in Pakistan (domestic destabilization)."

In other words, without defining any limits Pakistan intends to use its nuclear weapons to counter even a primarily conventional conflict situation if it feels threatened with military, political or economic defeat. However, there is a feeling in Pakistan that a nuclear response cannot be involved to deal with local contingencies and the nuclear threshold should be maintained at a high level.

Aformer foreign minister of Pakistan has opined that the destruction of even a single city would be an unacceptable risk for another country that contemplates a pre-emptive strike.

In an interview to CNN on June 1, 2002, Pakistani President Pervez Musharraf tried to allay the growing international fear of any nuclear war in the subcontinent by saying that, "I would even go to the extent of saying one shouldn't even be discussing these (nuclear war) things, because any sane individual cannot even think of going into this unconventional war, whatever the pressure." A few months earlier, while chairing the meeting of the NCAin October 2001, Pervez Musharraf reaffirmed the Pakistani strategic assets as the cornerstone of country's national security and that there will be no compromise on the nuclear programme. The statement had come in the light of increasing international concern about improving security and installing new safeguards on Pakistan's nuclear weapons after 9/11. Musharraf assured the world that the country's strategic capability was fully safeguarded. Such assertions need further examination, especially when Pakistan is considered as a potential source for terrorists to get access to technology and materials.

A. Q. Khan's televised confessional statement in February 2004 of being involved in international nuclear black-marketing drew unprecedented media attention. However, "A.Q. Khan got off lightly, sending disturbing messages about US and Pakistani attitudes toward proliferation."

And, "the most troubling question of all remains how and to what extent Pakistan's free-market approach to proliferation has allowed terrorist groups like Al Qaida to acquire nuclear materials and technology."

India's Nuclear Posture

Judging by the official pronouncements in the wake of the May 1998 tests, India appears set for a pragmatic course of action, including three basic components-construction of minimum deterrent with a NFU policy, participation in a possible Fissile Material Cutoff Treaty (FMCT) negotiations and the pursuit of arms control rather than disarmament. The Cabinet Committee on Security headed by the Prime Minister while approving the establishment of Nuclear Command Authority and 'alternate chains of command for retaliatory nuclear strikes in all eventualities', on January 4, 2003, summarised the nuclear doctrine as:

(i) building and maintaining a credible minimum deterrent;

(ii) a posture of NFU and nuclear weapons to be used only in retaliation against a nuclear attack on Indian territory or on Indian forces anywhere;

(iii) nuclear retaliation to be massive and designed to inflict unacceptable damage;

(iv) authorisation of retaliatory attack rests with the political leadership through the National Command Authority;

(v) non-use of nuclear weapon against non-nuclear weapon states;

(vi) in the event of a major attack against India, or Indian forces anywhere, by biological or chemical weapons, India will retain the option of retaliating with nuclear weapons;

(vii) a continuance of strict control on export of nuclear and missile-related materials and technologies, participation in the Fissile Material Cutoff Treaty negotiations, and continued observance of the moratorium on nuclear tests; and

(viii) continued commitment to the goal of a nuclear weapon-free world through global, verifiable and non-discriminatory nuclear disarmament.

As early as in 1994, India had proposed that India and Pakistan should jointly undertake not to be the first to use their nuclear capability against each other. Even after conducting the nuclear tests India expressed its readiness "...to discuss a 'no-first-use'agreement with that country, as also with other countries bilaterally, or in a collective forum." However, Gen. Musharraf thinks otherwise. Interviewed on NBC television in Washington on January 23, 2002, General Musharraf was asked to explain Pakistan's reluctance to follow India in adopting a policy of no-first-use of nuclear weapons. He replied: "When you talk of no-first-use, Pakistan has been offering denuclearisation of South Asia...so we are going far, far beyond them.

It is not an issue of no-first-use, but far beyond that... We want to denuclearise South Asia. Wewant to sign a No War Pact with them. Isn't that better? I(Musharraf) think the world community should insist on that. Pakistan is offering a much bigger deal."

The Indian Prime Minister rejected Pakistan's suggestion for a mutual rollback of their nuclear programme as India's nuclear programme is not Pakistan-specific. In fact, "the rationale for Pakistan's nuclear weapons programme continuously harped on is that Pakistan has always been quantitatively and technologically weaker than India in military terms. India's counter-argument is that, in terms of the ratio between defence responsibilities and the size of the armed forces, especially in terms of territorial defence from external aggression, this argument is not valid." As early as in 1974, Pakistan submitted a resolution at the 29th session of the UN General Assembly, which sought to endorse in principle the concept of a nuclear weapon-free zone in South Asia.

At that point of time, Pakistan was already running the nuclear weapon programme. It is worth remembering that then President Zulfikar Ali Bhutto had called a meeting of Pakistani scientists in Multan in January 1972 and had expressed his willingness to acquire nuclear weapon for Pakistan. But in the wake of India's May 1974 tests, Pakistan tried to gain an image of veiled peacemaker though lacking any sincerity. India itself had proposed a resolution in the same 29th session of the General Assembly in which it recognised that, "in appropriate regions and by agreement among the states concerned, the creation of nuclear-weapon-free zones could promote the cause of general and complete disarmament under effective international control."

India also considered in that proposal that "the initiative for the creation of a nuclear-weapon-free zone in the appropriate region of Asia should come from the States of the region concerned, taking into account its special features and geographical extent."

In reality, South Asia could not be treated in isolation for the purpose of creating a nuclear weapon-free zone, as it is only a sub-region and an integral part of the Southern Asian region. Hence, it is necessary to take into account the security of the region in its entirety. Unlike Pakistan, India's adherence to a NFU policy and its strategic assets are not country-specific. Therefore, any effort towards creating a minimum credible nuclear triad, including qualitative improvement in missile systems or other technological advancements, seems related to India's national security perspectives beyond, but inclusive, of Pakistan.

The Indian perspective is both global and regional in nature. India believes that: "As long as nuclear weapons exist, the threat of use of nuclear weapons, accidentally or inadvertently, will remain. Only global and complete nuclear disarmament, within a time-bound framework, can totally eliminate the danger of a nuclear war. This was the cornerstone of India's Action Plan for the elimination of nuclear weapons unveiled by late Prime Minister Rajiv Gandhi in 1988 at the Special Session of the General Assembly...While pursuing the goal of nuclear disarmament, it is desirable to take immediate steps for reducing nuclear danger. These could include measures to de-alert and de-target nuclear weapons, legally binding commitments on no-first-use of nuclear weapons and non-use of nuclear weapons against Non-Nuclear Weapon States."

India-Pakistan Nuclear CBMs

Former Indian External Affairs Minister Natwar Singh stated that: "A new dimension has been added since 1998 when both countries became nuclear powers. And now it is absolutely essential that we have best of relations. And the Manmohan Singh government has already made it clear that we look forward to continuing the process, we will take it forward and it will be multifaceted. And the differences we have will be ironed out through negotiations, friendly talks and cooperation." And at the end of the meeting of Foreign Ministers of India and Pakistan in New Delhi on September 5 and 6, 2004, to review the status of the Composite Dialogue, the duo agreed to take further the expert level meetings on conventional and nuclear CBMs, inter alia,to discuss the draft agreement on advance notification of missile tests."

In 1988, India and Pakistan agreed to "refrain from undertaking, encouraging or participating in, directly or indirectly, any action aimed at causing the destruction of, or damage to, any nuclear installation or facility in the other country." The term 'nuclear installation or facility' includes nuclear power and research reactors, fuel fabrication, uranium enrichment, isotopes separation and reprocessing facilities, as well as any other installations with fresh or irradiated nuclear fuel and materials in any form and establishments storing significant quantities of radioactive materials. And the two countries also agreed to inform on January 1 of each calendar year, of the latitude and longitude of its nuclear installations and facilities and whenever there is any change.

This practice is in regular use ever since it came into force from January 1, 1991, and the practice did not stop even during the crisis period of 2002. However, "each side has questioned the completeness of the other's list." Subsequently, a forward movement in nuclear CBMs was witnessed during the Indian Prime Minister's visit to Lahore in 1999.

The memorandum of understanding (MoU) signed by the foreign secretaries of the two countries at Lahore in 1999 mentioned that "The two sides shall engage in bilateral consultations on security concepts, and nuclear doctrines, with a view to developing measures for confidence-building in the nuclear and conventional fields, aimed at avoidance of conflict." The two countries agreed to provide each other with advance notification in respect of ballistic missile flight tests, and envisaged a bilateral agreement in this regard. India and Pakistan at Lahore also committed to continue to abide by their respective unilateral moratoriums on conducting further nuclear test explosions.

With a view to reaching bilateral agreements based on mutual deliberations and technical consultations, the two countries under the Lahore MoU included many significant issues such as national measures to reduce the risks of accidental or unauthorised use of nuclear weapons, notification in the event of any accidental, unauthorised or unexplained incident, prevention of incidents at sea in order to ensure safety of navigation by naval vessels and aircraft belonging to the two sides, review of the existing communication links (e.g., between the respective Directors-General of Military Operations), and periodic review of existing confidence-building measures. The two sides would also engage in bilateral consultations on security, disarmament and nonproliferation issues within the context of negotiations on these issues in multilateral fora. The expert level talks, led by Sheel Kant Sharma, and his Pakistani counterpart, Tariq Osman Hyder, during June 19-20, 2004, culminated in a joint statement on nuclear CBMs with some repetition of important issues under the Lahore MoU.

The joint statement recognises "the nuclear capabilities of each other, which are based on their national security imperatives, constitute a factor of stability." This implies that the two countries have moved beyond the earlier differing ambits of threat perceptions, for holding nuclear weapons in the respective states.

Instead of questioning the rationality of possessing nuclear weapons, the two countries now acknowledge nuclear weapons as a factor of stability in the region. The important issues covered in the joint statement are: upgradation of existing hotline between DGMOs; new dedicated and secure hotline between foreign secretaries to prevent misunderstanding, reduce risks relevant to nuclear issues; to conclude an agreement with technical parameters on pre-notification of missile flight testing; unilateral moratorium on nuclear tests unless a country decides that extraordinary events have jeopardised its supreme interests; bilateral discussions and further meetings to work towards the implementation of the Lahore MoU of 1999, among others.

The provision in the joint statement of June 20, 2004, that "both countries will continue to engage in bilateral consultations on security and nonproliferation issues within the context of negotiations on these issues in multilateral fora" seems to reflect the shared view of India and Pakistan to work together against the existing discriminatory international regimes and policies of disarmament. While agreeing to reaffirm a unilateral moratorium on further nuclear tests, the joint statement also shows consciousness for "their obligations to their peoples and the international community." It is perhaps indicative of the two countries endorsing international concerns related to nuclear security in South Asia.

The foreign secretaries of the two sides, Riaz Khokhar and Shyam Saran, who met in Islamabad during December 27-28, 2004, to review the progress made during the meetings of the Experts on Nuclear and Conventional CBMs, stated that they have, "narrowed further their differences on the draft agreement on pre-notification of flight testing of ballistic missiles, and agreed to work towards its early finalisation."

It is also reported that the Pakistani side has introduced 20 new proposals, including 'The Elements of a Strategic Restraint Regime (SRR)' comprising conflict resolution through a sustained, result-oriented dialogue; measures for nuclear restraint and conventional balance to be discussed at the political and experts level; objective of minimum credible deterrence; maintenance of nuclear weapons on low-alert status; no operational deployment of nuclear-capable ballistic or any other type of missiles/delivery systems; no acquisition or deployment of anti-ballistic missile systems; avoidance of a nuclear, missile, or conventional arms race; continuation of the national nuclear test moratoriums of both sides, as reaffirmed in the Joint Statement of June 20, 2004. But, in the progressive mode of consultations and addition of fresh proposals at every next meeting of expert groups, there remains little hope for any definitive conclusion of the agreement soon. The issues involving the technical parameters of advance notification and deployment strategy, however, are tricky aspects.

India and China

Together accounting for 2.5 billion people, China and India are today the engines of growth in the midst of rapid economic transformation in the global economy. In fact, driven by India and China, the emerging Asian economies are no longer witnessing a slump, as per a report by the UK financial services major Barclays. A slew of research reports and surveys reiterate the amazing growth story of these two Asian giants.

The Organisation for Economic Cooperation and Development (OECD) has projected early signals of revival in the Indian and Chinese economy. The Composite Leading Indicators (CLI) designed to provide early signals of turning points in business cycles, rose by 0.4 point for India in April 2009, while for China increased by 0.9 point. As per a report by the global financial services firm, BNP Paribas, India and China will be able to sidestep contraction in their growth rates this year, despite the ongoing global economic turmoil. The recovery in the emerging markets can be attributed to the fiscal measures taken by their respective governments, which would help them to post positive growth next year, the report said.

A study by the International Finance Corporation (IFC), the private lending arm of the World Bank, found that India's policies for the software sector and China's promotion of special economic zones (SEZs) for the manufacturing sector suggest that well-designed and sector-specific government policies can overcome weaknesses in investment climate and allow developing countries to compete globally in new fields.

Global investment firm, Moody's, says that driven by renewed growth in India and China, the world economy is beginning to recover from one of the worst economic downturns in decades. The Chinese GDP has risen by 7.9 per cent while that of India has grown by 6.1 per cent in the April-June 2009-10 period. Moody's has now revised India's growth forecast to 6.4 per cent for the current fiscal.

Trade

Trade has been the vital part of the strengthening bilateral economic relationship between the two countries. China has emerged as India's largest trading partner, replacing US in 2008-09. According to a reply filed by Mr Jyotiraditya Scindia, Minister of State for Commerce and Industry, in the Lok Sabha on July 27, 2009, bilateral trade engagement between India and China stood at US$ 33.77 billion in April to February 2008-09, an increase of nearly 7 per cent over US$ 31.6 billion in the year ago period. According to data available with the Union Ministry of Commerce and Industry, imports from China expanded 28 per cent and stood at US$ 26.5 billion in April to February period of 2008-09. India's major exports to China include ores, cotton yarn and fabric, organic and inorganic chemicals, precious stones, metals and machinery, while the items of imports from China include electrical machinery, organic chemicals, iron and steel, fertilisers and mineral fuel.

Investments

With increased mergers and acquisitions (M&A) both India and China are aggressively redrawing the global landscape through their M&A deals. According to a study by UK-based Chartered Management Institute, India and China (along with Brazil and Russia) would exert a greater influence on business markets and transform the business landscape by 2018. According to a survey by Deloitte Touche Tohmatsu (Deloitte) on venture capitalists (VCs) sentiment in the times of recession, China was scored as the most-favoured destination, followed by India.

The survey reveals that 50 per cent of global and non-India based Asian investors who plan to increase their investments over the next three years look at China as the favourite location. India follows its neighbour to get the second spot with 43 per cent of VCs expressing interests to invest in the country this year.

Increasing Synergies

Both India and China provide huge investment opportunities across a myriad of sectors. Significantly, many Indian and Chinese companies are collaborating to create a new competitive force.

- Shenyang IT, rated amongst China's Top 50 by Asia Pacific Region City, is keen to tie-up its US$ 7 billion IT business with India, particularly with Kerala.
- TKM, the wholly-owned subsidiary of TM International Logistics, the joint venture between Tata Steel and Germany's Martrade, has opened an office in Shanghai to undertake freight forwarding business.
- Bharat Heavy Electricals Ltd (BHEL) is looking at the option of picking up equity or even buying out forgings ventures in Eastern Europe and China.
- Two-wheeler maker, Bajaj Auto, has begun production of its bikes in China for exports to Nigeria, a potential market for low-cost and unbranded bikes.
- Even tourism departments are doing their bit to woo the Chinese. Orissa tourism department plans to combine the state's potential in eco-tourism, tribal tourism and Buddhist heritage sites to woo the Chinese tourists.

Future Perfect

Slowly and steadily two different core competencies seem to be emerging in the competitive environment between China and India. While China has become a world class manufacturing hub, characterised by economies of scale, India is climbing the value chain in quality at a rapid pace. In the retail sector, India has emerged as the most alluring market for investment, surpassing China. India has been ranked as the most attractive nation for retail investment among 30 emerging markets by US-based global management consulting firm, A T Kearney. Also, multilateral lending agency, Asian Development Bank (ADB) has approved the US$ 2.9 billion funding plan for India.

Indian Foreign Policy and China

The global political architecture is undergoing a transformation with power increasingly shifting from the West to the East, according to most political observers. The two most populous nations, China and India, are on their way to becoming economic powerhouses and are shedding their reticence in asserting their global profiles. Japan is gradually raising its military profile and the Southeast Asian economies are back in business after the setbacks of the 1997 financial crisis. Whether it is such hopeful prospects or the challenges ahead in the Korean peninsula, Taiwan, and Kashmir, it is clear that this new century will, in all likelihood, be an Asian century.

The future of this Asian century will to a large extent depend upon the relationship between the two regional giants, China and India. According to the United States National Intelligence Council Report titled "Mapping the Global Future," by 2020, the international community will have to confront the military, political and economic dimensions of the rise of China and India. This report likened the emergence of China and India in the early 21st century to the rise of Germany in the 19th and America in the 20th, with impacts potentially as dramatic. The import of their bilateral relationship is not lost on China and India. In one of his meetings with the Indian Prime Minister, Chinese Premier Wen Jiabao is reported to have remarked: "When we shake hands, the whole world will be watching." As of today, however, the trajectory of the India-China relationship remains as complex as ever and difficult to decipher despite positive developments in the last few years.

The puzzle that this chapter attempts to explore is the lack of a coherent Indian foreign policy approach vis-à-vis China despite the fact that China is India's nearest rival for geopolitical influence. According to standard realist theoretical paradigm in international relations, states respond to their structural conditions and do their utmost to tackle the most prominent challenges to their security. Yet, Indian foreign policy seems to have been unable to forge a coherent response towards a rising China that affects its security interests in many ways.

Cooperation or Conflict?

While realising fully well that it would take decades to seriously compete with the US for global hegemony, China has focused its strategic energies on Asia. Its foreign policy is aimed at enhancing its economic and military prowess to achieve regional hegemony in Asia. China's recent emphasis on projecting its rise as peaceful is aimed at allaying the concerns of its neighbours lest they try to counterbalance its growing influence. China's readiness to negotiate with other regional states and to be an economically "responsible" power is also a signal to other states that there are greater benefits in allying with China rather than opposing its rise in any manner.

China realises that it has thrived because it devoted itself to economic development while letting the US police the region and the world. America extending well into the 21st century, at least until China becomes a middle-class society and, if present trends continue, the world's largest economy.

However, while declaring that it will be focusing on internal socioeconomic development for the next few decades, China has actively pursued policies to prevent the rise of other regional powers, or at least to limit their development relative to itself. In case of India, this manifests itself in its cultivation of Pakistan as a close ally. From supplying nuclear and missile technologies to building its military infrastructure, China has d one all it can to help Pakistan be an effective counterweight to India. And this policy has largely succeeded. While India no longer seems to enjoy its earlier conventional superiority vis-à-vis Pakistan, possession of nuclear weapons by both nations ensures that any step that India takes to strengthen its nuclear weapons profile is viewed by the international community as highly d estabilising in the context of the fear of South Asia becoming a "nuclear flashpoint". China has thereby been successful in emerging as a "responsible" global player, despite its questionable nuclear and missile proliferation record, while the international community rails at India for making the world much more dangerous.

China's attempts to increase its influence in Nepal, Bangladesh, and Myanmar, its territorial claims on parts of India such as Arunachal Pradesh, its lack of support for India's membership to the United Nations Security Council and other regional and global organisations, all point towards China's attempts at preventing the rise of India as a regional and global player. It is this strategy that China has consistently pursued. In fact, this strategy has been so successful that some observers feel India is off China's diplomatic radar. This perception apparently is undergoing a revision as other major powers, especially the US, start courting India. The US is already looking at India as an important ally and the recently signed Indo-US civilian nuclear cooperation agreement is a testament to the growing strength of US-India ties. It is instructive that after US declared its ambition of helping India achieve the status of world power, China reacted swiftly and since then has been referring to India as a global power as opposed to a regional one, a formulation that China preferred before.

In contrast to China's well-laid out policy vis-à-vis India, India has from time to time oscillated from going ballistic over China to a sort of acquiescence. There appears to be no coherent long-term strategy vis-à Indian v is its most important neighbour. This is despite the fact that a growing volume of literature analysing Sino-Indian relations points toward the inevitability of a competitive rivalry between the two nations, which should alert Indian decision-makers of the need for a strategic approach vis-à-vis China.

In one of the most detailed studies of Sino-Indian relations in a historical perspective, John Garver makes a convincing case that India-China relations have, over the years, been shaped by a deep and enduring geopolitical rivalry. According to Garver; the rivalry is rooted in the "decades-long, multi-layered, and frequently sharp conflict over the two states' relations with the lands and peoples lying around and between them." Ashley Tell is takes this structura list approach further and argues that China and India as rising powers in Asia remain natural competitors, competing to increase their influence not only in South Asia but also outside South Asia proper. Tell is goes on to argue that India-China competition is not likely to mutate in to malignant rivalry in the near-term but if Indian and Chinese economic and military capabilities continue to grow at the current pace, there is a likelihood of this relationship turning into a dyadic rivalry.

This conclusion is supported by Sumit Ganguly who also contends that any dramatic improvement in Sino-Indian ties is unlikely and the relations between the two will remain competitive. Mark Frazier agrees but argues that precisely because so many sources of dispute exist between China and India, both sides have come to recognise the need to prevent tensions from leading to an overt rivalry. Therefore, according to Frazier, a quiet competition is the most likely possibility. Many in India have also reached similar conclusions. While there are differences on the exact nature that Sino-Indian competition might take in the future, there seems to be a broad consensus that a host of factors point towards a competitive Sino-Indian relationship. The underlying thrust of the above arguments is that whether India likes it or not, the inherent competition for regional influence will always underpin the realities of the relationship and therefore, India needs to shape its foreign policy accordingly. But the Indian policy seems one of over emphasising the promising future potentials in the relationship and de-emphasising troublesome past and present realities. It might then seem puzzling that a nation, such as India, that hopes to be a major global player is so insensitive about its closest competitor.

Constraints

There are a number of constraints that impede the development of a clear-eyed China policy in India. Some of these constraints reflect on the larger Indian foreign policy making while the others are China-specific.

Strategic Culture

Scholars of international politics have increasingly focused on culture as an important variable determining state behaviour in the international realm. Culture can refer both to a set of evaluative standards, such as norms or values, and to cognitive standards, such as rules or models defining what entities and actors exist in a system and how they operate and interrelate. It has been argued that the cultural environment affects not only the incentives for different kinds of state behaviour but also how states perceive themselves, or what is called state identity. Cultural elements of a state's domestic environment, thereby, become an important factor shaping the way national security interests are perceived by elites and the security policies of states. While critics have argued that culture does not matter in global politics and foreign policy and cultural effects can be reduced to epiphenomena of the distribution of power and capabilities, culture is clearly one of the variables shaping a state's foreign policy even if there are reasons to be cautious about its use in explaining political out comes.

A last air Ian Johnston argues that China has historically exhibited are latively consistent hard realpolitik strategic culture that has persisted across different time periods and continues to persist even in its present context when, according to him, China faces a threat environment that is most benign in several decades. China's strategic behaviour exhibits a preference for offensive uses of force, mediated by a keen sensitivity to relative capabilities and Chinese decision-makers seem to have internalized this strategic culture. Johnston also notes that Chinese decision-maker stend to see territorial disputes as high-value conflicts, due in part to a historical sensitivity to threats to the territorial integrity of the state. This is of direct consequence for the future of India-China relations. This strategic culture provides Chinese decision-makers a set of clear principles as well as a long-term orientation in designing foreign policy.

Andrew Scobell argues that China's foreign policy and its tendency to use military force are influenced not only by elite understandings of China's own strategic tradition but also by their understanding of the strategic cultures of other states. In this respect, it is important to recognise that Chinese strategists continue to consider India as a militaristic, unstable, and threatening power, with an ambition of separating Tibet from China. In their view, India seeks to dominate its neighbours and foment conflict between China and other nations. This puts India in the category of Chinese rivals along with the US and Japan— states that, according to Chinese strategic elites, have menacing designs on China's sovereignty and security.

In contrast, India's ability to think strategically on issues of national security is at best questionable. George Tan ham, in his landmark study on Indian strategic thought, points out that Indian elites have shown little evidence of having thought coherently and systematically about national strategy. He argues that this lack of long-term planning and strategy owes largely to India's historical and cultural developmental patterns. These include the Hindu view of life as largely unknowable, thereby being out sideman's control and the Hindu concept of time as eternal, there by discouraging planning. As a consequence, Tan ham argues that India has been on the strategic defensive throughout its history, reluctant to assert itself except within the subcontinent. India's former Minister for External Affairs, Jaswant Singh al so examined the evolution of strategic culture in Indian society and in its political decision-making class, with a particular reference to the post independence period. He finds Indian political elites lack the ability to think strategically about foreign policy and defence issues but he trains his guns on India's first Prime Minister, Jawaharlal Nehru, pointing to his "idealistic romanticism" and his unwillingness to institutionalise strategic thinking, policy formulation and implementation.

It is ironical, however, that even when Jaswant Singh was the External Affairs Minister, there is little evidence that anything of substance really changed in so far as India's China policy is concerned. For all the blame that Singh lays at Nehru's doorsteps, even Singh and his Bharatiya Janata Party-led government did not move towards the institutionalisation of strategic thinking, policy formulation, and implementation. Perhaps, the Indian strategic culture became too powerful a constraint for him to over come.

Lack of Institutionalisation

A major consequence of the lack of a strategic culture is the perceptible absence of institutionalisation of foreign policy making in India. Indian democracy is sustained by a range of institutions—from the more for mal ones such as the executive, legislative, and the judiciary, to the less formalin the broader civil-society. It is these institutions that in large measure have allowed Indian democracy to thrive and flourish for nearly 60 years despite a number of constraints that have led to the failure of democracy in many other societies. However, in the realm of foreign policy, it is the lack of institutionalisation that has allowed a drift to set in and the absence of a long-term orientation. Some have laid the blame on Nehru for his unwillingness to construct a strategic planning architecture because he single-handedly shaped Indian foreign policy during the formative years of the democracy. 22 Yet it is evident that even his successors failed to pursue institutionalisation in a consistent manner.

The Bharatiya Janata Party (BJP)-led National Democratic Alliance(NDA) came to power in 1999 promising that it would establish a National Security Council (NSC) to analyse military, economic, and political threatsto the nation and to advise the government on meeting these challenges effectively. While it did set up the NSC in the late 1990s and defined its role in policy formulation, it neglected the institutionalisation of the NSC and the building up of its capabilities to play the role assigned to it, there by failing to underpin national security policymaking with structural and systematic institutional arrangements. Moreover, as has been pointed out, the way the NSC is structured makes long-term planning impossible, there by negating the very purpose of its formation and its effectiveness remains hostage to the weight of the National Security Advisor (NSA) in national politics. The NSA has become the most powerful authority on national security and sidelined the institution of the NSC. Personality once again has prevailed over the institution. At times important national security decisions were taken in an *ad hoc* manner without utilising the Cabinet Committee on Security and the Strategic Policy Group (comprising key secretaries, service chiefs, and heads of intelligence agencies).

While the Congress-led United Progressive Alliance came to power in 2004 promising that it will make the NSC a professional and effective institution and blamed the NDA for making only cosmetic changes in the institutional arrangements, it has so far failed to make it work in an optimal manner whereby the NSC anticipates national security threats, coordinates the management of national security, and engenders long-term planning by generating new and bold ideas. An effective foreign policy institutional framework would not only identify the challenges but it would also develop a coherent strategy to deal with it, organise and motivate the bureaucracy and persuade and inform the public. The NSC, by itself, is not a panacea as witnessed in the inability of the NSC in the US to successfully mediate in bureaucratic wars and effectively coordinate policy. But the lack of an effective NSC in India is reflective of India's ad hoc decision-making process in the realm of foreign policy. The fundamental problem, perhaps, is that those holding the levers of power succumb to the temptation of controlling institutions and awarding loyalists with assignments, sidelining competence. India cannot emerge as a global power or even a regional one unless it designs appropriate institutions to manage its national assets concomitant to India's vision of itself as a major player in the international system.

In the specific case of India's China policy, this lack of effective institutionalisation of policy-making has made it difficult for India to assess the implications of a rising China in its neighbourhood. In the absence of an effective strategic planning architecture, India's China debate has remained just that, a debate, with no attempt at the highest echelons of foreign policy-making to evolve a coherent strategy towards China.

India's China Debate

The Indian political establishment is fond of arguing that there is a distinct continuity that defines Indian foreign policy. One can relate this easily to the standard structural-realist theory of international politics, according to which states fashion their foreign policies in response to the systemic constraints imposed by the international system, and domestic politics is not an important variable in this process. In a certain sense, this holds true for Indian foreign policy in general. There have been relatively few dramatic shifts in Indian foreign policy over the years and these shifts have been engendered by larger systemic forces, such as the end of the Cold War and the disappearance of the Soviet Union.

In so far as India's China policy is concerned, there is visible continuity in the official position of India. There is a consensus across Indian political spectrum for improving bilateral ties with China and for resolving Sino-Indian differences through dialogue. However, this official policy hides a broader debate in India about how to deal with China. It has been pointed out that there are three broad views in India on how to deal with China and they have been classified as the pragmatists, the hyperrealists, and the appeasers. The pragmatists view China as a long-term threat and as a competitor but argue that this competition can be managed by engaging China economically and balancing against China by emerging as a major power in the international system. The hyperrealists view China as a clear and present danger and would like India to contain China by for gin galliances around China's periphery and by strengthening its military capabilities. The appeasers view China as a friendly and benevolent neighbour and would like India to engage it whole-heartedly since China, in their opinion, is not a threat to India in any way.

Along similar lines, Steven Hoffman has also delineated Indian perceptual positions on China. He has outlined three ideal types which he classifies as the Mainstream position, China-Is-Not-Hostile position, and China-Is-Hostile position. These ideal types closely correlate with the pragmatists, the appeasers, and the hyperrealists of the above-mention edtypology. The mainstream Indian perspective on China, according to Hoffman, views China as a potential threat to Indian security threats but hopes that effective Indian diplomacy can avert any major problems in the future. The China-Is-Not-Hostile perspective holds that China is a rational and peace-loving state that does not have malevolent intentions vis-à-vis India. In marked contrast, the China-Is-Hostile position views China as a short and long-term strategic rival of India and calls for Indian diplomatic assertiveness vis-à-vis China.

The common perception in the early years of independent India was that India had lost its great power status due to internal strife and discord, coupled with a stagnating economy which did not keep pace with the technological advancements of its competitors. It was assumed that the global balance maintained by the superpowers through the Cold War could be used to contain external dangers and thus military preparedness could wait. This belief was shattered by the 1962 border conflict with China. The India-Pakistan war of 1965 revealed the extent of Sino-Pakistan collusion and the unwillingness of the superpowers to pull India's chest nuts out of the fire. Subsequent enhanced reliance on a single superpower limited India's choices till a paradigm shift took place with the collapse of the Soviet Union. This experience also conditions the domestic debate in India: The Communists caution against an alliance with any power which limits India's ability to foster mutual trust and forge amicable relations with its neighbours while the Congress has drawn attention to thee mergence of a global market and a globalising polity that makes a policy of universal global engagement most appropriate. The debate is clothed in clichés easily understood by their respective constituencies.

This debate has been going on for quite some time. Though the multiplicity of views reflects Indian democracy at its best, in many ways it also impedes the formulation of a long-term strategy. The consequence is that the Indian government, realising that there are a plethora of views on China, has taken the path of least resistance, a policy that keeps most groups satisfied, if not happy, even though it is a policy only in name.

Power Matters

The success and failure of a nation's foreign policy is largely a function of its power and the manner in which that power is wielded. Power and its pursuit lie at the heart of inter-state relations. A state's power in the international system can be defined as a function of the material capabilities that it possesses. Despite all the talk of India as a rising power, on all indicators of power, economic and military, India remains behind China in terms of capabilities. While India's economic and military capabilities have no doubt increased substantially in recent times, with its GDP being fourth in the world in purchasing power parity and its military the third largest in the world, China's capabilities have continued to remain ahead of India's. More importantly, India is yet to master the ability "to integrate the creation, deployment and use of military instruments in support of national objectives." Military power, more often than not, affects the success with which other instruments of statecraft are employed. As has been observed by Robert Art, military power always lurks in the back ground of interstate relations, even when nations are at peace with each other. It affects the influence that states exert over one another, thereby shaping political outcomes. In stark contrast to India, China has shown a willingness to use force quite readily in pursuit of its national goals while always insisting that it is defensive in nature. Chinese leaders tend to rationalize even their offensive military operations as purely defensive and measures of last resort (this logic has also been applied to the 1962 Sino-India war), to an extent where defence can even include a pre-emptive strike.

Indian foreign policy's failure to achieve its objectives vis-à-vis China has a lot to do with India's as yet underdeveloped power capabilities. China's rising power and the effectiveness with which it has wielded it has allowed it to achieve most of its strategic objectives vis-à-vis India. In fact, one of the reasons why China does not consider India to be its rival is because of its low opinion of Indian capabilities. Power matters and in international politics, weakness begets failure while strength begets strategic clout. Unless India achieves higher rates of economic growth and modernises its military, both quantitatively and qualitatively, and learns to use its military instruments in pursuit of national objectives, its foreign policy will struggle to achieve the results it desires.

Outcome: Does it Serve Indian Interests?

As a consequence of various constraints that have impeded that evolution of a long-term China policy in India, Indian foreign policy remains mired in confusion. Leaving aside the question of the ability of the Indian elites to think strategically on national security, in the case of India's China policy, one is not even sure if the Indian political and foreign policy establishment understands the basic forces that shape and configure global politics. India's inability, or rather unwillingness, to see the world as it is instead of as it should be, has become the major bane of foreign policy. India's lack of direction in its China policy is clearly revealed by the manner in which it has dealt with China in the past few years. While Sino-Indian bilateral relations have apparently improved, it is not clear if India has any idea as to what ends it wants to harness this improvement and what its strategic objectives with respect to China are. This has resulted in policy flip-flops that have undermined India's regional and global diplomatic stature.

Former Indian Defence Minister George Fernandes described China as India's "potential enemy number one" and former Prime

Minister Atal Bihari Vajpayee explained to the world powers that Indian nuclear tests were a response to the threat posed by Chinese nuclear weapons and Sino-Pakistan nuclear and missile collaboration. But some five years later, China became a "good neighbour" for the same Indian government when Prime Minister Vajpayee visited Beijing. What brought about this remarkable transformation, of course, remains unclear till date. The Man mohan Singh government came to the office declaring that it wants to have friendly relations with China, which, of course, is a reasonable foreign policy objective. But without a clear articulation of India's national security objectives, such declarations remain just pious rhetoric that has never been in short supply in India-China relations. Pursuit of friendly relations with China seems to have become an end in itself when it should be a means towards achieving India's larger strategic objective of emerging as a major regional and global player. Diplomacy without an overarching conceptual frame work of foreign policy often becomes a technical exercise in splitting differences, thus acquiring shades of what many might consider appeasement.

India's China policy is in many ways symptomatic of a larger misunderstanding in the Indian political establishment with regard to what the nation's foreign policy should be. For the left-liberal strand, foreign policy is merely an extension of domestic policy. As such since India is as secular, democratic, and peace-loving nation, India's pursuit of its relations with other states should merely be a reflection of these virtues. This has shaped much of the moral rhetoric in foreign affairs in India for the better part of the last 50 years and still continues to shape the understanding of global affairs within the major political formations on the left of the Indian political spectrum. The Indian discourse on foreign policy, in the words of one of the most astute observers of Indian foreign policy, "has remained frozen in a rhetorical trap, reminiscent of our class X essays in the earnest, third-worldist, allegedly nonaligned seventies." A vivid example of this attitude is the rather extreme positions on national security taken by the Communist Parties consistently. While emphasising their fraternal ties with China's ruling Communist Party time and again, they have called for an end to all military cooperation with the US and

Israel, asking the Indian government to return to a policy of genuine nonalignment. Their complete silence on Chinese activities adversely affecting Indian national security interests even as they continue to denounce the US as a global imperialist has befuddled many.

Prime Minister Man mohan Singh has also articulated a vision of Indian foreign policy, according to which foreign policy exists to push pragmatic economic goals, especially as India integrates more and more with the global economy, and also to build a world of open inclusive nations. This understanding of Indian foreign policy unambiguously identifies India with other liberal democracies of the world. The Prime Minister also suggested that the global environment has never been more conducive for India's economic development than it is today and the world wants to help India to achieve its full potential. He argued that India should engage other great powers such as the US and China to the fullest and neither should be treated as an adversary. While there is much to commend in this articulation of Indian foreign policy agenda, particularly the exhortation that India should rise and take full advantage of the opportunities presented by the changing global economic milieu, it is rather naïve in its assertion that foreign policy is nothing more than an outcome of economic policy and that international politics is nothing but a sum total of global trade and economic cooperation. It is in fact an offshoot of the liberal fallacy that assumes that only if nations were to trade more with each other, the world would become more prosperous and peaceful. In the case of Sino-Indian relations, many have argued that once economics becomes the driving factor, it will us her in a 'paradigm shift' in Sino-Indian bilateral relations. The understanding here being that in the short-term there is no threat to Indian interests from China and it is only a potential long-term threat or challenge to vital Indian interests. There is also the attendant belief that by embedding India-China relations into an expanding structure of economics ties future problem scan be averted. In many ways, this has become the dominant narrative of Sino-Indian relations in recent years.

K. Subrahmanyam has argued that China's desire for increasing its bilateral trade with India and collaboration in sectors such as information technology can be effectively leveraged by India in shaping China's attitudes vis-à-vis India. In a recent study, Jairam Ramesh, Minister of Environment and Forest, has come up with the concept of "Chi-India" that denotes synergy between the two Asian giants. He views closer economic cooperation between China and India as the best way to build trust and friendship, leading to a long-lasting peace between the two states. The problem with these assumptions is that not only is there little empirical evidence to prove that more trade leads to peace and tranquillity, but also that while politics and economics are certainly inter-related, the international economic system rests upon the international political order and not vice-versa. Indian foreign policy cannot be conducted on the naïve assumption that greater economic integration with the world would somehow solve all its foreign policy problems.

At the other end of the political spectrum, the Indian right, because of its preoccupation with establishing a "Hindu" nation and minority bashing, has extended its narrow sectarian view to foreign policy. The consequence has been its obsession with Pakistan as evil incarnate in its foreign policy agenda and its inclination to view the world in black and white, friends and enemies, evil and noble. While undoubtedly pursuing pragmatic economic and foreign policies when in power, the Indian right, as represented by the BJP, seems to be under tremendous pressure to revert back to its extremist views, now that it is out of power. Where India's multiculturalism and pluralism should be leveraged as India's strengths in negotiating with an increasingly polarised outside world, the Indian right, with its resistance to India's plural heritage, has been more interested in turning India into a mirror image of Pakistan.

Then there is the great Indian bureaucracy which suffers from the same myopia that Henry Kissinger long back diagnosed for the US foreign service— that it views its role as merely a solver of concrete issues as they come about and a negotiating instrument rather than one of shaping events and conceptualising strategy.

Shaped by these forces, Indian foreign policy has merely been one of responding to events around it rather than anticipating them and evolving coherent long-term strategies to deal with them in the best interests of the country. A nation's foreign policy, to be effective, should ultimately rest on philosophical assumptions as to the nature of world order and the relationship of order to progress and national interest. In the absence of such a conceptual framework, incoherence would loom large as the diplomatic back and forth would become an end in itself and rather than shaping events, the state would end up reacting to developments around it as in the case of Indian foreign policy. The greatest casualty of this larger foreign policy malaise has been India's China policy. From *Hindi-Chini bhaibhai* to potential enemy number one to great friend, India just does not know how to deal with its neighbourhood dragon that has played its cards so skilfully vis-à-vis India. It can be argued that successive Indian governments have, in fact, been following a coherent policy towards China, i.e., cooperation with China to build Indian capability till such time when India is able to challenge China's primacy openly. If indeed this is the guiding framework, then India is in for a rude shock, as the current Chinese policy towards India will essentially preclude India's emergence as a global or even regional power of any reckoning.

There is nothing really sinister about China's attempts to expand its own influence and curtail India's. China is a rising power and as such will do its utmost to prevent the rise of other power centres around its periphery. This is not very different from the stated US policy of preventing the rise of other powers that might threaten its position as a global hegemon. Just as the US is working towards achieving its strategic objective, China is pursuing its own strategic agenda. In many ways, it is natural for China to view India as a potential rival: for foreign capital, export markets, political influence, and aspirations for regional leadership.

There is also nothing extraordinarily benign in China's attempts to improve its bilateral relations with India in recent times. After limiting India's influence in various ways, China would not like to see India coming close to the US in order to contain China. In this geopolitical chessboard, while both the US and China are using India towards their own strategic ends, India has ended up primarily reacting to the actions of others. And the primary reason for this is the failure to recognise the forces that drive international politics in general and come up with a coherent strategy towards China, in particular.

With the US largely preoccupied with its war on terror and Iraq, China has increasingly asserted its pre-eminence in Asia. It has started to act like a traditional great power, pursuing its regional interests in a proactive manner and transforming its diplomatic relations with smaller neighbours. According to informed observers, this points to a well-conceived grand strategy at play – a strategy that would make it possible for China "to continue its economic growth, technological modernisation, and military build-up without provoking other countries to a costly rivalry."

However, notwithstanding China's attempts at reassuring its neighbours, China's growing power and muscle flexing as in the Taiwan Straits has led other regional powers to re-evaluate their strategic options. Japan has recently sought to broaden the scope of its security ties with the US and for the first time has explicitly discussed joint US-Japanese cooperation in the event of a crisis in the Taiwan Straits. In the face of a rising China that offers new opportunities, some in Australia have demanded that the government review its 50-year-old treaty with the US. China's rise has also engendered a cautious wariness in Russia, despite Moscow's improving ties with Beijing. There is nothing surprising in China wielding its increasing economic and military clout in the region to gradually extend its influence and most other regional powers seem to have realised this. The only exception seems to be India, which seemingly believes that only if the two nations would trade more, all problems in their bilateral relationship would take care of themselves.

It is the structure of global politics that by definition makes Sino-Indian competition inevitable. There are two options for India – either play the game of global politics by the rules laid down by its structure or resign itself to a secondary status in the global hierarchy. Given that Indian decision-makers are already talking of India as a global player in the making, they cannot but take the rules of the game that is global politics, seriously. Of course, a Sino-Indian competition that can be diplomatically managed would be in everyone's interest. But historically, rising powers have tried to reshape their strategic environment to reflect new realities of power and this has provoked conflicts. Many in India share the idea that only if India provokes China would China threaten India. This might seem comforting as it gives India a false sense of control over the unfolding of events. But China could be provoked by its own strategic environment if that is not seen to be commensurate with its rising prowess and expectations, regardless of India's actions. India's weakness, in that case, would do more harm than good.

The best that India can do is to first put its own house in order. India needs to develop its economic and military might without in any way being apologetic about it. It needs to clearly articulate its national interests and engage China on a host of issues, from the border problem to the alleged dumping of cheap Chinese goods in the Indian market. India needs to recognise that appeasing China is neither desirable nor necessary even as a direct confrontation with China is not something India can afford, at least in the near future. A stable foundation for the future of India-China relations cannot be laid by feigning total ignorance of Chinese activities that have adversely affected Indian national interests in the past. In all likelihood, Chinese attitudes towards India will change radically in India's favour as the US strategy of strengthening India as a balancer in the Asian balance of power gathers momentum. This should present India a strategic opportunity to recalibrate its China policy and leverage its relationship with one power vis-à-vis the other.

India is a rising power in Asia and it needs to demand its rightful place in the interstate hierarchy. But it will garner that respect only if it starts behaving in a manner appropriate to a major Asian power. India and China are the two major powers in Asia with global aspirations and some significant conflicting interests. As a result, some amount of friction in their bilateral relationship is inevitable. The geopolitical reality of Asia makes sure that it will be extremely difficult, if not impossible, for *Hindi-Chini to be bhai-bhai* (brothers) in the foreseeable future. If India and China continue to rise in the next few years, a security competition between the two regional giants will be all but inevitable. If India is serious about its desire to emerge as a major global power, then it will have to tackle the challenge of China's rise. A rising China will not tolerate a rising India as its peer competitor. Even if a rising India does not have any intention of becoming a regional hegemon, China will try its best to constrain India as it has already done to a large extent. And it is that containment that India has to guard against. China's intentions vis-à-vis India may seem entirely peaceful at the moment but that is largely irrelevant in the strategic scheme of things. India cannot have a foreign policy shaped by the assumed kindness of its neighbours. A nation's foreign policy requires the ability of its leaders to think in the long term. India cannot and should not wear rose-tinted glasses on Sino-Indian relations just because things seem to be going smoothly at present.

This reality should be accepted by the Indian policy-makers, rather than wished away. India should make a serious attempt to manage the frictions by expanding the zone of cooperation with China even as it tries to steadfastly pursue its national interests. It needs to display the confidence to craft a foreign policy that best serves its national security interests without always looking over the shoulders to make sure that China is not displeased. Again, India can learn a lot by examining how China has managed its relationship with the US in the last two decades.

While India certainly needs to engage China in an effort to reconcile security and political perspectives, it is naïve to assert, as many do, that India should first be sensitive to China's concerns, real or imaginary, before defining its foreign policy goals and strategic agenda. Indian foreign policy agenda should be driven by only India's national security imperatives. India needs to be more pro-active, consistent, and realistic when engaging China. China is not a malevolent, sinister international entity out there to demolish India but a state which is simply pursuing its own strategic interests in a hard-headed fashion on its way to its status of a great power. It is time for India to realise that India's great power aspirations cannot be realised without a similar cold-blooded realistic assessment of its own strategic interests in an anarchic international system where there are no permanent friends or enemies, only permanent interests. But for this to happen, the Government of India will have to formulate a clear China policy and, more importantly, a broader national security strategy. Ad-hocism just won't do. This needs to be the top priority of the government if it wants India to emerge as a global power of any reckoning. India should recognise that a merely tactical foreign policy approach without the backing of a sound strategy will lead to nowhere.

China and India Policy Dominate Global Boardrooms

'Globalization and the opportunities it presents in Asia' was the theme of a presentation by V. Thyagarajan, Senior Vice President and Regional Director of Glaxo Smith Kline Asia Pacific at the recent CIMA CEO Forum in Colombo. A panel discussion comprising Prakash Schaffter, moderator and Managing Director-Janashakthi Insurance Co, Nihal Fonseka, Colombo Stock Exchange Chairman and CEO-DFCC Bank, Jeremy Huxtable, Managing Director/CEO – Suntel, Keith Modder, Managing Director – Virtusa, Dave Ranasinghe, Managing Director – Bodyline and Mourad Mankarios, Principal Coach – Singapore Institute of Management, followed after the presentation.

Excerpts of Mr. Thyagarajan's Presentation

Globalization has been around for a long time but there are recent enablers which have really given it a spur. First and foremost, in my view, the end of the Cold War and the subsequent fall of communism was an important turning point because it moved the debate away from ideology and pushed what works best when dealing with the market economy. That was the first trigger and enabler for globalization to take place. This led to several trade agreements, the WTO, the value of FTA in many parts of the world clearly increasing the dependence between countries on the trade front and enabled globalization to take place. Technology and innovations taking place was an important enabler because it impacted people's lives. Not just information technology but the kind of communications for example had big changes taking place.

Internet

The Internet has clearly transformed the way we operate today. There is nothing that is happening in one part of the world that is not known elsewhere. People move from one part of the world to the other. Sri Lankans are working in different parts of the world, people are moving across the EU; migration enables globalization because people with global mindsets are different.

There are a few key trends which are cemented now. Money flows; you can sit in any part of the world, invest your money in any part of the word, this enables money and ideas to flow and business in different part of the world to flow. Markets are becoming global. The demand for products have become global. Manufacturing and production are clearly a global phenomenon. A good example is from my own industry, the pharmaceutical industry; there was a time when countries required pharmaceutical companies to have a factory in the country as a license to market the product. This was a huge inefficiency because we had factories all over the world operating at 20 to 30% capacity. Today, we have global manufacturing centres which supply to different parts of the world that is much more efficient and beneficial. The same thing can be said for services. A trend which is clearly established is that talent has become global.

Rise of China, India

The rise of China and India is talked about everywhere. This has made a big impact not only in Asia but globally. Today, in no boardroom around the world is there a board meeting without a discussion on the China strategy or the India strategy. Investors want CEOs to explain the China strategy or what are you doing in India. This is because in the last 20 years or so, China has been growing by 10 percent per annum, it is a tremendous economic power. India, more recently is also growing significantly. The size of these countries in terms of population and sheer economic might is having a big impact not only on these countries itself but also on Asia. The South East Asian Tigers along with Korea and Taiwan became global much earlier. They followed a model of economic development which was export-led, they sought markets outside their own boundaries for many reasons. Many of them are small countries with a few exceptions and they saw being global ahead. They have lessons from which we can learn. As I said earlier, it's not just an economic impact but there are tremendous social and cultural implications. These countries have vast populations and it does raise tensions and questions of inclusive development.

Trickle Down Approach

In China and India, the impact of poverty from being a trickle down approach. If you travel around small towns in India, you can see the impact of technology and simple indicators. Some years ago, you had to stand in a queue and wait five or six years to get a telephone connection. Today, people get landlines and it's quite amazing to see everyone in rural India having mobile phones which is recent craze.

There is a tremendous impact on poverty. Agriculture incomes are going up and per capita income is beginning to inch up. The other impact is the economic reform, regardless of the political view of the party in power. Reforms need to be compelling otherwise businesses won't survive. This is happening across the board, in China which is a communist country, in Vietnam, in India with a coalition government. Economic reform is necessary. The centre is shifting towards the east. This may sound optimistic but economic growth is really coming from Asia rather than the traditionally developed European and US centred approach.

The importance of China in world affairs, not just in economic terms is there for everybody to see. This wasn't the case a few years ago. Now the US was the single base superpower and does worry about what China thinks. China's views on policies are clearly sought and recognized because it represents a big chunk of the world. It has become the manufacturing centre of the world from safety pins to aircrafts. You can go to any part of the world and look at the label and find made in China. It is definitely an incredible share of the manufacturing world. Their trade reserves are huge and their foreign exchange reserves exceed trillions of dollars. This gives them a power which is beyond China. Their ability to invest this is significant, the amount of sovereign funds, a significant proportion of American bonds are held by the Chinese and they are beginning to invest in different parts of the world. Clearly it is a different situation than it was 20 years ago. This has a clear impact not only for China but for all Asian economies. This is spurring demand for products that China manufactures and this is an example for others in the region to follow.

Sleeping Giant Wakens

The next example is India, my country. The best way to encapsulate what is happening in India is the sleeping giant is slowing waking up. Economic reform has been a recent phenomenon. The biggest champions of economic growth is the minister of West Bengal which is a communist government. Showcase India in a way which was unexpected. Nobody expected this to take place. It was the Y2K fear and trend which brought the IT industry to the fore. It was small industry with 2 or 3 million people which has now put India on the world stage. It has become the service centre of the world. You can see it in big cities. There are four metros, Chennai, Mumbai, Kolkata and Delhi. These are big cities now. Tier 2 cities are also beginning to see the impact of purchasing power which is visible if you travel to India. It spurs demand for consumer power and durables and the biggest brand names in the world. There was time when companies used to focus on the top layer of the segment, top 10 percent. Now the strategies are changing and unlocking the purchasing power of the middle. The number of Indian companies going global in terms of being competitive globally are going up and have now become so competent.

Global Indian Talent

Lots of Indians are studying in the US. Even CEO's of global corporations are Indian. It has an impact on the strategies of these companies. More recently, trade between India and China increased tenfold and India is recognizing that it is not 'China or India' but 'China and India'.

Singapore

This is an interesting example for Sri Lanka. There is outstanding leadership in Singapore. Competence, calibre, high quality governance and leadership, political stability which is so key and enabled the country to focus on economic development. There is no other resource Singapore has besides its people and because of its size and leadership that has a global vision, they have a global mindset. The Singapore market is a global market. Size is no obstacle to excellence. The country has the best airport and airline in the world and it has nothing to do with its size. Size is not an issue at all. Malta is no bigger than Singapore and how it reinvented itself by talking to the EU — its transition from a low tech manufacturing centre to a service centre. A small country that took the opportunity to convert and reinvent itself. It focuses heavily on financial services and computing. All these strategies have seen a significant surge in investment between 2000 and 2008 and has an impact on jobs, on the economy growing and demand etc... more recently, many Arab countries are looking at Malta as a bridge into Europe and as this have can have implications for Sri Lanka.

India and Global Strategy

Indian IT companies are transforming the way they do business at home and globally. Mindset has to change. Attitudes have to change. Political instability impact is quite significant on social and cultural issues and there is a lot of debate around inclusive development. In many parts of Asia, there are countries where there are disparities in income and globalization is only aimed at people at the top. There are significant tensions at the other end of the social spectrum which is a huge challenge and not easy to go about. In developed countries, in the US, the rhetoric of the candidates for the presidential nomination on the democratic side, is very much this. Clearly, it is something which worries and concerns people across the world.

Sri Lanka – Moving Forward

Inter-dependency is significantly higher than before. It is here to stay. What are the implications of globalization for Sri Lanka? Look at the strengths Sri Lanka has and things here to focus on. Could Sri Lanka be a bridge to India. Sri Lanka and India ties have to be developed more strongly. But I think the political situation is key to any development.

China's Policy of Subduing India's Quest for Power

Subduing India's quest for power is one of China's many goals in modernizing its armed forces. A US Congressional report which says, China is developing a capability to project air and naval forces beyond its coastal areas, has among its goal "subduing India's quest for power", securing unification of Taiwan, preventing Japan's rise as the strongest Asian power, ensuring Chinese influence over the Korean peninsula and supporting Beijing's claims in the east and south China seas. China's foreign and defence policy initiatives, military analysts say, are quite obviously designed to marginalise India in the long-term and reduce India to the status of a subregional power. For many decades now, despite Indian protestations to that country, China has been pursuing a carefully orchestrated plan for the strategic encirclement and containment of India and has been gradually enlarging its sphere of influence towards South East Asia and the Bay of Bengal. China's strategic manoeuvring and its intransigence in resolving the long-standing territorial and boundary dispute with India are a source of soft potential conflict.

China continues to be in occupation of approximately 30 thousand square kilometres of Indian territory in Aksai Chin since the 1962 war and lays claim to large areas of Indian territory in the eastern sector. Pakistan has also ceded a part of occupied Kashmir to China through this China built the Karakoram highway that now provides a strategic land link between China and Pakistan.

Despite the Border Peace and Tranquility Agreement (BPTA) of 1993, the Confidence Building Measures (CBMs) in the Military Field agreed in 1996 and over a dozen meetings of the Joint Working Group and the Experts Group, even the LAC is yet to be demarcated. Political observers say, perhaps the real reason that compels China to drag its feet in resolving its dispute with India is to enable Pakistan to continue to destabilize India through its proxy war without fear of major military retaliation due to the specter of a two front war. The only conclusion that can reasonably be drawn is that China is deliberately stalling further progress on these substantive issues as its suits China to put them on the back burner for the time being.

India is also watchful of China's increasing military involvement in Myanmar which has the potential to impinge on India's trade and maritime interests. China's wooing of Nepal and Bhutan, its sale of sophisticated military technology to Pakistan, Bangladesh and Myanmar, and the possibility it acquiring naval bases, and overland and air-routes to such bases in the countries around India, are areas of concern for India's security. Even through China's navy is still decades away from acquiring the long-range capability necessary to operate with some degree of assurance and freedom in the Indian Ocean, these aspects need to be constantly monitored and vectored into India's calculations.

Since the Gulf WAr of 1991, China has stepped up its efforts to modernize the People's Liberation Army (PLA). The PLA army has been engaged in raising a large number of rapid deployment divisions and in improving mobility and logistics support capability, while simultaneously upgrading its ability to undertake operations, improve air defence capability and institute state-of-the art command and control systems. In this context, Chinese aspirations to gradually upgrade the PLA navy, to acquire deep penetration strike and strategic lift transport aircraft for the PLA air force and to obtain mid-air refueling capability for long range operations, are also relevant. All these endeavours aim ai creating a modern fighting force capable of undertaking swift offensive operations in area away from China's borders in keeping with China's strategy of fighting a limited war under high-tech conditions. It is noteworthy that the upgradation of the military logistics infrastructure in Tibet is continuing at a steady pace. China has been actively engaged in building new roads, supply lines and airfields close to the Indian frontier.

Policy to Box Resurgent India

In establishing close political and military nexus with Pakistan directed against India, China is seeking to box India into the geographical confines of South Asia to stultify its stature as an emerging global power. As remarked by P.R. Chari, Director, Institute of Peace and Conflict Studies, New Delhi, since the United States too is interested in bolstering the entity of Pakistan, despite its drift into social chaos and financial bankruptcy, an axis of powers-Pakistan, China and the US, with palpable anti-India compulsions is visible. Undoubtedly, China has developed close military relationship with Pakistan since 1965 largely designed to restrain Soviet expansion into the Indian Ocean via Afghanistan, but Pakistan has used the weapons, nuclear and missile technology acquired from China to bolster its defences against India and to allow it to be used by China to erode India's stature as a regional military and economic power.

India, aspiring to become a global power, is increasingly perceived as a potential giant on the strength of an expanding economy and market especially by the major industrial nations. In the Asian context, India is undoubtedly a force to be reckoned with and its demonstrated nuclear capability has enhanced its military stature even if the G-7 countries had been condemnatory of its underground nuclear weapons tests in may, 1998. Over the two years, much to the chagrin of China which is insisting on India [and Pakistan] honouring the UN Security Council Resolution and sign CTBT, the international community is gradually reconciling itself to the reality, though there is an understandable concern that the embittered Indo-Pak relationship may end up in a nuclear holocaust. Japan, Australia, Germany, Russia and even the US after the visits by President Clinton and Mr. Vajpayee to each other's country, are inclined to lift sanctions imposed after the Pokhran II nuclear tests. The Clinton visit to India in March last year has, apart from generating warmth in Indo-American relations, aroused rethinking on the part of countries like Japan and Britain to reassess their bilateral ties with India. A global partnership and security dialogue between India and Japan is something which China will carefully evaluate for its strategic impact on Asian security. There is, therefore, no scope of the Russian blueprint of strategic partnership between Moscow, New Delhi and Beijing in matters of international security and the establishment of a multipolar world of peace, security and development. Such a strategic partnership is envisaged by Russian President Putin who has visited China and India and spoke out his mind on this idea to the leaderships there.

It is plainly evident that the strategic direction of India's missile and nuclear programme is against China, however strong the denials of such a fear expressed by Defence Minister George Fernandes after Chinese protestations in the past. China's current nuclear posture of "creeping proliferation" would eventually include China. India could also profitably reevaluate its policy of dealing with Taiwan in the present gingerly fashion and deepen its relations with Vietnam as part of an extra-regional strategy.

5

Disarmament, Nuclear Proliferation, India's Security Issues

For India, Disarmament or Equal Security

India's nuclear policy remains firmly committed to one basic tenet: In a world of nuclear proliferation, our national security lies either in global disarmament or in the exercise of the principle of equal and legitimate security for all. This has been the basis of India's consistent campaign for nuclear disarmament in the past five decades. No other country in the world has exercised the kind of restraint that India demonstrated for nearly a quarter of a century after the first Pokhran test of 1974, despite the fact that India has faced a situation, unparalleled in the world, with two nuclear powers in its immediate and troubled neighbourhood.

The 1990s, however, brought about a qualitative deterioration in India's security environment. This resulted, in the first instance, from the complicity of the "permanent five" guardians of the nuclear nonproliferation regime in the spread of nuclear know-how in India's neighbourhood, which they ignored or overlooked. Indeed, as seen from India, nuclear technologies began to serve as commodities of strategic, political and economic commerce. For India, nonproliferation efforts began to appear curiously selective.

The deterioration was also a result of new strategic alignments. After the end of the Cold War, a new nuclear club came into existence, stretching from Vancouver to Vladivostok. Spreading across the globe, from the eastern rim of Asia back across continents to the Pacific Northwest, this new security structure left a gap-a vacuum-in South Asia. Because it is exclusive, selective and inadequate, this protective umbrella, from a South Asian point of view, is also inherently discriminatory. Large parts of the world today enjoy the benefit of the extended deterrence of the nuclear weapon powers. But India does not. Since this large majority does not share either India's history or its security concerns, closing the gap has not been a priority for it. Again, not so for India.

That is why, in the flood of commentary on our decision to test nuclear weapons, there have been so many ill-informed assessments of India's security predicament. Paradigms of security relevant to others are transposed to us. The people of India, one-sixth of humanity, are seen merely as objects of the security perceptions of others. We are assigned a particular place in the world order and not treated as subjects responding to our own interests. While the present nuclear powers justify nuclear weapons even against perceived threats from non-nuclear states, a regime of international nuclear apartheid becomes operational whenever India claims a place in the sun.

India's decision to conduct nuclear tests was a step taken in our national interest. By exercising this option, India only brought the existing nuclear reality, hitherto ignored, into the open. It sought to move toward, and has gained, some strategic autonomy. That is India's due. Thus, in the absence of any viable alternative, India, through a limited series of tests, has only reasserted that either the international nuclear security paradigm be reviewed or that it be made inclusive. India cannot accept a semicolonial and inferior status as a nation whose security prescriptions are determined for it by others.

We appeal to the international community-particularly to the nuclear weapon powers and all countries that derive their security through nuclear-deterrent protection extended to them-to join us in re-examining the present international security regime. We must find ways and means of moving toward global nuclear disarmament, step by step. In the wake of India and Pakistan's tests, there have been many calls by the international community for restraint in further development of the nuclear option. India has made several assurances and offers displaying precisely such restraint. We have stated clearly that we will not be the first to use nuclear weapons. We have announced a moratorium on further testing, and conveyed our willingness to convert that moratorium into a de jure obligation. We are ready to engage in meaningful discussions on a fissile material cut off treaty in the Conference on Disarmament. And we have already announced our accession to the Chemical Weapons Convention. We have also announced strict adherence to, and a stringent tightening of, export control measures on nuclear, missile, chemical-and biological-weapons-related technologies.

But the present model of nuclear nonproliferation based only on differential standards of security is not viable. What is required is a balance of rights and obligations in the entire field of disarmament and nonproliferation. The way ahead is through the evolution of a universal security paradigm for the entire globe. In the nuclear realm, as in all others, humanity is indivisible.

Movement in India for Nuclear Disarmament

Preamble

After the five nuclear weapon tests of May 11 and 13, the BJP-led government has declared India a nuclear weapons power. This decision in no way increases India's security and is not in the interest of its people. By qualitatively escalating the arms race in the subcontinent, it makes a war with our neighbours likelier and the possibility of mutual annihilation through a nuclear exchange very real. The tests and the consequent rhetoric by senior government leaders introduce a new spiral of suspicions and tensions with our neighbours which will increase, not decrease, nuclear insecurities all around.

These tests were a complete departure from a settled national consensus. There was a national consensus in favour of elimination of all nuclear weapons; there was a national consensus that in the absence of any tangible movement towards global disarmament, India must keep its nuclear option open. This consensus has now been breached in the pursuit of narrow political ends and in the name of a fake national consensus supporting nuclear weapons that is now belied in Parliament and on the streets. These decisions by the Government to move towards nuclear weapons are therefore reprehensible and deserve to be unequivocally condemned. The Indian Government's dangerous move towards nuclear weaponisation has now brought forth a similar Pakistani response which also needs to be condemned.

The tests and the dynamic that they have initiated will also adversely affect the prospect for global disarmament which had improved with increasing public opinion against nuclear weapons. India, which always called for nuclear disarmament and did not wish to be a party to a discriminatory global nuclear regime, is now seen to be only demanding to join the Nuclear Weapons Club. According to the current strategic thinking of the BJP, "nuclear apartheid" is acceptable as long as we are among the discriminators: the Select Six as opposed to the Select Five! We strongly condemn the hypocritical behaviour associated with the attainment of nuclear weapon status by the Indian government. We believe that nuclear weapons are not safe in the hands of any nation. We also deplore sanctions imposed by nuclear weapons-states which show no commitment to genuine nuclear disarmament. But this does not exonerate the BJP in any way.

The BJP-led coalition has also reversed India's long-standing policy of denying legitimacy to nuclear weapons. Nuclear weapons are uniquely evil and have no legitimate role to play as strategic armaments or as deterrents. They are weapons of mass destruction. The sheer scale of their impact, even if only a "few" such weapons are ever used, is simply unconscionable.

Hiroshima and Nagasaki are horrific examples of the destructive potential of nuclear weapons. Nuclear weapons cannot distinguish between combatants and civilians. They impose suffering of the most horrible kind on their victims, including on the yet-unborn through trans-generational effects. Civil and medical defence against them is impossible. They are uniquely evil in their capacity to exterminate all life on this planet.

The International Court of Justice has unequivocally condemned nuclear weapons. Calling them "the ultimate evil," its President pronounced the decision of the Court on July 8, 1996, declaring the threat and use of nuclear weapons "generally contrary to rules of international law applicable in armed conflict." In its historic decision, the Court unanimously called on all states to "bring to a conclusion" negotiations leading to "disarmament in all its aspects."

Our Principles and Objectives

1. *We are deeply and firmly committed to universal nuclear disarmament.*

We reject the argument that we must live forever with such weapons or that the nuclear genie cannot be put back into the bottle. We, as ethical and rational human beings can make this choice: the responsibility is ours. There is a special obligation on the nuclear weapons-states and nuclear-capable states to rapidly move towards universal nuclear disarmament.

2. *Nuclear weapons, possessed no matter by which country or government, do not increase, but reduce, national security.*

The Club of nuclear weapons-states has always been a collection of hypocrites who claim that their possession of these weapons is the best insurance for global peace, while their acquisition by others would be a threat! India has now put in its application for joining this Club, albeit as a junior member.

The Cold War era has conclusively shown that national nuclear posturing aggravates existing rivalries and hostilities and creates new ones. It is dangerous to use external threats as diversionary tactics, as the present government seems to be doing through nuclear weaponisation.

A nuclear weapons regime is by its very nature secretive and elitist, and thus profoundly anti-democratic. It further promotes and deepens the ugly militarisation of everyday life and thinking that is already taking place in India. The ideology of nuclearism which is currently being touted as nuclear nationalism is inseparable from the promotion of an ideology of masculinist aggressiveness. Today, this can be identified as the hallmark of communal nationalism. This has nothing in common with India's pluralist tradition.

National nuclear race creates a false sense of pride and imposes continuing and rising economic, social and political costs. The social and economic costs of nuclearisation, both through missed opportunities and direct weapons manufacture and deployment, can be crippling. Nuclear weapons are incompatible with rational development goals. They represent a wasteful diversion from the true and fundamental security needs of ordinary people. In India the high costs of development of a nuclear arsenal, of its maintenance, storage, constant upgradation and expansion, will impair our ability to redress our basic ills such as sharp inequalities, casteism, communalism and sexism.

3. India must declare that it will never use nuclear weapons under any circumstances.

The government's initial position that it will only use such weapons for "defence", not for aggression, allows their first use. The vague claim for "defence purposes" can justify any act, and does not distinguish between nuclear and non-nuclear conflicts. The government's subsequent contradictory offer of conditional no-first-use is inadequate. The use of nuclear weapons is wholly immoral and unacceptable and indefensible under all circumstances. India must also seek no use pledge from all nuclear weapon states.

4. India and Pakistan must put an end to all nuclear testing.

There is no justification for any further testing by either India or Pakistan. The Pakistani retaliatory tests must not be used to rationalise more Indian tests, let alone open deployment of nuclear weapons.

5. No production and no deployment of nuclear weapons, either by India or Pakistan. Above all, no arming of planes, missiles and other delivery vehicles with nuclear weapons, and no deployment of such delivery vehicles.

Unlike in 1974, the 1998 tests are connected to a programme of weaponisation of bombs of different sizes and yields. They suggest that India is even thinking of producing battlefield nuclear weapons like nuclear-tipped artillery shells, etc. This raises the chances of their being used, leading to dangerous nuclearisation of conventional military exchanges, possibly triggering a full-scale nuclear exchange. There must be complete transparency in the nuclear-related regime. In order to decide about its own security, the public must always know fully what is done by the powerful who talk in the name of the people but are determined to keep information and power to themselves alone.

If India and Pakistan do not deploy nuclear weapons, we may still escape a nuclear arms race. Maintaining the firebreak between tests and open deployment or operationalisation of India's nuclear capability has become crucial. If this firebreak is established—and holds—we can still prevent a futile descent into headlong nuclear hostility, tension and rivalry and therefore into a spiral of ever-growing insecurity.

India can still salvage some credibility as a serious campaigner for global nuclear disarmament if it refrains from open deployment.

India's Security Threat Environment

The intelligence apparatus in India faces challenges on four main fronts (being the world largest democracy and that too in a region where there no other single stable democracy comes with a price):

1) There has been a sea change in the perception of what constitutes Indian "national space." The definition is much broader now and issues such as economics, media, and science that were for some time considered removed from the realm of intelligence targeting are now indivisible parts of it. At the very least concepts such as Economic-Warfare, Cyber-warfare, and Media-Offensive, etc... have served to increase intelligence targeting needs.
2) There is a change in the tenor of revisionist sentiment within the country. Revisionists today are able to use sophisticated resources to aggressively project their views. In some cases this leads to advanced forms of terrorism. It can also exacerbate the existing fissures and divisions in society i.e. caste, religion, ethnicity, and economic disparity. Intelligence agencies today are under a lot of pressure to predict and thus help contain revisionism.
3) The nature of organized crime has changed and its infiltration into society is growing. The merger of the local crime syndicates with narcotics distributors and arms smugglers has increased their destabilizing influence on society. This element often interacts with the elements mentioned in point 2, and produces extremely serious threats to national security. Intelligence targeting of these elusive and dangerous criminals is a difficult task especially as it involves crossing national borders.

4) Increased nuclear and missile technology proliferation to India's hostile neighbours has imposed more demanding requirements on all three aspects of intelligence targeting, i.e. collection, collation and dissemination. The need in this casė to provide accurate and actionable intelligence assessments regarding these threats is paramount.

The changed environment clearly places great strain on the intelligence services, so severe are the demands that in the case of the Central Intelligence Bureau (CIB) that the task force on Internal Security has gone so far as to recommend that the charter of the IB be re-written. It is also quite clear that an emphasis is needed on the use of technical means of handling intelligence and the task force on Intelligence Apparatus was asked to look into ways of merging TECHINT into the entire intelligence collection system.

External

Threats-China

- India considers recurring Sino-Indian border clashes a potential threat to its security. Negotiations since the 1962 Sino-Indian border war have to resolve the conflicting border claims, and each side improved its military and logistics capabilities in the disputed regions. Since the war, China has continued its occupation of the Aksai Chin area, through which it built a strategic highway linking Xizang and Xinjiang autonomous regions. China had a vital military interest in maintaining control over this region, whereas India's primary interest lay in Arunachal Pradesh, its state in the northeast bordering Xizang Autonomous Region. In 1987, although India enjoyed air superiority, rough parity on the ground existed between the two military forces, which had a combined total of nearly 400,000 troops near the border. The Indian Army deployed eleven divisions in the region, backed up by paramilitary forces, whereas the PLA had fifteen divisions available for operations on the border. After a 1986 border clash and India's conversion of Arunachal Pradesh from union territory to state, tensions between China and India escalated. Both sides moved to reinforce their capabilities in the area, but neither ruled out further negotiations of their dispute. Most observers believe that the mountainous terrain, high-altitude climate, and concomitant logistic difficulties made it unlikely that a protracted or large-scale conflict would erupt on the Sino-Indian border.

Threats-Pakistan

The Indo-Pakistani War of 1947

In 1947-48, Pakistan and India fought the first of their three wars involving the Muslim-majority territory of Kashmir, which both claimed and whose Hindu Maharajah opted for India at partition. The conflict ended in stalemate and Kashmir remains disputed territory divided by a heavily-defended Line of Control (LoC) where since 1948 UN observers have investigated reported violations.

The Indo-Pakistani War of 1965

Other than ideology and Kashmir, the main source of friction between Pakistan and India in the 1960s was the distribution of the waters of the Indus River system. As the upper riparian power, India controlled the headworks of the prepartition irrigation canals. After Independence India had, in addition, constructed several multipurpose projects on the eastern tributaries of the Indus. Pakistan feared that India might repeat a 1948 incident that curtailed the water supply as a means of coercion. A compromise that appeared to meet the needs of both countries was reached during the 1950s; it was not until 1960 that a solution finally found favour with Ayub Khan and Jawaharlal Nehru.

The 1965 war began as a series of border flare-ups along undemarcated territory at the Rann of Kutch in the southeast in April and soon after along the ceasefire line in Kashmir. The Rann of Kutch conflict was resolved by mutual consent and British sponsorship and arbitration, but the Kashmir conflict proved more dangerous and widespread. In the early spring of 1965, UN observers and India reported increased activity by infiltrators from Pakistan into Indian-held Kashmir. In mid-1965 Pakistan sent guerrilla forces into the Indian part of Kashmir in the hope of stirring up a rebellion that would either oust the Indians or at least force the issue back onto the international agenda. Pakistani forces did not find as much support among the Kashmiri population as they had hoped, and no uprising by Kashmiris against India took place. Fighting spread, and by August India had retaken Pakistani-held positions in the north while Pakistan attacked in the Chamb sector in southwestern Kashmir in September. A process of escalation culminated in a full-scale Indian offensive toward Lahore on September 6. Fighting, frequently very bitter, continued until a UN-sponsored ceasefire took hold on September 23. Both sides had tacitly agreed not to let the war spread to the East Wing of Pakistan. Each country had limited objectives, and neither was economically capable of sustaining a long war because military supplies were cut to both countries by the United States and Britain.

The war was militarily inconclusive; each side held prisoners and some territory belonging to the other. Losses were relatively heavy—on the Pakistani side, twenty aircraft, 200 tanks, and 3,800 troops. Pakistan's army had been able to withstand Indian pressure, but a continuation of the fighting would only have led to further losses and ultimate defeat for Pakistan. Most Pakistanis, schooled in the belief of their own martial prowess, refused to accept the possibility of their country's military defeat by "Hindu India" and were, instead, quick to blame their failure to attain their military aims on what they considered to be the ineptitude of Ayub Khan and his government.

The Indo-Pakistani War of 1971

By 1971, the largely Punjabi army was in a politically untenable position in East Pakistan, which had voted overwhelmingly for an autonomist party. Once it became clear that a compromise between the civilian leaders of West Pakistan and East Pakistan was unattainable, Yahya Khan was forced to choose between the two sides, and his actions were seen by the Bengalis of the East Wing as favouring the interests of West Pakistan, which were hardly distinguishable from those of the armed forces. Yahya Khan decided to postpone indefinitely the convening of the new National Assembly, which would have been dominated by Bengalis. Within days, unrest spread throughout East Pakistan. Bengalis went on strike and stopped paying taxes. Bengali autonomists became separatists. Army elements in East Pakistan were strengthened in the spring of 1971 and were used to suppress Bengali recalcitrance. The task was undertaken with ferocity; killing, rape, looting, and brutality were widespread and resulted in the flight of nearly 10 million refugees to India over six months.

The army was generally successful during the spring and summer of 1971 in restoring order in East Pakistan, but increasing Indian support of the anti-government Bengali guerrillas known as the Mukti Bahini (Liberation Force) began to shift the balance. When Indian troops finally intervened directly in December, there was no hope of stopping them. On December 3, Pakistani forces began hostilities in the west with attacks on Indian airfields. They had little success, and within twenty-four hours India had seized air superiority, launched attacks against West Pakistan, and blockaded the coast. Pakistani forces in East Pakistan surrendered to the Indian army on December 16, and India offered a cease-fire. In the face of superior force on all fronts, Pakistan had little choice but to accept the breakup of the country and the independence of Bengalis in Bangladesh (the former East Pakistan).

Operation Brass Tacks

There were periods of considerable tension between Pakistan and India in later years. In November 1986, India launched its largest maneuver ever, Operation Brass Tacks, menacingly close to the Pakistan border. The Pakistan Army responded with threatening countermovements, and in early 1987 there was serious concern that war might break out. India accused Pakistan of aiding Sikh insurgents in India's state of Punjab. Pakistan denied this accusation, but some people thought that Operation Brass Tacks might have been a means to strike at alleged bases in Pakistan's Punjab Province. The India-Pakistan hot line was brought into use, and Zia skillfully seized the initiative by traveling to India to view a cricket game, using the opportunity to meet with Indian leaders to defuse the situation.

Siachen Glacier

Among the major disputes between the two countries, only that over the Siachen Glacier, which is located in a remote area of northern Kashmir where boundaries are ill defined, has led to fighting in recent years. The two armies had been in desultory but very costly (primarily because of exposure to the elements) high-altitude combat there since 1984, when Indian forces moved into previously unoccupied territory at the extreme northern end of the Kashmir Line of Control.

Transborder

Jammu and Kashmir

Background: A United Nations resolution, adopted after the 1948 war between India and Pakistan over disputed Kashmir, allows the people of Kashmir to join either India or Pakistan. The United Nations had urged both countries to hold a plebiscite in Kashmir allowing people to choose which country they wanted to join following the removal of Pakistani military forces, but the plebiscite was never held. New Delhi regards Kashmir as an integral part of India while Islamabad insists that the dispute should be settled according to the terms of the resolution. Both countries reject total independence for Kashmir.

Jammu and Kashmir has been a target of externally sponsored religion-based terrorism for the last five years. The aim is to divide people on the basis of sectarian affiliation and undermine the secular fabric and territorial integrity of India. Kashmiri militant groups have committed serious abuses, including the deliberate targeting of Kashmir Hindus by fundamentalists, terrorist groups and foreign mercenaries. The persecution by Muslim extremists of the Hindu minority and the systematic religion-based extremism of terrorist elements has resulted in the exodus of 250,000 members of the Hindu and other minorities from the Kashmir Valley to other parts of India. Fundamentalists and terrorists have also targeted and assassinated Muslim intellectuals and liberal Muslim leaders in Jammu and Kashmir. As a consequence, as many as 50,000 Muslims have also been compelled to flee the Valley to seek safety in other parts of India.

In addition to political killings and kidnappings of politicians and civilians, terrorists engaged in extortion and carried out acts of random terror that killed hundreds of Kashmiris. Terrorist acts by Kashmiri groups have also taken place outside Jammu and

Kashmir. Many of the terrorists are not Indian citizens, but are of Afghan, Pakistani and other nationalities. Militants in Jammu and Kashmir continue to use kidnapings to sow terror, seek the release of detained comrades, and extort funds. According to the Government, terrorists in Jammu and Kashmir kidnaped 422 persons during 1997, of whom 181 were killed by their captors, 82 were released, and 158 remained unaccounted for. The July 1995 kidnaping of American, British, German, and Norwegian nationals by terrorists remains unresolved. The Norwegian captive was beheaded in August 1995. A captured terrorist stated that the remaining hostages—one American, two Britons, and a German—were murdered by their captors in December 1995. There has not been a verifiable contact with the hostages for more than 2 years. In Jammu and Kashmir, the judicial system barely functions due to threats by militants against judges, witnesses, and their family members, because of judicial tolerance of the Government's heavy-handed antimilitant actions, and the frequent refusal by security forces to obey court orders.

Threats-Sri Lanka/Tamil: As of August 1997 there were about 65,000 Tamil refugees from Sri Lanka living in 115 camps in India, including approximately 6,000 who fled the upsurge in fighting in Sri Lanka during 1996 and 338 suspected of militant activities, who are detained in special camps. An estimated 30,000-60,000 more Sri Lankan Tamils are not registered as refugees and are living outside the camps. The Government states that there are some 57,000 Sri Lankan Tamil refugees in camps in India and a few thousand more living outside the camps.

Threats-Andhra Pradesh/Naxalite

In India today there are many Maoist parties and organizations that either predate the Communist Party of India (Marxist-Leninist) or emerged from factions when the CPI-ML split after the death of Charu Majumdar. Three of them, the CPI-ML (People's War), CPI-ML (Party Unity), and the Maoist Communist Centre (MCC), are currently engaged in armed struggle. An inter-connected "Naxalite belt" stretches across central India, comprising Bihar, MP, Orissa, Andhra Pradesh, Maharashtra and parts of Tamil Nadu. Those parts which were connected to the neighbouring states came under the influence of Naxalism. Its members are called Naxalites after the eastern Indian town of Naxalbari, where their movement originated in 1967.

The 25 May 1967 peasant uprising at Naxalbari in Darjeeling district of West Bengal began under the leadership of revolutionary communists belonging to the Communist Party of India-Marxist [CPI(M)]. The uprising was brutally suppressed by the CPI(M)-led United Front government of West Bengal at the behest of the Congress government at the Centre. In reaction, communist revolutionary ranks rebel against the leadership of the party. The rebellion soon assumes an all India dimension. Entire state units of CPI(M) in Uttar Pradesh and Jammu and Kashmir and considerable sections in Bihar and Andhra Pradesh joined this rebellion. On 22 April 1969 they formed the Communist Party of India (Marxist-Leninist).

Since 1980 clashes between police and Naxalite Maoist revolutionaries have taken place in northwestern Andhra Pradesh. In areas under their control, Naxalites dispense summary justice in "people's courts" which in some cases condemn to death suspected police informers, village headmen, and others deemed to be "class enemies" or "caste oppressors." The Naxalites extort money from business firms, and railway services in one area had to be canceled in July and August due to PWG destruction of stations, track and signaling equipment. Over the past few years, hundreds of policemen and suspected Naxalites have been killed, according to press reports and human rights organization. As of September police had killed 102 Naxalites in approximately 80 "encounters." Seventeen years of guerrilla-style conflict have led to serious human rights abuses by both sides. Human rights groups allege that "encounters" are usually faked by the police to cover up the torture and subsequent murder of Naxalite suspects, sympathizers, or informers. These groups cite as evidence the refusal of police to hand over corpses of suspects killed in "encounters," which are often cremated before families can view the bodies. Andhra police have contributed to the establishment of an armed vigilante group known as the "Green Tigers," whose mission is to combat Naxalite groups in the state. The NHRC is investigating some 285 reported cases so-called "fake encounter deaths" allegedly committed by the Andhra police in connection with anti-Naxalite operations.

Threats-Assam

Insurgency and increased ethnic violence have taken a heavy toll in Assam, and led to the installation of a "unified command" of civilian, military and paramilitary forces in the state. While there were numerous allegations of human rights violations directed against security forces, public attention has begun to focus on the actions of insurgents of the United Liberation Front of Assam (ULFA) and the Bodo Security Force in Assam. The kidnaping of NGO environmental activist Sanjay Ghosh in July 1997 and his death at the hands of his United Liberation Front of Assam (ULFA) captors led to wide public criticism. On August 6, the ULFA confirmed that Ghosh died in captivity; he had been "arrested and tried" by the ULFA on July 4. The Chief Minister of Assam and a High Court judge in Meghalaya survived attempts to kill them during the year. According to the Union Home Ministry's 1996-97 report, a total of 201 persons were killed in Assam between April 1996 and March 1997. The ULFA was responsible for 107 deaths, and the National Democratic Front of Bodoland (NDFB) was responsible for 174 deaths during this period. However, Mass, a human rights organization in Assam with a credible record, claims that during the period January 1 through July 21, a total of 202 people were killed in the state (of which 68 died at the hands of security forces and 57 were killed by the ULFA). Compilation of reports of killings from the press suggests that the numbers may be even higher.

Threats-Northeast/Nagaland

Extensive, complex patterns of violence continued in the seven states of northeastern India. The main insurgent groups in the northeast include two factions of the National Socialist Council of Nagaland (NSCN) in Nagaland; Meitei extremists in Manipur; and the all Tripura Tiger Force (ATTF) and the National Liberation Front of Tripura (NLFT) in Tripura. The proclaimed object of many of these groups is to break out of the Indian union, creating new, independent nations. Their stated grievances against the Indian Government range from charges of neglect and indifference to the endemic poverty of the region, to allegations of active discrimination against the tribal and non-tribal peoples of the region by the centre. The oldest of these conflicts, involving the Nagas, started with India's independence in 1947. On August 1, a ceasefire between the Government and the ISAC-Muivah faction of the NSCN went into effect and has been largely observed by the Government and all insurgent groups in the state. However, factional feuds among rival Naga insurgent groups claimed an estimated 120 lives during the first 3 months of the ceasefire. The Government extended the ceasefire for another 3 months on November 1, unilaterally including even those armed groups in Nagaland which had not been party to the original ceasefire.

Threats-Sikhs in Punjab

Sikhs in Punjab are the majority community. The problems that arose in Punjab were due to the religion-based terrorist elements, externally encouraged, who sought to widen the communal divide between the Sikhs and other communities for their political ends. In the course of time, as many Sikhs fell victims to the terrorist bullets and bombs as Hindus. This defeated the aim of the terrorists of communalizing the Punjab polity. The people of Punjab have rejected terrorist violence and have demonstrated their faith in the democratic process by electing representatives to the State and national legislatures in elections held during 1992. Peace has returned to Punjab.

Nuclear Weapons

India's nuclear weapons program was started at the Bhabha Atomic Research Centre in Trombay. In the mid-1950s India acquired dual-use technologies under the "Atoms for Peace" nonproliferation program, which aimed to encourage the civil use of nuclear technologies in exchange for assurances that they would not be used for military purposes. There was little evidence in the 1950s that India had any interest in a nuclear weapons program, according to Joseph Cirincione of the Carnegie Endowment for International Peace. Under the "Atoms for Peace" program, India acquired a Cirus 40 MWt heavy-water-moderated research reactor from Canada and purchased from the U.S. the heavy water required for its operation. In 1964, India commissioned a reprocessing facility at Trombay, which was used to separate out the plutonium produced by the Cirus research reactor. This plutonium was used in India's first nuclear test on May 18, 1974, described by the Indian government as a "peaceful nuclear explosion."

According to the Bulletin of Atomic Scientists, India began work on a thermonuclear weapon in the 1980s. In 1989, William H. Webster, director of the CIA, testified before the Senate Governmental Affairs Committee that "indicators that tell us India is interested in thermonuclear weapons capability." India was purifying lithium, producing tritium and separating lithium isotopes. India had also obtained pure beryllium metal from West Germany.

Testing

After 24 years without testing India resumed nuclear testing with a series of nuclear explosions known as "Operation Shatki." Prime Minister Vajpayee authorized the tests on April 8, 1998, two days after the Ghauri missile test-firing in Pakistan.

On May 11, 1998, India tested three devices at the Pokhran underground testing site, followed by two more tests on May 13, 1998. The nuclear tests carried out at 3:45 pm on May 11th were claimed by the Indian government to be a simultaneous detonation of three different devices-a fission device with a yield of about 12 kilotons (KT), a thermonuclear device with a yield of about 43 KT, and a sub-kiloton device. The two tests carried out at 12:21 pm on May 13th were also detonated simultaneously with reported yields in the range of 0.2 to 0.6 KT.

However, there is some controversy about these claims. Based on seismic data, U.S. government sources and independent experts estimated the yield of the so-called thermonuclear test in the range of 12-25 kilotons, as opposed to the 43-60 kiloton yield claimed by India. This lower yield raised skepticism about India's claims to have detonated a thermonuclear device.

Observers initially suggested that the test could have been a boosted fission device, rather than a true multi-stage thermonuclear device. By late 1998 analysts at Lawrence Livermore National Laboratory had concluded that the India had attempted to detonate a thermonuclear device, but that the second stage of the two-stage bomb failed to ignite as planned.

TEST	*DEVICE*	*DATE*	*YIEL Dclaimed*	*YIEL Dreported*
	Fission device	18 May 1974	12-15 kiloton	4-6 kiloton
Shakti 1	Thermonuclear device	11 May 1998	43-60 kiloton	12-25 kiloton
Shakti 2	Fission device	11 May 1998	12 kiloton	??
Shakti 3	Low-yield device	11 May 1998	0.2 kiloton	low
Shakti 4	Low-yield device	13 May 1998	0.5 kiloton	low
Shakti 5	Low-yield device	13 May 1998	0.3 kiloton	low

India's Nuclear Arsenal

Though India has not made any official statements about the size of it nuclear arsenal, the NRDC estimates that India has a stockpile of approximately 30-35 nuclear warheads and claims that India is producing additional nuclear materials. Joseph Cirincione at the Carnegie Endowment for International Peace estimates that India has produced enough weapons-grade plutonium for 50-90 nuclear weapons and a smaller but unknown quantity of weapons-grade uranium. Weapons-grade plutonium production takes place at the Bhabha Atomic Research Centre, which is home to the Cirus reactor acquired from Canada, to the indigenous Dhruva reactor, and to a plutonium separation facility.

According to a Jan. 2001 Department of Defence report, "India probably has a small stockpile of nuclear weapon components and could assemble and deploy a few nuclear weapons within a few days to a week." A 2001 RAND study by Ashley Tellis asserts that India does not have or seek to deploy a ready nuclear arsenal. According to a report in Jane's Intelligence Review, India's objective is to have a nuclear arsenal that is "strategically active but operationally dormant", which would allow India to maintain its retaliatory capability "within a matter of hours to weeks, while simultaneously exhibiting restraint." However, the report also maintains that, in the future, India may face increasing institutional pressure to shift its nuclear arsenal to a fully deployed status.

Nuclear Non-Proliferation: An Indian Perspective

The global nuclear nonproliferation regime is facing some serious challenges. But we need to put these current challenges in perspective. Though the challenges facing the nonproliferation regime today might seem as if they are unprecedented, we must also not forget that from its inception, the regime has faced such challenges. Indeed, historically, the existence of such challenges has provided the impetus to strengthen and tighten the regime. India's first nuclear test in 1974 led to establishment of the Nuclear Suppliers Group (NSG); revelations about Iraq's success in hiding its nuclear wea-pons program led to the Additional Protocol; North Korea's withdrawal from the nuclear Non-Proliferation Treaty (NPT) led to proposals to eliminate the right to withdrawal clause in the Treaty, though this particular proposal has not yet been accepted.

Nevertheless, the nonproliferation regime does face a crisis today. For the first time, a non-nuclear member state, North Korea, has with-drawn from the Treaty and gone nuclear, and another non-nuclear member state, Iran, is threatening to do the same. Such non-compliance with the basic purpose of the treaty can lead other NPT non-nuclear weapon states (NNWS) to also seek their own nuclear weapons, thus unravelling the treaty. The NSG waiver granted to India for international nuclear com-merce despite India building a nuclear arsenal and not being a signatory to the NPT is also seen as a challenge to the nonproliferation regime. Meanwhile, little progress has been made on nuclear disarmament, a key objective of the NPT, another issue that agitates NNWS.

But the most important challenge that the nonproliferation regime faces is the breakdown in the consensus about nonproliferation. The global nuclear nonproliferation regime was established and strengthened in the first several decades after the NPT came into force in 1970 because the major powers, the key actors in international regime creation, management and sustenance, broadly agreed on the need for the regime and its key objectives and provisions. Over the last decade, that consensus has broken down. Washington's policies have been an important factor in this decline, but other major powers have not helped much either because they have allowed differences with the US on other political issues to spill over into nonproliferation issues. This has given violators and non-complying members space to exploit and weaken the regime. Hopefully, the next US administration will recognize the need for global consensus and work towards it. Equally hopefully, other powers will recognize that they would ultimately lose if the regime completely collapses and thus act in concert with the US to shore up the regime. India is severely constrained from doing much to help the regime. India, not being a member of the NPT, has been outside the nonproliferation regime, and indeed a target of the regime. With the NSG waiver and the additional IAEA safeguards in place, India is now moving towards a *modus vivendi* with the regime. And India has strong interest in preventing further nuclear proliferation. The challenge that India and the nonproliferation regime face is in finding a way for India to support and strengthen the regime even while staying outside many of the formal institutions of the regime.

India's Nuclear Policy

Though India conducted a nuclear test in 1974, the Indian nuclear weapons program was more or less shut down for the next decade and half. Though some developmental work continued at a low level, the decision to build nuclear weapons was taken only around 1988-1989. The Indian decision to go nuclear appears to have been taken reluctantly: Indian intelligence had been warning for about a decade that Pakistan was making steady progress on its nuclear weapons program, and both the international community in general, and the nonproliferation regime more specifically seemed unable or unwilling to stop Pakistan's nuclear pursuit. In addition, there were clear indications that China was aiding Pakistan's efforts. India's efforts at nuclear disarmament made no headway either, with the Rajiv Gandhi Action Plan receiving little support from the powers that mattered. These conditions appear to have left Indian decision-makers believing that they had little choice but to restart the Indian nuclear program.

The Indian decision to conduct a second series of tests in 1998 and declare itself openly a nuclear weapon state is more complex. As the nonproliferation order tightened, with the NPT being extended indefinitely and the CTBT (Comprehensive Test Ban Treaty) threatening to eliminate an Indian nuclear option, various

Indian governments sought to slip the noose by conducting nuclear tests. Such efforts were thwarted either due to internal political problems or because preparations for nuclear tests were discovered. India's 1998 tests were thus a response to fears that India would be permanently consigned to a position of nuclear inferiority, especially vis-à-vis China.

In the decade since the 1998 nuclear tests, India's weapons program has made slow but steady progress. India's size and conventional military capability are sufficient to handle most threats that it faces, which also reduces the pressure to deploy nuclear weapons in more adventurous roles.

Early fears about a nuclear arms race between India and Pakistan and China now appear to have been exaggerated. India has shown little concern with the state of the nuclear balance between itself and its two nuclear neighbours, concentrating instead on building up a relatively small but capable nuclear arsenal. India's doctrine of no first use and a credible minimum force structure represents a prudent investment, in line with India's general view that nuclear weapons are political instruments with little value other than as a deterrent for other nuclear forces. It must be noted, however, that India's nuclear forces are currently not capable enough to deter China because India does not have a missile with sufficient range to target all regions of China. Therefore India's nuclear force, especially its missile force, should be expected to grow slowly both in qualitative and quantitative terms over the next decade.

The US-India Nuclear Deal

The US-India nuclear deal was essential to India because India's traditional approach towards nuclear cooperation had reached a dead-end. Traditionally, India sought international nuclear cooperation, even while maintaining a nuclear weapons program, by agreeing to partial safeguards on nuclear imports. This strategy allowed India to supplement its domestic nuclear power capability with international cooperation, as long as there were willing international partners. However, when the rules of international nuclear commerce changed from partial safeguards (safeguards only on the specific imported item) to full-scope safeguards (safeguards on the entire nuclear program as a condition for any nuclear commerce), India was faced with the choice of either giving up its nuclear weapons program, or giving up on international nuclear commerce. Not surprisingly, India chose the latter. What the US-India nuclear deal does is give India the option yet again to both keep its nuclear weapons program while also preserving its access to international nuclear commerce. The issue had become even more vital for India because India's explosive economic growth has put much greater strains on its electricity generation capacity, leading to peak power shortages of as much as 11 percent. Now that the nuclear deal is complete, and India has the necessary waiver from the NSG that permits other nuclear powers such as France and Russia to supply India with civilian nuclear technology, India is expected to significantly enhance its civilian nuclear power sector with international cooperation.

The nuclear deal is unlikely to have major impact on India's nuclear weapons program. In the last two decades, ever since India went nuclear in the late 1980s, India has only built a few dozen nuclear warheads. Most estimates suggest that India has enough fissile material for about 65-110 warheads, with some estimates suggesting even lower numbers. If we assume a median of 85 warheads, it would suggest that India has only built, on average, about four warheads a year. This suggests that India feels no great pressure to rapidly increase its arsenal. The suggestion, by some arms control experts, that access to foreign nuclear fuel will free India's domestic fuel resources for weapons does not hold much water because India has much larger stockpiles of fuel (about one ton) that it could have converted for weapons if it had wanted to do so. In other words, the small size of the Indian nuclear force is the consequence of deliberate choice rather than because of any fissile material shortage.

India's Nonproliferation and Arms Control Policies

Over the last several decades, India has emphasized nuclear disarmament rather than nuclear nonproliferation. New Delhi's position on the spread of nuclear weapons was a complex one. On the one hand, India always saw such spread of nuclear weapons as a danger. Its decision not to sign the NPT despite taking part in the negotiations was a difficult one, reached after New Delhi concluded that signing the treaty would adversely affect Indian security especially because neither Washington nor Moscow appeared willing to provide any form of extended deterrence cover for India's security. In other words, India never accepted the idea that nuclear proliferation was legitimate, unlike, for example, China in the 1950s and 1960s.

Therefore, though New Delhi refused to sign the NPT, it also refused to help other states such as Libya with nuclear technology.

New Delhi was also quite meticulous about ensuring that its nuclear weapons technology did not reach other non-nuclear weapon states. Though there have been some concerns raised that India might have illegally acquired some technologies and materials, and that it may have been careless in ensuring the security of some of its nuclear technology, the Indian record in protecting its technology from leaking is far better than that of most other nuclear powers.

In the process, New Delhi built up a reputation as a 'responsible nuclear power' that became an unexpected bonus in dealing with the international community, especially as India sought a waiver from NSG guidelines. India squared this circle of both opposing the NPT and opposing nuclear proliferation by taking the position that though each country should be free to decide on how to meet its security needs, states that did sign the NPT had an obligation to live up to their commitments. Thus, on both North Korea and Iran, India's position has been to argue that because these countries voluntarily accepted the NPT, they have an obligation to live up to their treaty commitments.

India's response to the threat of nuclear proliferation was to take an active part in nuclear disarmament diplomacy, seeing the elimination of nuclear weapons as both a way of dealing with the threat of proliferation as also a way of avoiding the unpleasant decision about building its own nuclear weapons. India also was at the forefront in pressing that *all* commitments in the NPT be honoured, including the Article 6 obligation towards nuclear disarmament, rather than focusing only on the spread of nuclear weapons to non-nuclear states.

Thus, a favorite Indian argument about nuclear proliferation was to point out that what mattered was not just horizontal proliferation (or the expansion of the nuclear weapons club) but also vertical proliferation (the expansion of the arsenals of the existing members of the club).

Nevertheless, as the global nuclear nonproliferation regime comes under increasing threat due to noncompliance or even outright violations by countries such as Iran and North Korea, India will have to increasingly face up to the needs of fashioning a more appropriate approach to the nonproliferation regime. In addition to focusing on nuclear disarmament and noncompliance by NWS (Nuclear Weapon States), India will also have to come up with meaningful and effective ways of dealing with noncompliance by NNWS (Non-Nuclear Weapon States), something that India had previously ignored. One of the disadvantages that India faces in making this policy transition is that India is not a member of the NPT and it is unlikely to become one unless India's *de facto* NWS status is accepted as *de jure* status by the NPT members. This is unlikely. But the alternative – India giving up its nuclear weapons and joining the treaty as a NNWS – is equally unlikely. In essence, then, India's relationship with the treaty in unlikely to undergo any formal changes though India can be expected to play a more active diplomatic role in trying to keep the NPT system together.

As stated earlier, India is likely to continue stressing nuclear disarmament as a way of resolving the problems of nuclear proliferation. Though India's disarmament drive is sometimes seen a cynical ploy to divert attention from its unwillingness to accede to the NPT, a good number among India's political and administrative elite appear sincerely committed to the goal of a nuclear-weapon free world. This may very well be because no serious cost-benefit analysis has been undertaken within the government of the implications of nuclear disarmament on India's security interest. If so, it would not be the first time: India originally supported both the NPT and the CTBT without realizing the full import of these treaties on India's security. India would eventually refuse to accede to either treaty. Nevertheless, India does strongly support a Nuclear Weapons Convention with the objective of eventual comprehensive nuclear disarmament. Even after openly declaring itself as a nuclear weapon state, India has reiterated its commitment to comprehensive nuclear disarmament.

Global Governance of Nonproliferation

If efforts at comprehensive global nuclear disarmament are to succeed, arms control and disarmament institutions need to be strengthened. This is easier said than done. It would be difficult even to agree on the principles for such institutions. The Conference on Disarmament (CD) and its predecessor entities were clearly the key forum for global nonproliferation negotiations and were responsible for the most successful global arms control measures, including the NPT. But, unfortunately, the CD has been deadlocked for more than a decade now, with member-states unable even to agree on a work agenda. The CD's consensus rule is generally blamed for this deadlock, but it is unlikely that this rule will be or can be changed.

This deadlock has serious consequences: negotiations on the Fissile Material Cut-Off Treaty (FMCT), the key next step in global nuclear arms control, has been held up. The FMCT negotiations are likely to be challenging, given the disagreements among some key parties on important issues such as whether the treaty should have verification elements (the US has opposed verification measures, while most others want it), and whether existing fissile material stocks should be counted in the treaty (some states including Pakistan want existing stocks included, while many states including the NWS only want to cutoff future production). But until serious negotiations start, it is unlikely that the disagreements on these issues can be resolved, which will delay the treaty and quite possibly, suggest the need to move the treaty to some other forum.

Indeed, there are now more calls for moving critical arms control treaties away from the CD altogether because of the inability of the CD to get anything done.

Two key arms control measures, the Ottawa Treaty banning land mines, and the Convention on Cluster Munitions have been negotiated outside the CD. If the CD continues to be unable even to decide on what their annual agenda should be, frustration with the CD process can only increase. On the other hand, despite the problems with the CD, it remains the indispensable forum for nuclear arms control negotiations. Neither the Land Mines treaty nor the Convention on Cluster Munitions are appropriate examples because neither of these initiatives include the key nuclear weapon powers. Such a non-CD model might be useful when like-minded countries come together, leaving out states that are likely to present serious obstacles. But clearly such a model will not work in dealing with nuclear arms control and disarmament. The primary obstacle in nuclear arms control talks are the nine nuclear weapon states and their touchiness on issues they consider vital to their national security. Moving to an *ad hoc* body outside the CD will be of little help.

If the CD is deadlocked, the situation is little better in other fora such as the UN First Committee on Disarmament and International Security, which is essentially a talk shop with little real initiative being shown by the various member states, and with no progress on any issue. In any case, with all member states included, the First Committee is not exactly nimble. Even the UN Disarmament Commission, which was intended to be a forum for less formal and more open discussion of disarmament issues has become stultified with member-states stating well-known national positions rather than suggesting possible ways finding middle ground for breaking deadlocks and making progress.

The problems afflicting these nuclear arms control institutions create serious difficulties when trying to deal with the challenges currently facing the NPT and the nuclear nonproliferation regime. Broadly, these challenges include preventing noncompliance and break-out by NNWS, fulfilling of the full treaty obligations by NWS, and establishing other supporting treaties and norms to support the nuclear nonproliferation order, such as the FMCT, CTBT and various technology control regimes.

Preventing noncompliance by NNWS signatories to the NPT, especially cases of such states trying to build nuclear weapons, is the key problem. Though the NPT has not been able to prevent the spread of nuclear weapons, it has, until recently, prevented the spread of nuclear weapons to signatory NNWS. Three of the four states that built nuclear weapons after the treaty was established were not NPT signatory states. Thus, the only real failure the NPT has had is with North Korea, a signatory NNWS state that built a nuclear weapon and then withdrew from the treaty. But if North Korea does not return to the NPT fold, or if another state in a similar situation such as Iran were to build nuclear weapons, then the pressures on NPT would be far greater than that posed by India, Pakistan or Israel. This is because other states in the neighborhood of Iran and North Korea will feel the pressure to respond by building their own nuclear weapons. But all such states are signatory NNWS and they will be able to build their nuclear weapons only by violating their NPT commitments. In other words, these states will also have to leave the NPT to build their own nuclear weapons, or will have to violate the treaty by covertly building their arsenals. In either case, this would represent the beginning of the unravelling of the treaty.

The treaty itself can do little about noncompliance: non-compliance needs to be addressed by the UN Security Council and other interested institutions and parties. But these institutions depend on nation-states which have the capability to monitor noncompliance, such as the U.S. The International Atomic Energy Agency (IAEA), which is mandated to monitor the nuclear programs of member-states, does not, in many cases, have the resources to satisfactorily fulfil its safeguards mandate. In addition, the IAEA can only report noncompliance to the UN Security Council, which has to take a political call on what is to be done.

A key problem that the UNSC faces in dealing with issues of noncompliance is that there is often little political consensus on what could be done to handle such cases. That lack of consensus is visible in the case of both North Korea and Iran. In both cases, the issues of disagreement appear to be not so much about the specifics of the individual case (on which there is broad agreement) but on how these countries should be handled, with China and Russia generally favouring a softer approach than the US. It is difficult to not see in Chinese and Russian opposition to the American approach a broader concern with US foreign policy and strategy which reveals itself as a reluctance to go along with American approach to these problems, and sometimes as outright opposition. Washington is not entirely blameless: over the last decade the US has eschewed the essential task of creating consensus on a broad range of international issues that has created these conditions of non-cooperation by other major powers. The US, as the hegemonic power, needs to pay greater attention to its responsibilities. Fortunately, there are signals that the US has realized the need for creating such consensus. The next US administration will have to expend greater efforts in creating the climate for consensus that is vital to dealing with the challenges facing the nuclear nonproliferation regime.

The NWS will also have to do more to live up to their NPT commitments. This includes taking real measures towards nuclear disarmament, rather than constantly citing their reduced nuclear arsenals – the result of post-Cold War nuclear arms control measures rather than a step towards nuclear disarmament – as an indication of their commitment towards nuclear disarmament. Nobody underestimates the difficulties of the process towards nuclear disarmament, but the NWS could start by agreeing to that goal, and undertaking other measures such as reducing the salience of nuclear weapons in their military doctrines, de-alerting their nuclear forces, eliminating their remaining tactical nuclear weapons, and withdrawing their nuclear forces to their homeland as a way of indicating their commitment towards nuclear disarmament.

Regional Nonproliferation Initiatives

Along with global measures, regional measures to reduce the nuclear risk may seem a logical step. A number of regional nuclear-weapons free zones (NWFZ) exist, and there has been a long-standing proposal for a similar measure in South Asia. India has rejected such proposals, though, oddly, it has offered to accept some other NWFZ, such as the Bangkok Treaty. Globally, though, the idea has gained greater support.

Nevertheless, it is not clear that the five accepted NWS are fully committed to the concept of such NWFZ. For such zones to be effective, it must prohibit the testing, deployment and transit of nuclear weapons through that region. If it cannot do this effectively, it becomes a nonproliferation measure which targets the regional states rather than a step towards global nuclear disarmament. There is little indication that such zones have lived up to this standard or that NWS have treated such zones seriously. Their nuclear armed ships regularly traverse areas that are supposedly nuclear weapons free with little hindrance. Regional members to such arrangements have little capacity to monitor such transit and even less capacity to control or prevent such transit. In essence, such zones are paper arrangements whose key provisions are routinely violated by the NWS.

In addition, there are other weaknesses to such treaties and proposals. Though such treaties can reduce bilateral nuclear insecurities among neighbours, they do little to contain extra-regional nuclear threats. This is most clearly visible in South Asia. India will be unlikely to accept any South Asian regional nuclear arms control proposal that leaves it vulnerable to China. And China is unlikely to accept any controls on its nuclear weapons programs given its concerns about the US. In other words, nuclear politics cannot be isolated as a regional problem when extra-regional concerns are present.

Finally, there is little to suggest that these measures have in any way aided nuclear arms control or disarmament. These measures, by themselves, have put little pressure on the nuclear powers to find ways to reduce the salience of nuclear weapons in their military strategies. The best that can said about these proposals is that they have supported the existing norm about the illegitimacy of nuclear weapons.

Overall, India's approach to nuclear arms control and disarmament has been at either the bilateral or the global levels rather than at the regional level. At the bilateral level, India and Pakistan have concluded a number of agreements to reduce the nuclear risk, including an agreement to not attack each others' nuclear facilities, to not test ballistic missiles towards each other, to control military movements near their border and hotline agreements to enhance communication in crisis.

At the global level, India has proposed disarmament approaches as well as risk reduction measures such as de-alerting of nuclear forces. In contrast, there have been few regional measures that India has either proposed or accepted.

Conclusion

India has always had an uneasy relationship with the global nuclear nonproliferation regime. On the one hand, it has seen the nonproliferation regime as a discriminatory order that unfairly targeted NNWS while allowing the NWS to maintain their nuclear arsenals. On the other hand, India has always seen the spread of nuclear weapons as a danger and has been careful about ensuring that its own nuclear technology has not spread to other NNWS. Though the current crisis in the nuclear nonproliferation regime is serious, and a breakdown of the regime can affect India also, New Delhi has only limited means to tackle the problem.

The key requirement to deal with the crisis in the nonproliferation regime is consensus among the major powers, a consensus that goes beyond boilerplate policy statements and includes concerted action by all major powers in the recognition that if they do not act, they could all face serious difficulties. If North Korea is not denuclearised, Japan's current nuclear calculus could change, setting off chain-reaction all over East Asia, a prospect that China cannot ignore. A similar chain reaction could take place in the Middle East if Iran's nuclear ambitions are not controlled, something that will directly impact on both China and Russia. The US has the greatest responsibility: it must reinvigorate the nonproliferation consensus, but to do this, it must also lead a global consensus on major international issues that go beyond nuclear proliferation. Without such a consensus, institutional tinkering will be useless and the current nuclear nonproliferation challenges cannot be met.

6

India and United Nations

Introduction

The United Nations, since its birth in 1945, has proved to be a unique experiment for the world community of nations. Born as an "embodiment of the will of the peoples of the world', the United Nations has served as a repository of collective wisdom and a forum for joint action for each of its Member States, in their search for a better, safer, healthier and a more prosperous existence.

As a founder member of the United Nations, India has been a firm supporter of the Purposes and Principles of the United Nations, and has made significant contributions to the furtherance and implementation of these noble aims, and to the evolution and functioning of its various specialized programmes. It stood at the forefront during the UN's tumultuous years of struggle against colonialism and apartheid, its struggle towards global disarmament and the ending of the arms race, and towards the creation of a more equitable international economic order. At the very first session of the UN, India had raised its voice against colonialism and apartheid, two issues which have been among the most significant of the UN's successes in the last half century. India exulted in the UN's triumph, and saw in the UN's victory, a vindication of the policy relentlessly pursued by it from its initial days at the world forum.

Today, as we stand at the beginning of the 21st century, new challenges are before us. Freed from the shackles of the Cold War, the UN stands poised to grapple with the changes which the world has witnessed over the years. Today's challenges, be they political, economic, social, environmental or demographic, are global, impinging on the affairs of all States and making the interdependence of peoples so much greater. If this demands a greater dependence on the UN as the only democratic, universal forum for the community of nations, it also demands a strengthening of the UN itself and its revitalization. The ongoing reform process is primarily aimed towards these ends. A revitalized and strengthened United Nations and a more representative Security Council will enable this unique organisation to face the challenges of the 21st century more effectively. As the United Nations strives to find solutions to these issues, India pledges to work, with abiding faith and hope, towards UN's success, and to assume greater responsibilities that the world community expects from it.

Development

The UN cannot avoid its development responsibilities. Much needs to be done-the international community has to go a long way in meeting the ODA target of 0.7 per cent of GDP agreed nearly a quarter century ago. According to the report of the Development Assistance Committee of the Organization for Economic cooperation and Development, overseas aid from 21 richest OECD countries fell from 0.25 per cent of combined national income in 1996 to 0.22 per cent in 1997. According to the same report, development aid has fallen by 20 per cent in real terms since 1992. India is one of the largest contributors to the core resources of UNDP and a significant contributor to those of UNFPA and UNICEF. India is also a major contributor to the core resources of and the World Food Programme. India's contribution to these funds is higher than that of many OECD countries. We hope that the developed countries will also increase their contributions to untied and apolitical resources for development.

India has contributed US $ 100,000 to the UNCTAD Trust Fund for the least Developed countries. It has also been contributing US $ 50,000 per annum to the ITC Global Trust Fund since its inception in 1996. It also makes substantial voluntary contributions to UNEP, Habitat, UN Drug Control Programme, UNRWA, UNIFEM UN Volunteers etc.

UN Peacekeeping

Time and again, India has risked the lives of its soldiers in peacekeeping efforts of the United Nations, not for any strategic gain, but in the service of an ideal. India's ideal was, and remains, strengthening the world body, and international peace and security.

Indian troops have taken part in some of the most difficult operations, and have suffered casualties in the service of the UN. Professional excellence of the Indian troops has won universal admiration. India has taken part in the UN peacekeeping operations in four continents. Its most significant contribution has been to peace and stability in Africa and Asia. It has demonstrated its unique capacity of sustaining large troops commitments over prolonged periods. Presently, India is ranked as one of the largest troop contributors to the UN. India has also offered one brigade of troops to the UN Standby Arrangements. Over 55,000 Indian Military and Police personnel have served under the UN flag in 35 UN peace keeping operations in all the continents of the globe.

India provided a paramedical unit to facilitate withdrawal of the sick at wounded in Korea. After the ceasefire, India became the Chairman of the Neutral Nations Repatriation Commission. One brigade group of the Indian Army participated in the operation in Korea, authorized by the UN General Assembly through Uniting for Peace resolution. Indian troops provided guards for the prisoners of war. The Chairman of the Neutral Nations Repatriation Commission was Lt. Gen. K.S. Thimmaya and the Commander of the Custodian Force to take custody of the Prisoners of War (numbering over 22,000) was Maj. Gen. S.P.P. Thorat.

India also contributed to peace in the Middle East. The United Nations Emergency Force (UNEF) was created in 1956 following cessation of hostilities between Egypt and Israel. India provided an infantry battalion, which accounted for the bulk of the UN force. Over 11 years, from 1956 to 1967, more than 12,000 Indian troops took part in UNEF.

Pursuant to the Geneva Accord, an International Control Commission (ICC) for Indo-China was set up in 1954. India was the Chairman of the Commission, which implemented the ceasefire agreement between Vietnam, Laos, Cambodia and France. India provided one infantry battalion and supporting staff until the ICC was wound up in 1970. The UN faced one of its worst crises when war between the government and the secessionist forces broke out in Congo. The UN operation in the Congo, ONUC, was unique in many ways. The operation involved heavy casualties. It was also the first time that the UN undertook an operation in an intra-State, rather than an inter-State conflict. The operation upheld the national unity and territorial integrity of the Congo. The Indian contingent lost 39 men in action in the Congo. The performance of the Indian troops was distinguished by their discipline, self-restraint and humanitarian concern.

Indian Army provided a Force Commander and observers for the Observer Mission in Yemen in 1963-64 (UNYOM). India also participated in the UN operation in Cyprus (UNFICYP). India provided three Force Commanders to UNFICYP, Gen. K.S. Thimmaya, Lt. Gen. P.S. Gyani and Lt. Gen. Dewan Prem Chand. The UN set up a Military Observer Group to monitor the situation on Iran-Iraq border. India provided military observers during the period 1988-90.

Following the end of the Gulf War, the UN established the UN Iraq-Kuwait Observer Mission (UNIKOM). Indian observers continue to participate in the operation. UN operation in Namibia is considered one of the success stories of the United Nations. Lt. Gen. Prem Chand of India was the Force Commander. Indian military observers in Namibia were responsible for the smooth withdrawal of foreign troops, elections and subsequent handing over of the authority to the government.

UN established the ONUMOZ to restore peace and conduct elections in Mozambique. India provided a large contingent of staff officers, military observers, independent headquarters company, and engineering and logistics company. The operation has ended successfully. In recent times, one of the biggest peace keeping operations which was completed successfully was the UN operation in Cambodia. India provided an infantry battalion, military observers and a field ambulance unit.

India has also regularly sent military observers to various UN operations. This includes ONUCA (Central America) in 1990-92, ONUSAL (El Salvador) in 1991 and UNOMIL (Liberia) in 1994. The UN Operation in Somalia is considered one of the most difficult and challenging operations the UN has ever attempted. Indian naval ships and personnel were involved in patrolling duties off the Somali coast, in humanitarian assistance on shore, and also in the transportation of men and material for the United Nations. The objective was humanitarian relief. The Indian contingent successfully combined the often conflicting roles of coercive disarmament and humanitarian relief to the civilian population. With stand-alone capacity, the Indian brigade had operational responsibilities for one-third of Somalia viz. 1,73,000 sq. km area of responsibility, the largest ever held by any contingent. In spite of such a large areas of operations, there were minimum civilian casualties in the area of responsibility of the Indian contingent. The Indian contingent dug a large number of wells, constructed schools and mosques, and ran mobile dispensaries and relief camps, which provided veterinary care, and medical and humanitarian relief to a large number of Somalis and their livestock. In spite of suffering casualties the Indian contingent exercised utmost restraint in firing in self defence. It also organized and carried out rehabilitation and resettlement of thousands of refugees and helped to repatriate them to their homes. The Indian contingent played a vital role in reviving the political process by organizing reconciliation meetings. The last remaining units of the Indian contingent were repatriated from Somalia on board Indian naval ships from Kismayo port. India demonstrated its capacity to provide an integrated force, comprising land and naval forces as well as air support. India provided a contingent comprising one infantry battalion and support elements to the UN assistance mission in Rwanda to help ensure security for the refugees, and to create conditions for free and fair elections. After successful completion of the assignment, the Indian contingent was repatriated in April 1996.

The Indian army has participated in the successive phases of the UN mission in Angola since 1989. The Indian contingent comprised one infantry battalion group, one engineer company, staff officers and military observers. The contingent has made a sizeable contribution towards construction of quartering camps. The Indian contingent was also involved in rebuilding bridges over the Conga, Rio Quisaju, Rio Mugige and Rio N'hia Rivers. One high risk task was the demining of the main arterial road connecting Lobito and Huambo and repairing a 60 mile stretch of the road. The Indian contingent has also built a 3,300 feet airstrip at Londuimbali. The Deputy Force Commander was an Indian army officer. India also participated in the UN Observer Mission in Angola (MONUA), which succeeded UNAVEM III.

The Chief Military Observer of the UN Observer Mission in Sierra Leone (UNOMSIL) was also an Indian army officer. India provided a medical unit and civilian police personnel to UNOMSIL. After the upgradation of the UN Mission in Sierra Leone in November-December 1999, India provided two infantry battalion groups, a quick reaction company, a field engineering company, a level III medical facility, a special forces company, an artillery battery, transport and attack helicopters and the backbone of the force headquarters in Freetown. Maj. Gen. V.K.Jetley was the first UN Force Commander in Sierra Leone.

India has also provided an infantry battalion to the UN Interim Force in Lebanon (UNIFIL). The Force Commander of UNIFIL is Maj.Gen. L.M. Tewari. India is also currently participating in the UN Mission in Ethiopia and Eritrea (UNMEE) with an infantry battalion, a Force Reserve Company and a Field Engineer Construction Company.

Recent peacekeeping operations have tended to be multi-dimensional, and include police monitors and election observers. India has contributed police personnel and election observers to the UN peacekeeping operations in Cambodia, Mozambique and Angola. India provided 123 police personnel to UN mission in Haiti (Phase II). India has also provided police monitors for the UN International Police Task Force in Bosnia and Herzegovina, Sierra Leone (UNOMSIL), Western Sahara (MINURSO) and Kosovo (UNMIK). In addition, two companies of CRPF have deployed in UNMIK as Special Police units. The Police Commissioner of MINURSO is an Indian Police Officer, Mr. O.P. Rathor. India sent Lt. Gen. Satish Nambiar, as the Force Commander of UNPROFOR in former Yugoslavia in 1992-93.

India has also provided senior staff to assist the UN Secretary-General at the UN Headquarters. Major Gen. I. J. Rikhye served as Military Advisor to the UN Secretary General from 1960 to 1969.

India also hosted a UN Regional Training Workshop for Peacekeeping Operations in New Delhi during January 20-26, 1996 in which 17 countries of the Asia-Pacific region participated. Mr. Kofi Annan, the then Under Secretary General for Peacekeeping visited India in this connection. India also held an International Seminar on UN Peacekeeping in March 1999 in which over 70 countries participated. The United Services Institution (USI) of India hosted another seminar in New Delhi in September 2000 in collaboration with the Swedish National Defence College. A Centre for UN Peacekeeping (CUNPK) was set up under the aegis of USI in New Delhi in 2000. UN Secretary General Kofi Annan visited the Centre in March 2001 during his visit to India.

India has considerable experience in demining activities and has made significant contributions to the de-mining work in various missions in Rwanda, Mozambique, Somalia, Angola and Cambodia. Experienced Indian Army Engineers have been employed for training of selected personnel from the host countries to execute mine clearance programmes as also to generate awareness of the problem among the local people. Indian Army has also undertaken mine clearance projects in support of repatriation and rehabilitation programmes of the UNHCR.

India has also provided opportunities for training to military officers from different countries. India has, at present, army training teams in six countries: Seychelles, Laos, Mauritius, Botswana, Zambia and Bhutan. India has also offered diverse courses to service personnel at various military training institutions across the country. This includes officers from Bangladesh, Bhutan, France, Germany, Japan, Jordan, Kazakastan, Kenya, Korea, Laos, Malaysia, Maldives, Mauritius, Myanmar, Namibia, Nepal, Nigeria, Oman, Saudi Arabia, Singapore, South Africa, Sri Lanka, Sudan, Tanzania, Thailand, UAE, UK, USA, Vietnam, Zambia and Zimbabwe. Cadets from countries such as Maldives, Palestine, Bhutan, Nepal, Sri Lanka and also many African States receive pre-commission training at the National Defence Academy, Khadakvasla and the Indian Military Academy, Dehradun. Over 100 Indian soldiers and officers have sacrificed their lives while serving in UN peacekeeping operations.

Disarmament

Since independence, India has consistently pursued the objective of global disarmament based on the principles of universality, non-discrimination and effective compliance. Given the horrific destructive capacity of nuclear weapons, India has always believed that a world free of nuclear weapons would enhance both global security and India's own national security. Thus India has always advocated that the highest priority be given to nuclear disarmament as a first step towards general and complete disarmament.

As early as 1948, India called for limiting the use of atomic energy for peaceful purposes only, and the elimination of atomic weapons from national armaments. India was the first country to call to an end to all nuclear testing in 1954. This was followed up in subsequent decades by many other initiatives, for example, on the Partial Test Ban Treaty, and the call for international negotiations on nuclear nonproliferation. In 1978, India proposed negotiations for an international convention that would prohibit the use or threat of use of nuclear weapons. This was followed by another initiative in 1982 calling for a "nuclear freeze"-i.e. prohibition on the production of fissile material for weapons, on production of nuclear weapons, and related delivery systems. At the special sessions of the United Nations General Assembly on disarmament, India put forward a number of serious proposals including the 1988 Comprehensive Plan for total elimination of weapons of mass destruction in a phased manner. It was a matter of regret that the proposals made by India along with several other countries did not receive a positive response and instead, a limited and distorted nonproliferation agenda, meant above all to perpetuate nuclear weapons was shaped.

India was compelled by considerations of national security to establish and adopt a policy of keeping its nuclear option open while it continued to work for global nuclear disarmament. India's nuclear capability was demonstrated in 1974. India exercised an unparalleled restraint in not weaponising its nuclear capability. It is relevant to recall, that during this period, when we voluntarily and totally desisted from testing, over 35,000 nuclear weapons were developed through a series of tests by states possessing nuclear weapons. This has happened even as Article VI of the Non-Proliferation Treaty committed the Nuclear Weapons States, party to the NPT, to take steps in good faith for nuclear disarmament. India was obliged to stand apart on the CTBT in 1996 after having been actively engaged in the negotiations for two and a half years precisely because the issues of nonproliferation, global disarmament and India's concerns about her security and strategic autonomy were ignored.

India's continued commitment to nuclear disarmament and nonproliferation is clear from the voluntary measures announced by India after undertaking a limited series of underground nuclear tests last year. India remains committed to converting its voluntary moratorium into a de jure obligation accordance with our long held positions disarmament, and in response to the desire of the international community that the CTBT should come into effect in September 1999. India has declared that it will maintain minimum credible nuclear deterrent and will not engage in an arms race. India has declared a no-first-use doctrine. We are willing to strengthen this commitment by undertaking bilateral agreements as well as by engaging in discussions for a global no-first-use agreement. India believes that a global no-first-use agreement would be the first step towards the delegitimization of nuclear weapons. India remains the only state possessing nuclear weapons to unambiguously call for a Nuclear Weapons Convention to ban and eliminate nuclear weapons just as the Biological Weapons Convention (BWC) and the Chemical Weapons Convention (CWC) have banned the other two categories of weapons of destruction.

Nuclear Disarmament and Nonproliferation

In 1996, India, along with the members of the Group of 21 countries, put forward proposal, submitted to the Conference on Disarmament (CD), of a Programme of Action calling for a phased elimination of nuclear weapons (1996-2020). India has unambiguously indicated its commitment the establishment of an ad hoc committee in the Conference on Disarmament in Geneva to negotiate global nuclear disarmament. India is also the only state with nuclear weapons, which responded positively to certain aspects of the 8-Nation initiative on disarmament, entitled

"Towards a Nuclear Weapon Free World", put forward in June 1998 by Brazil, Egypt, Ireland, Mexico, New Zealand, South Africa and Sweden.

At the NAM Summit in Durban, at India's initiative, NAM agreed that an international conference be held, preferably in 1999, with the objective of arriving at an agreement, before the end of this millennium, on a phased programme for the complete elimination of all nuclear weapons. The call for the elimination of nuclear weapons was reiterated once again by Prime Minister in his address to the UN General Assembly in 1998. India remains committed to cooperating with like minded states to attain this goal. India also introduced a resolution in the 53rd General Assembly calling for reducing nuclear danger by de-alerting nuclear weapons.

India is fully committed to the goal of curbing nuclear proliferation in all its aspects. It was at India's initiative that the item "nonproliferation of nuclear weapons" was included in the agenda of the UN in 1964. In 1965, India along with other like-minded countries submitted a joint memorandum towards achieving a solution to the problem of proliferation; it included the conclusion of an international nuclear nonproliferation treaty. However, the NPT as it emerged from these negotiations, was flawed and discriminatory, seeking to create a permanent division between the nuclear 'haves' and 'have-nots'.

India believes that the indefinite and unconditional extension of the NPT in May 1995 has only served to legitimize nuclear arsenals of the NPT states possessing nuclear weapons into perpetuity, thus posing a major obstacle to the goal of global nuclear disarmament. The NPT Preparatory Commission (PrepCom) meetings held in 1997 and 1998 have also clearly demonstrated the reluctance on the part of the states possessing nuclear weapons to take steps towards a speedy process of global nuclear disarmament.

India has developed wide-ranging expertise in nuclear technology and ensured through a stringent and effective system of export controls that there is no proliferation of these technologies for weapons purposes. India's record in this matter is, in fact, better than some of the NPT signatories. At the same time, we are against ad hoc regimes or cartels which restrict high technology in an arbitrary, unequal and patently discriminatory manner. They need to be universalised, made transparent and equitable.

Comprehensive Nuclear Test Ban Treaty

India's commitment to a comprehensive ban on nuclear testing dates back to 1954 when Jawaharlal Nehru called for a "standstill agreement" whereby testing of all nuclear weapons was to be immediately suspended, pending an agreement on their complete prohibition. It was again at India's initiative that the item "Suspension of Nuclear and Thermo-Nuclear Tests" was included in the agenda of the UN in 1959.

During the course of the negotiations in the Conference on Disarmament (CD) in Geneva on the CTBT, India put forward a number of proposals consistent with the mandate adopted by the CD in 1994. These proposals were aimed at ensuring that the CTBT would be truly comprehensive and would be part of the step-by-step process of eliminating all nuclear weapons. However, these proposals were regrettably ignored and instead, Article XIV on Entry into Force requiring India to join the treaty before it became operational was adopted in violation of basic treaty law. India was thus forced to declare its opposition to the CTBT as it emerged.

After concluding a series of tests on May 13, 1998, India immediately announced a voluntary moratorium on further underground nuclear test explosions. In announcing this moratorium, India accepted the core obligation of a test ban and also addressed the general wish of the international community. India also announced its willingness to move towards a de jure formalization of the voluntary undertaking.

India is now engaged in discussions with key interlocutors on a range of issues, including the CTBT. India is prepared to bring these discussions to a successful conclusion. For the successful conclusion of talks, creation of a positive environment by India's interlocutors is a necessary ingredient. India expects that other countries, as indicated in Article XIV of the CTBT, will adhere to this Treaty without conditions.

Fissile Material Cutoff Treaty (FMCT)

India supports the ban on production of fissile material for nuclear weapons purposes. This demand has been articulated by India in the UN through concrete proposals like the Action Plan which it presented in 1988. India also co-sponsored a UN General Assembly resolution (48/75 L) in 1993, which called for an early commencement of negotiations for the prohibition of the production of fissile material for nuclear weapons or other nuclear explosive devices. India has joined the consensus in the Conference on Disarmament on establishing an ad hoc committee to negotiate a FMCT. India believes that this is an integral part of the nuclear disarmament process. It would also go a long way in arresting problems of illegal transfers of nuclear material. India supports efforts for negotiations on a universal, non-discriminatory and verifiable fissile material cutoff treaty that would prohibit the future production of fissile material for weapons purposes but would permit such production for civilian uses.

Negative Security Assurances (NSAs) and Nuclear Weapon Free Zones (NWFZs)

India has always maintained that NSAs provide illusory benefits, and that the real security assurance is complete elimination of nuclear weapons, and also that in the interim, if NSAs are to be given, they should be provided through an international, comprehensive, legally-binding and irreversible agreement. Similarly, consideration of security assurances in the narrow strait-jacket of Nuclear Weapon Free Zones (NWFZS) cannot do justice to the wide variety of concerns that emanate from the global nature of the threat posed by nuclear weapons. As a responsible state possessing nuclear weapons, India has stated that it does not intend to use nuclear weapons to commit aggression or for mounting threats against any country. India respects the sovereign choice exercised by states not possessing nuclear weapons in establishing NWFZs on the basis of agreements freely arrived at among the states of the region concerned. At the fifth session of the ASEAN Regional Forum in Manila, India stated that it fully respects the status of the Nuclear Weapon Free Zone in South East Asia and is ready to convert this commitment into a legal obligation.

India will remain responsive to the expressed need for commitments to other nuclear weapon free zones as well.

Chemical Weapons Convention (CWC)

Convention has India is an original signatory to the Chemical Weapons Convention, having signed it on 14 January 1993, and was among the first 65 countries to have ratified the Treaty. The universal and non-discriminatory character of the CWC are primarily responsible for the large number of signatories and the equally large numbers of ratifications. The implementation of the CWC involves a combination of voluntary declarations and mandatory verification arrangements aimed at ensuring compliance in a transparent and universal manner. A National Authority (NA) has been set up to oversee implementation of the Convention in India.

As the first Chairperson of the Executive Council of the Organization for Chemical Weapons (OPCW), India guided the deliberations of the organization during its crucial first year. Implementation of all obligations assumed by India to the Convention and related activities have proceeded satisfactorily. India believes that the provisions of the Convention require to be implemented in a non-discriminatory manner. National implementing legislations containing provisions which undermine the Convention hold out the prospect of leading to matching responses by other-states parties thereby leading to an unnecessary dilution of the spirit and the confidence reposed in the CWC by a great majority of countries party to the CWC. Similarly, the existence of technology denial regimes such as the Australia Group remains an aberration when seen against the large number of ratifications the enjoyed so far.

Biological and Toxin Weapons Convention (BTWC)

India ratified the Biological Weapons Convention in 1974. India has participated in all four Review Conferences of the Biological and Toxin Weapons Convention (BTWC) and in the meetings of the Group of Governmental Experts. India is currently participating in the negotiations of the Ad hoc Group of the States Parties of the BTWC with the aim to strengthen the convention by a protocol, including possible verification measures. India maintains that these measures should be non-discriminatory and avoid any negative impact on scientific research, international cooperation and industrial development.

Anti-Personnel Landmines (APLS)

India is fully committed to the eventual elimination of anti-personnel landmines and achievement of the objective of a nondiscriminatory and universal ban on APLS.

A beginning can be made with a ban on export and transfer of APLS, that would enjoy an international consensus, and by addressing humanitarian. concerns and legitimate defence requirements of states. India is sensitive to the humanitarian aspects of the landmine crisis and the need for a strong international response.

Aware that APLs have been used indiscriminately in conflicts not of an international nature, India has called for a ban on their use in all internal conflicts. India follows a conscious policy of not exporting APLS. India has also been contributing to UN demining efforts since the Congo peacekeeping operations in 1963. An officer of the Indian Army is presently deployed with the UN Mine Action Centre in Bosnia. India is presently in the process of ratifying amended Protocol II of the 1980 Inhumane Weapons Convention (CCW), which deals with anti-personnel landmines. India stands ready to negotiate a ban on the export and transfer of landmines in the Conference on Disarmament.

Transparency in Conventional Weapons Transfers and Small Arms

India is committed to strengthening the norm of transparency in conventional armaments in general, and greater participation in the UN Register of Conventional Arms in particular. India has reported to the Register annually since 1994.

The issue of proliferation of, and illicit trafficking in, small arms has moved up the agenda of the international community on disarmament issues. India is acutely aware of this problem and intends to participate actively in international search for effective solutions, including a proposed international conference to discuss the issue of illicit trafficking in small arms in all its aspects.

Environment

India is among the top 12 mega centres of the world in terms of its genetic diversity. It has a wide range of geoclimatic conditions and a rich and varied flora and fauna, as well as a long standing tradition of environmental sensibility and concern that goes to the very roots of its millennia-old culture. Harmony with nature has been an integral part of the ethos of Indian society.

The then Prime Minister of India, Mrs. Indira Gandhi, was the sole foreign head of state or government to participate in the United Nations Conference on Human Environment held in Stockholm in June 1972, at a time when international concern over environmental issues was yet to fully crystallise. At that session she emphasised that the environmental concerns cannot be viewed in isolation from developmental imperatives.

India considers environmental and developmental issues to be closely intertwined. It fully supports international cooperation in the field of the environment so as to effectively deal with global environmental problems. It is committed to a global partnership that simultaneously seeks to protect the environment while addressing the development requirements and aspirations of the developing countries.

India has consistently played an important role in the evolution of an international consensus to tackle major global environmental issues. It was an active participant in the process leading up to and culminating in the convening of the United Nations Conference on Environment and Development in Rio de Janeiro in June, 1992. The Rio Conference affirmed the importance of sustainable development, which encompasses both development and environmental protection.

Agenda 21, adopted by the Rio meet, provides a blueprint on how to make development socially, economically sustainable. Despite constraints, India has initiated several activities and programmes in the context of Agenda 21, which are consistent with its national goals and objectives. India is a party to numerous multilateral environmental conventions which contribute to the protection of the environment and to sustainable development. These include the Framework Convention on Climate Change, the Convention on Biological Diversity, the Vienna Convention on the Protection of the Ozone Layer, the Montreal Protocol on Substances that Deplete the Ozone Layer, the Ramsar Convention on Wetlands of International importance, the Basel Convention on the Transboundary Movement of Hazardous Wastes, the Convention on Combating Desertification, and the Convention on the International Trade in Endangered Species of Wild Flora and2 Fauna.

India is also an active member of the Commission on Sustainable Development that was set up after the Rio Conference to monitor the implementation of Agenda 21.

India is among the leading countries in the vanguard of efforts directed at environmental protection. It has in position an elaborate framework of environmental legislation for the conservation of forests, preservation of wildlife and the control of water, air and soil pollution.

It has a network of protected areas converting 84 national parks and 447 wildlife sanctuaries. India has also introduced the Eco-Mark label for environment-friendly products, requires the undertaking of Environment Impact Assessment before commencing major industrial projects, has in 2position functioning Environmental Tribunals as well as an effective system of Environmental Audit.

At the Special Session of the UN General Assembly held in June 1997 to review the progress made five years after the Rio meet, India expressed its disappointment over the lack of fulfillment at the international level of commitments voluntarily undertaken by the industrialised countries at Rio. On its part, India reiterated its commitment to the global partnership established at Rio de Janeiro.

UN Reform Process

Reform and improvements are an intrinsic part of any organization which has to serve the needs of a changing environment. The United Nations is no exception. India supports a strengthened and revitalized United Nations with its various organs functioning within their mandates in accordance with the

UN Charter. India supports an enhanced role for the United Nations in development and development cooperation dialogue. India firmly believes that development should be central to UN's agenda and be pursued in its own right. It is an indispensable prerequisite to the maintenance of international peace and security.

India has actively participated in all reforms and restructuring exercises that could enhance the capacity of the UN in the fulfilment of its primary tasks.

India actively supported the establishment of UNICEF on a permanent basis, the creation of the UN Development Programme, establishment of UNEP and restructuring of the UN in the economic and social fields.

It was also represented in the High Level Expert Group established by the UN Secretary-General in the mid-nineties on the financing of the UN. It participated constructively in the discussions on the Agenda for Peace and the Agenda for Development. India was also one of the co-Chair of the Working Group on Strengthening of the United Nations.

India has been supportive of the UN Secretary-General Mr. Kofi Annan's reform proposals. While some of these have been agreed and implemented, discussions continue on others. An important proposal is the holding of the Millennium Assembly. India believes that the Millennium Assembly must identify concrete goals for the promotion of development cooperation and disarmament and must also provide the United Nations with the required resources to effectively tackle these challenges.

India shares the concerns for improving efficiency, avoidance of duplication, and the minimization of waste in the functioning of the entire UN system. While efforts for these objectives need to be intensified, India believes that the Member States should pay their contributions unconditionally, in full and on time, as delays in payments have caused an unprecedented financial crisis in the UN system. Contributions of the Member States should have, as their fundamental underpinning, the capacity to pay principle. Financial reforms hold the key to the future of the world body. Without sufficient resources, the UN's activities and role would suffer.

The United Nations as a universal forum should have as its guiding principles transparency, non-discrimination, consensus, and equal respect for the dignity of all individuals, societies and nations. Be it world trade, environment and development, resolution of the global debt crisis, or economic assistance for the poorest members of the world community, these values have to be the touchstone of global initiatives and actions.

The composition of the Security Council has remained largely static, while the UN General Assembly membership has expanded considerably. This has undermined the representative character of the Council. An expanded Council, which is more representative, will also enjoy greater political authority and legitimacy.

In 1965, the membership of the Security Council was expanded from 11 to 15. There was no change in the number of permanent members. Since then, the size of the Council has remained frozen. Even more dramatic than the increase in the number of Member States of the UN, is the change in composition of the General Assembly. The overwhelming majority of the UN General Assembly members today are developing countries. They are also, most often the objects of the Council's actions. They must have a role in shaping those decisions which affect them. The present composition of the Security Council, particularly the permanent members' category, is weighted heavily in favour of industrialized countries. This imbalance must be redressed in an expansion of the Council, by enhancing the representation of developing countries in both permanent and non-permanent members' categories. Activities of the Security Council have greatly expanded in the past few years. The success of Security Council's actions depends upon political support of the international community. Any package for restructuring of the Security Council should, therefore, be broad-based. In particular, adequate presence of developing countries is needed in the Security Council. Nations of the world must feel that their stakes in global peace and prosperity are factored into the UN's decision making.

Any expansion of permanent members' category must be based on an agreed criteria, rather than be a pre-determined selection. There must be an inclusive approach based on transparent consultations. India supports expansion of both permanent and non-permanent members' category. The latter is the only avenue for the vast majority of Member States to serve on the Security Council. Reform and expansion must be an integral part of a common package.

Charter Member: India and the United Nations

India is a charter member of the United Nations and participates in all of its specialized agencies. It has contributed troops to UN peacekeeping efforts in the Korea, Egypt and Congo in earlier years and in Somalia, Angola and Rwanda in recent years, and more recently Haiti. India has been a member of the UN Security Council six terms, most recently from 1991 to 1992.

Activities

UN General Assembly

India has traditionally played an active role in the United Nations General Assembly. In 1953, the chief delegate of India at the time, Vijaya Lakshmi Pandit was elected first woman President of the UN General Assembly.

As a founder member of the United Nations, India has been a firm supporter of the Purposes and Principles of the United Nations, and has made significant contributions to the furtherance and implementation of these noble aims, and to the evolution and functioning of its various specialized programmes. It stood at the forefront during the UN's tumultuous years of struggle against colonialism and apartheid, its struggle towards global disarmament and the ending of the arms race, and towards the creation of a more equitable international economic order.

At the very first session of the UN, India had raised its voice against colonialism and apartheid, two issues which have been among the most significant of the UN's successes in the last half century. India exulted in the UN's triumph, and saw in the UN's victory, a vindication of the policy relentlessly pursued by it from its initial days at the world forum. India has also played an active role in the deliberations of the United Nations on the creation of a more equitable international economic order. It has been an active member of the Group of 77, and later the core group of the G-15 nations. Other issues, such as environmentally sustainable development and the promotion and protection of human rights, have also been an important focus of India's foreign policy in international forums.

UN Security Council

India has been elected six times to the UN Security Council, and is the country that has served for the most number of years as an elected member. India is currently seeking a permanent seat on the United Nations Security Council. It is a member of the G4, an organization composed of Brazil, Germany, Japan, and India, all nations who are currently seeking permanent representation. According to their plan the UN Security Council would be expanded beyond the current fifteen members to include twenty-five members. This would be the first time that permanent status has been extended to a South Asian nation and supporters of the G4 plan suggest that this will lead to greater representation of developing nations rather than the current major powers.

India has the world's second largest population and is the world's largest liberal democracy. It is also the world's twelfth largest economy and fourth largest in terms of purchasing power parity. Currently, India maintains the world's third largest armed force. India is the third largest contributor of troops to United Nations Peacekeeping missions after Pakistan and Bangladesh.

Financial Contribution

India is one of the main contributors to the UN regular budget. Indian contribution to United Nations Democracy Fund was USD $15 million for the 2009..

Representation

India maintains a permanent mission to the UN, currently headed by Ambassador Nirupam Sen.

7

India and SAARC

SAARC South Asian Association for Regional Cooperation

The South Asian Association for Regional Cooperation (SAARC) was established when its Charter was formally adopted on 8 December 1985 by the Heads of State or Government of Bangladesh, Bhutan, India, Maldives, Nepal, Pakistan and SriLanka.

News Analysis

The Association provides a platform for the peoples of South Asia to work together in a spirit of friendship, trust and understanding. It aims to promote the welfare of the peoples of South Asia and to improve their quality of life through accelerated economic growth, social progress and cultural development in the region.

Cooperation in the SAARC is based on respect for the principles of sovereign equality, territorial integrity, political independence, noninterference in internal affairs of the Member States and mutual benefit. Regional cooperation is seen as a complement to the bilateral and multilateral relations of SAARC Member States. Decisions are taken on the basis of unanimity. Bilateral and contentious issues are excluded from the deliberations of SAARC. The SAARC Secretariat is based in Kathmandu. It coordinates and monitors implementation of activities, prepares for and services meetings, and serves as a channel of communication between the Association and its Member States as well as other regional organizations. The Secretariat is headed by the Secretary General, who is appointed by the Council of Ministers from Member Countries in alphabetical order for a three-year term. Mr. Q.A.M.A. Rahim from Bangladesh is the current Secretary General. The previous Secretaries General were from Bangladesh, India, Maldives, Nepal, Pakistan and Sri Lanka. The next Secretary General is to be from Bhutan.

The availability of real time maritime intelligence from South and South East Asian countries has been a key factor in the Sri Lankan navy's recent stunning successes against the intrepid and innovative naval wing of the LTTE. (Intelligence Key To Navy's Success: Source, *Hindustan Times*, Correspondent or Reporter, Oct 31, 2007) Pakistan said Monday that it would go ahead with the multi-billion Iran-Pakistan-India (IPI) gas pipeline project. (Pak Vows To Go Ahead With Iran Gas Pipeline F.P. Report, *Frontier Post*, Correspondent or Reporter, Oct 30, 2007)

Pakistan will join hands with India to combat extremism and work with other SAARC countries to develop a mechanism for exchanging information to curb terrorism and drug trafficking, interior minister Aftab Ahmed Khan Sherpao has said. (Indo-Pak Strategy Soon, *Tribune*, Correspondent or Reporter, Oct 29, 2007) There was solid basis for New Delhi's response to the blasts in Karachi. The two countries are in the process of evolving a mechanism for police cooperation against terrorism and it is in India's interest to make Benazir conform to the.... (India Should Not Be Cynical, *Pioneer*, Radha Kumar, Oct 27, 2007)

The SAARC members on Thursday decided to strengthen cooperation in combating terror and crime, with a meeting of home ministers, chaired by Union Home Minister Shivraj Patil, agreeing to a bi-annual meeting of police chiefs. (SAARC Members Vow To Combat Terror, *Indian Express*, Correspondent or Reporter, Oct 26, 2007)

Saarc countries on Thursday decided to have regular exchange of information to combat terrorism and to work towards establishing a convention for mutual legal assistance in criminal matters. (SAARC Nations Agree To Work Together To Combat Terror, *Times of India*, Correspondent or Reporter, Oct 26, 2007)

Viewing terrorism as a "serious threat" to South Asia's peace and development, SAARC countries today decided to have regular exchange of information to combat the menace and push efforts for establishing a convention for mutual legal assistance... (SAARC Vows To Combat Terror, *Hindu*, Correspondent or Reporter, Oct 26, 2007)

Home Ministers of SAARC countries on Thursday said terrorism remained a serious threat to peace and development in the region and called upon the member-states to strengthen institutional mechanisms to fight it effectively. (Terrorism A Serious Threat: SAARC, *Hindu*, Correspondent or Reporter, Oct 26, 2007)

Acknowledging that terrorism remains a serious threat to sustainable peace and development of South Asia, SAARC countries underlined the need to give an added push to evolving a treaty on mutual legal assistance with the home or interior ministers... (SAARC Nations For Evolving Treaty On Mutual Legal Aid, *Tribune*, A N Sudarsan Rao, Oct 26, 2007)

After the Karachi bloodbath on October 19 the global condemnation of the terrorists' act and commiseration for Pakistan and Ms Benazir Bhutto was on the expected lines. (Cooperate To End Terrorism, *Tribune*, Gen V.P. Malik (retd), Oct 26, 2007)

Home Secretaries of SAARC countries on Wednesday resolved to move forward in the matter of mutual assistance to check terrorism and trans-border crimes and expressed the need for better cooperation among police organisations of member-countries. (SAARC Ministers On Mutual Assistance To Check Terrorism, *Pioneer*, Correspondent or Reporter, Oct 25, 2007)

Agreeing to share information to check trans-border crimes, police chiefs from SAARC nations on Tuesday suggested a database that could help security agencies combat terrorism, narcotics smuggling and cyber crime. (SAARC Meet: New Database To Combat Terrorism, *Indian Express*, Correspondent or Reporter, Oct 24, 2007). Member countries of the South Asian Association for Regional Cooperation on Tuesday proposed the creation of a database among them for a coordinated action against terrorism, drug trafficking, cyber crimes and financial frauds. (S. Asian Terror Database Proposed, *Dawn*, Jawed Naqvi, Oct 24, 2007)

High-voltage talks are on this week to counter terrorism in the subcontinent, and it may just be coincidental that the move comes in the wake of explosions in Ajmer, Ludhiana and Karachi. (Edits, *Statesman*, Editorial, Statesman, Oct 24, 2007)

India and Pakistan today agreed to work together for identifying measures to beef up the anti-terror mechanism in the light of information shared earlier by the two on terrorist incidents and terror-related activities. (India, Pakistan Agree To Work On Anti-Terror Mechanism, *Statesman*, Correspondent or Reporter, Oct 23, 2007)

The second annual meeting of the SAARC home ministers will begin here tomorrow to hammer out a treaty on mutual legal assistance in criminal matters, forming a regional police forum and evolving a comprehensive mechanism for tackling terror...... (SAARC Home Ministers' Meeting Today, *Tribune*, Correspondent or Reporter, Oct 23, 2007)

India will host the second meeting of SAARC Interior/Home Ministers from Tuesday preceded by second meeting of SAARC Home Secretaries and the sixth SAARC Cooperation on Police Matters. (India To Host SAARC Ministerial Meet, *Pioneer*, Correspondent or Reporter, Oct 23, 2007)

The Pakistani link to the recent terror strikes in Hyderabad, Ajmer and Ludhiana came to the fore on Monday as India sought Pakistan's help in tracking down suspects who are believed to have cross-border links. (At Anti-Terror Meet, India Seeks Pak'S Help In Tracking Bombers, *Indian Express*, Correspondent or Reporter, Oct 23, 2007)

India and Pakistan will hold the second meeting of the Joint Anti-Terrorism Mechanism (JATM) here on Monday, during which Islamabad is expected to raise the issue of Samjhauta Express blast inquiry report. (Second Round Of Indo-Pak Jatm Talks On Monday, *The Economic Times*, Correspondent or Reporter, Oct 22, 2007)

With the British government more or less towing the American line on Iran albeit indirectly and the American pressure on India to clear its stand on the "errant" Iranian President, it looks like from SAARC (South Asian Association for Regional.... (India, Afghan And The Nam, Deccan Herald, Deepali Gaur Singh, Oct 10, 2007)

Climate Change: India to Sign Treaty with SAARC Nations

Marking a shift from its earlier position of staying within the United Nations Framework Convention on Climate Changes, India now appears ready to collaborate with various countries on climate change. On top of the list are the US, China and Japan. In a bid to present itself as a leader on climate change issues in the SAARC region, India is set to sign a treaty on environment with SAARC countries, the draft text of which is ready, *The Indian Express* has learnt. India has also discussed the possibility of a bilateral cooperation with Japan on thermal technology which cuts down on greenhouse gases.

Minister of Environment and Forests Jairam Ramesh met Japanese Environment Minister Sakihito Ozawa on Monday on the issue. SAARC Environment Ministers are at present in New Delhi. On Tuesday, the SAARC delegates are expected to release a joint environmental statement.

Ministry officials said the cooperation will chiefly be in the regions of forestry, biodiversity and wildlife and coastal management. Ramesh, speaking to *The Indian Express*, indicated that India needed to look beyond the Kyoto Protocol. "India has multiple messages to give on climate change, and India cannot be Doctor No," he said. "We are engaging with China, Japan and the US on climate change." This includes, he said, "being open to the discussion of a bilateral with Japan on climate change technologies." The focus is on reducing greenhouse gases through better coal-based thermal power technologies. "We are discussing with Japan coal-based power generation with less greenhouse gases. Japan is helping us with that."

In yet another shift, India seems set to be a donor in the issue of tackling climate change. It will give one-time grants for forestry and coastal management, Ramesh said. "We are looking at assuming a prominent role for climate change and environment in South Asia. The draft for a new environment agreement is also ready from India's side. The crux will be technology and financial transfer. Climate change is becoming a very important issue for SAARC, the theme of the April 2010 SAARC meet at Thimpu will be climate change. We are making one time grants of one million dollars to the SAARC forestry Centre, Thimpu, and one million dollars to SAARC Coastal Management Zone, Maldives.," he said. On a bilateral agreement with the US, Ramesh said: "We are open to it. The PM will discuss this with US President Barack Obama next month. The discussions are likely to be on energy security."

Bangladesh–India Relations

Both Bangladesh and India are part of what is known as the Indian subcontinent and have had a long common cultural, economic and political history. The cultures of the two countries are similar; in particular Bangladesh and India's states West Bengal and Tripura are all Bengali-speaking. However, since the partition of the Indian subcontinent in 1947, India emerged as an independent state and Bangladesh (as East Bengal, later rename to East Pakistan in 1956) was allocated as a part of Pakistan. Following the bloody Liberation War of 1971, Bangladesh gained its independence and established relations with India. The political relationship between India and Bangladesh has passed through cycles of hiccups. The relationship typically becomes favourable for Bangladesh during periods of Awami League government.

Historical Background

During the Partition of India after independence in 1947, the Bengal region was divided into two: East Bengal (present-day Bangladesh) and West Bengal. East Bengal was made a part of the Islamic Republic of Pakistan due to the fact that both regions had an overwhelmingly large Muslim population, more than 86%. In 1955, the government of Pakistan changed its name from East Bengal to East Pakistan.

There were some confrontations between the two regions though. Firstly, in 1948, Muhammad Ali Jinnah declared that only Urdu would the sole official language of the entire nation, though more than 95% of the East Bengali population spoke Bengali. And when protests broke out in Bangladesh on February 21, 1952, Pakistani police fired on the protesters, killing hundreds. Secondly, East Bengal/East Pakistan was allotted only a small amount of revenue for its development out of the Pakistani national budget. Therefore, a separatist movement started to grow in the isolated province. When the main separatist party the Awami League, headed by Sheikh Mujibur Rahman, won 167 of 169 seats up for grabs in the 1970 elections and got the right to form the government, the Pakistan president under Yahya Khan refused to recognize the election results and arrested Sheikh Mujibur Rahman. This led to widespread protests in East Pakistan and in 1971, the Liberation War, followed by the declaration (by Sheikh Mujibur Rahman on 7 March 1971) of the independent state of Bangladesh.

India under Indira Gandhi fully supported the cause of the Bangladeshis and its troops and equipment were used to fight the Pakistani forces. The Indian Army also gave full support to the main Bangladeshi guerrilla force, the Mukti Bahini. Finally, on 26 March 1971, Bangladesh emerged as an independent state. Since then, there have been several issues of agreement as well as of dispute.

Areas of Agreement

1. India played a central role in the independence of Bangladesh. About 250,000 Indian soldiers fought for, and 20,000 losing their lives for the cause of an independent Bangladesh. India sheltered over 10 million refugees who were fleeing the atrocities of the occupying West Pakistan Army. India and its ally Bhutan were the first countries to recognize Bangladesh as an independent nation. Bangladeshis have some awareness of their obligation and gratitude towards India.
2. Sheikh Mujibur Rahman's first foreign visit as Prime Minister and the Founding Father of the newly born nation was to India and it was then decided Indo-Bangladesh relations would be guided by principles of democracy, socialism, nonalignment and opposition to colonialism and racism. Indira Gandhi too visited Bangladesh in 1972 and assured that India would never interfere in the internal affairs of the country.
3. In 1972, both the countries signed a 'Treaty of Friendship and Peace'. An Indo-Bangladesh Trade Pact was also signed.
4. The mainstream party Awami League is generally considered to be friendly towards India.

Areas of Contention

1. A major area of contention has been the construction and operation of the Farakka Barrage by India to increase water supply in the river Hoogly. Bangladesh insists that it does not receive a fair share of the Ganga waters during the drier seasons, and gets flooded during the monsoons when India releases excess waters.
2. There have also been disputes regarding the transfer of Teen Bigha Corridor to Bangladesh. Part of Bangladesh is surrounded by the Indian state of West Bengal. On 26 June 1992, India leased three bigha land to Bangladesh to connect this enclave with mainland Bangladesh. There is dispute regarding the indefinite nature of the lease.
3. Terrorist activities carried out by outfits based in both countries, like Banga Sena and Harkat-ul-Jihad-al-Islami. Recently India and Bangladesh had agreed to jointly fight terrorism.
4. The Sharing of Ganges Waters was also a matter of dispute.

Bhutan–India Relations

The bilateral relations between the Himalayan Kingdom of Bhutan and the Republic of India have been traditionally close. With independence in 1947, India inherited the suzerainty over Bhutan enjoyed by the British Raj. Although modified and modernised since, India remains influential over Bhutan's foreign policy, defence and commerce.

Background

For much of its history, Bhutan has preserved its isolation from the outside world, staying out of international organisations and maintaining few bilateral relations. Bhutan became a protectorate of British India after signing a treaty in 1910 allowing the British to "guide" its foreign affairs and defence. Bhutan was one of the first to recognize India's independence in 1947 and both nations fostered close relations, their importance augmented by the annexation of Tibet in 1950 by the People's Republic of China and its border disputes with both Bhutan and India, which saw close ties with Nepal and Bhutan to be central to its "Himalayan frontier" security policy. India shares a 605 kilometres (376 miles) border with Bhutan and is its largest trading partner, accounting for 98 percent of its exports and 90 percent of its imports.

1949 Treaty

On August 8, 1949 Bhutan and India signed the Treaty of Friendship, calling for peace between the two nations and non-interference in each other's internal affairs. However, Bhutan agreed to let India "guide" its foreign policy and both nations would consult each other closely on foreign and defence affairs. The treaty also established free trade and extradition protocols.

The occupation of Tibet by Communist China brought both nations even closer. In 1958, the then-Indian Prime Minister Jawaharlal Nehru visited Bhutan and reiterated India's support for Bhutan's independence and later declared in the Indian Parliament that any aggression against Bhutan would be seen as aggression against India.

The period saw a major increase in India's economic, military and development aid to Bhutan, which had also embarked on a programme of modernisation to bolster its security. While India repeatedly reiterated its military support to Bhutan, the latter expressed concerns about India's ability to protect Bhutan against China while fighting a two-front war involving Pakistan.

Despite good relations, India and Bhutan did not complete a detailed demarcation of their borders until the period between 1973 and 1984. Border demarcation talks with India generally resolved disagreements except for several small sectors, including the middle zone between Sarpang and Geylegphug and the eastern frontier with the Indian state of Arunachal Pradesh.

Distancing from India

Although relations remained close and friendly, the Bhutanese government expressed a need to renegotiate parts of the treaty to enhance Bhutan's sovereignty. Bhutan began to slowly assert an independent attitude in foreign affairs by joining the United

Nations in 1971, recognising Bangladesh and signing a new trade agreement in 1972 that provided an exemption from export duties for goods from Bhutan to third countries. Bhutan exerted its independent stance at the Non-Aligned Movement (NAM) summit conference in Havana, Cuba also in 1979, by voting with China and some Southeast Asian countries rather than with India on the issue of allowing Cambodia's Khmer Rouge to be seated at the conference. Unlike in Nepal, where its 1950 treaty with India has been the subject of great political controversy and nationalist resentment for decades, the nature of Bhutan's relationship with India has not been affected by concerns over the treaty provisions. From 2003 to 2004, the Royal Bhutanese Army conducted operations against anti-India insurgents of the United Liberation Front of Assam (ULFA) that were operating bases in Bhutan and using its territory to carry out attacks on Indian soil.

2007 Treaty

India renegotiated the 1949 treaty with Bhutan and signed a new treaty of friendship in 2007. The new treaty replaced the provision requiring Bhutan to take India's guidance on foreign policy with broader sovereignty and not require Bhutan to obtain India's permission over arms imports. In 2008, Indian Prime Minister Dr. Manmohan Singh visited Bhutan and expressed strong support for Bhutan's move towards democracy. India allows 16 entry and exit points for Bhutanese trade with other countries (the only exception being the PRC) and has agreed to import a minimum of 5,000 megawatts of electricity from Bhutan by 2020.

India–Maldives Relations

Bilateral relations between the Republic of India and the Republic of Maldives have been friendly and close in strategic, economic and military cooperation. India contributed to maintaining security on the island nation and has forged an alliance with respect to its strategic interests in the Indian Ocean.

Background

The Maldives is located south of India's Lakshadweep Islands in the Indian Ocean and approximately 700 kilometres from Sri

Lanka. Both nations established diplomatic relations after the independence of Maldives from British rule in 1966. Since then, India and Maldives have developed close strategic, military, economic and cultural relations. India has supported Maldives' policy of keeping regional issues and struggles away from itself, and the latter has seen friendship with India as a source of aid as well as a counter-balance to Sri Lanka, which is in proximity to the island nation and its largest trading partner.

Development of Bilateral Relations

India and Maldives officially and amicably decided their maritime boundary in 1976, although a minor diplomatic incident occurred in 1982 when the brother of the President of Maldives Maumoon Abdul Gayoom declared that the neighbouring Minicoy Island that belonged to India were a part of Maldives; Maldivies quickly and officially denied that it was laying claim to the island. India and Maldives signed a comprehensive trade agreement in 1981. Both nations are founding members of the South Asian Association for Regional Cooperation (SAARC), the South Asian Economic Union and signatories to the South Asia Free Trade Agreement. Indian and Maldivian leaders have maintained high-level contacts and consultations on regional issues.

Operation Cactus

In November 1988 speedboats carrying 80 armed militants of the People's Liberation Organisation of Tamil Eelam landed in Maldives and along with allies who had infiltrated the country, began taking over the government. The plot, planned in Sri Lanka by the Tamil nationalist group was believed to be an attempt by a Maldivian businessman and politician opposed to the regime of the President of Maldives Maumoon Abdul Gayoom to gain control while the PLOTE sought a safe haven and base for its activities.

The militants took control of the airport in Male, the national capital, but failed to capture the President of Maldives Maumoon Abdul Gayoom, who had fled and asked for military aid from India on November 3. The then-Indian Prime Minister Rajiv Gandhi ordered 1,600 troops to aid the Maldivian government. In a military operation codenamed "Operation Cactus," Indian forces arrived within 12 hours of the request for aid being made, squashed the coup attempt and achieved full control of the country within hours. 19 PLOTE militants were killed and 1 Indian soldier wounded.

India's intervention was endorsed by other nations such as the United States, Soviet Union, Great Britain and its neighbours Nepal and Bangladesh. Its speedy and decisive victory and the restoration of the Maldivian government brought both nations even closer in friendship and cooperation. In wake of internal security crises and tensions with Sri Lanka, Maldives saw its relationship with India as a source of future security.

Commercial Relations

Since the success of Operation Cactus, the relations between India and Maldives have expanded significantly. India has provided extensive economic aid and has participated in bilateral programs for the development of infrastructure, health, civil aviation, telecommunications and labour resources.

It established the Indira Gandhi Memorial Hospital in Male, the capital of Maldives, expanded telecommunications and air links and increased scholarships for Maldivian students. While India's exports to Maldives during 2006 were worth Rs. 384 crores, imports were worth less than Rs. 6 crores. The State Bank of India has contributed more than USD 500 million to aid the economic expansion of Maldives. India and Maldives have announced plans to jointly work to expand fisheries and tuna processing.

Military Relations

On 7 March 2005 Defence Attaché's Office (DAO) was established in the High commission of the Republic of Maldives in India by making Lt.Colonel Abdulla Shamaal as first defence attaché. This was the first Defence Attaché's office set up abroad. Given, that defence relations is a major component of the Indo-Maldives bilateral relations and both counties have a long record of strengthening their defence ties through a wide range of activities, such as Military Joint Exercises, exchange of visits of senior officers of the Armed forces, training of large number of defence services personnel from the Maldives at Indian defence establishments, provision of military aid, and intelligence and information sharing, the necessity for a DAO was felt. Hence, the DAO was instituted to further strengthen and consolidate the already existing bilateral defence relations in a mutually beneficial manner. As a result, the DAO functions as the primary mechanism integrated in the resident Mission of the Republic of Maldives in New Delhi, India to guide direct and coordinate defence ties between the two countries.

On April 2006 Indian Navy gifted a Trinkat Class Fast Attack Craft of 46m length to Maldives National Defence Force's Coast Guard

India start the process to bring the island country into India's security grid. The move comes after the moderate Islamic nation approached New Delhi earlier this year over fears that one of its island resorts could be taken over by terrorists given its lack of military assets and surveillance capabilities. India is also signing an agreement later this year which includes following things.

- India will permanently base two helicopters in the country to enhance its surveillance capabilities and ability to respond swiftly to threats. One helicopter from the Coast Guard is likely to be handed over during Antony's visit while another from the Navy will be cleared for transfer shortly.
- Maldives has coastal radars on only two of its 26 atolls. India will help set up radars on all 26 for seamless coverage of approaching vessels and aircraft.
- The coastal radar chain in Maldives will be networked with the Indian coastal radar system. India has already undertaken a project to install radars along its entire coastline. The radar chains of the two countries will be interlinked and a central control room in India's Coastal Command will get a seamless radar picture.
- The Indian Coast Guard (ICG) will carry out regular Dornier sorties over the island nation to look out for suspicious movements or vessels. The Southern Naval

Command will overlook the inclusion of Maldives into the Indian security grid.

- Military teams from Maldives will visit the tri-services Andaman Nicobar Command (ANC) to observe how India manages security and surveillance of the critical island chain.

Indo-Nepalese Relations

Relations between India and Nepal are close yet fraught with difficulties stemming from geography, economics, the problems inherent in big power-small power relations, and common ethnic, linguistic and cultural identities that overlap the two countries' borders. New Delhi and Kathmandu initiated their intertwined relationship with the 1950 Indo-Nepal Treaty of Peace and Friendshipý and accompanying letters that defined security relations between the two countries, and an agreement governing both bilateral trade and trade transiting Indian soil. The 1950 treaty and letters stated that "neither government shall tolerate any threat to the security of the other by a foreign aggressor" and obligated both sides "to inform each other of any serious friction or misunderstanding with any neighboring state likely to cause any breach in the friendly relations subsisting between the two governments." These accords cemented a "special relationship" between India and Nepal that granted Nepal preferential economic treatment and provided Nepalese in India the same economic and educational opportunities as Indian citizens.

Independent Political History

1950-1970

In the 1950s, Nepal welcomed close relations with India, but as the number of Nepalese living and working in India increased and the involvement of India in Nepal's economy deepened in the 1960s and after, so too did Nepalese discomfort with the special relationship. Tensions came to a head in the mid-1970s, when Nepal pressed for substantial amendments in its favour in the trade and transit treaty and openly criticized India's 1975 annexation of Sikkim which was considered as part of Greater

Nepal. In 1975 King Birendra Bir Bikram Shah Dev proposed that Nepal be recognized internationally as a zone of peace; he received support from China and Pakistan. In New Delhi's view, if the king's proposal did not contradict the 1950 treaty and was merely an extension of nonalignment, it was unnecessary; if it was a repudiation of the special relationship, it represented a possible threat to India's security and could not be endorsed. In 1984 Nepal repeated the proposal, but there was no reaction from India. Nepal continually promoted the proposal in international forums, with Chinese support; by 1990 it had won the support of 112 countries.

1970-1980

In 1978 India agreed to separate trade and transit treaties, satisfying a long-term Nepalese demand. In 1988, when the two treaties were up for renewal, Nepal's refusal to accommodate India's wishes on the transit treaty caused India to call for a single trade and transit treaty. Thereafter, Nepal took a hard-line position that led to a serious crisis in India-Nepal relations. After two extensions, the two treaties expired on March 23, 1989, resulting in a virtual Indian economic blockade of Nepal that lasted until late April 1990. Although economic issues were a major factor in the two countries' confrontation, Indian dissatisfaction with Nepal's 1988 acquisition of Chinese weaponry played an important role. treaty and letters exchanged in 1959 and 1965, which included Nepal in India's security zone and precluded arms purchases without India's approval. India linked security with economic relations and insisted on reviewing India-Nepal relations as a whole. Nepal had to back down after worsening economic conditions led to a change in Nepal's political system, in which the king was forced to institute a parliamentary democracy. The new government sought quick restoration of amicable relations with India.

1990s

The special security relationship between New Delhi and Kathmandu was reestablished during the June 1990 New Delhi meeting of Nepal's prime minister Krishna Prasad Bhattarai and

Indian prime minister V.P. Singh. During the December 1991 visit to India by Nepalese prime minister Girija Prasad Koirala, the two countries signed new, separate trade and transit treaties and other economic agreements designed to accord Nepal additional economic benefits.

Indian-Nepali relations appeared to be undergoing still more reassessment when Nepal's prime minister Man Mohan Adhikary visited New Delhi in April 1995 and insisted on a major review of the 1950 peace and friendship treaty. In the face of benign statements by his Indian hosts relating to the treaty, Adhikary sought greater economic independence for his landlocked nation while simultaneously striving to improve ties with China.

21st Century

In 2005, after King Gyanendra took over, Nepalese relations with India soured. However, after the restoration of democracy, in 2008, Prachanda, the Prime Minister of Nepal, visited India, in September 2008. He spoke about a new dawn, in the bilateral relations, between the two countries. He said, "I am going back to Nepal as a satisfied person. I will tell Nepali citizens back home that a new era has dawned. Time has come to effect a revolutionary change in bilateral relations. On behalf of the new government, I assure you that we are committed to make a fresh start." He met Indian Prime minister, Manmohan Singh, and Foreign Minister, Pranab Mukherjee. He asked India to help Nepal frame a new constitution, and to invest in Nepal's infrastructure, and its tourism industry.

In 2008, Indo-Nepali ties got a further boost with an agreement to resume water talks after a 4 year hiatus. The Nepalese Water Resources Secretary Shanker Prasad Koirala said the Nepal-India Joint Committee on Water Resources meet decided to start the reconstruction of breached Kosi embankment after the water level goes down. During the Nepal PM's visit to New Delhi in September the two Prime Ministers expressed satisfaction at the age-old close, cordial and extensive relationships between their states and expressed their support and cooperation to further consolidate the relationship. The two issued a 22-point statement highlighting the need to review, adjust and update the 1950 Treaty of Peace and Friendship, amongst other agreements. India would also provide a credit line of up to 150 crore rupees to Nepal to ensure uninterrupted supplies of petroleum products, as well as lift bans on the export of rice, wheat, maize, sugar and sucrose for quantities agreed to with Nepal. India would also provide 20 crore as immediate flood relief.

In return, Nepal will take measures for the "promotion of investor friendly, enabling business environment to encourage Indian...investments in Nepal."

Furthermore, a three-tier mechanism at the level of ministerial, secretary and technical levels will be built to push forward discussions on the development of water resources between the two sides. Politically, India acknowledged a willingness to promote efforts towards peace in Nepal. Indian External affairs minister Pranab Mukherjee promised the Nepali Prime Minister Prachanda that he would "extend all possible help for peace and development."

In 2008, the Bollywood film *Chandni Chowk to China* was banned in Nepal, because of a scene suggesting the Gautama Buddha was born in India. Some protesters called for commercial boycott of all Indian films.

Indo-Pakistani Relations

Indo-Pakistani relations are grounded in the political, geographic, cultural, and economic links between the Republic of India and the Islamic Republic of Pakistan the two largest countries of South Asia. The two countries share much of their common geographic location, and religious demographics (most notably Hinduism, Islam, Sikhism, Buddhism); yet diplomatic relations between the two are defined by numerous military conflicts and territorial disputes. However, attempts to warm relations have been made.

Much of South Asia came under direct control of Great Britain in the late 18th century. The British Raj over the Indian subcontinent lasted for almost 150 years. 95% of the people living in South Asia practised either Hinduism and Islam. The Muslim League, headed by Quaid e Azam Mohammad Ali Jinnah, proposed the Two Nation Theory in the early 20th century. According to the theory, Muslims and others shared little in common, and British India should be divided into two separate countries, one for the Muslims and the other for the Hindu majority, which he feared would suppress the Muslim minority. The campaign gained momentum in early 1940s and by the end of World War II, British India's partition looked inevitable. The Partition of India in 1947 created two large countries independent from Britain: Pakistan as two wings in the East and West, separated by India in the middle. Soon after Independence, India and Pakistan established diplomatic relations. Subsequent years were marked by bitter periodic conflict, and the nations went to war four times. The war in 1971 ended in defeat and another partition of Pakistan. The eastern wing split off as a new country named Bangladesh, while the western wing continued as Pakistan.

There have been some improvements in relations since the mid-2000s. Most notably, Pakistan released an Indian man accused of being a spy in 2008: he had been detained since 1975. But relations soured slightly after the 2008 Mumbai Terrorist Attacks by an alleged group partially consisting of Pakistani based militants.

Seeds of Conflict

Millions of Muslims and Hindus were killed in communal riots following the partition of the British Empire. Millions of Muslims living in India and Hindus and Sikhs living in Pakistan emigrated in one of the most colossal transfers of population in the modern age. Both countries accused each other of not providing adequate security to the minorities emigrating through their territory. This served to increase tensions between the newly-born countries.

According to the British plan for the partition of British India, all the 680 princely states were allowed to decide which of the two countries to join. With the exception of a few, most of the Muslim-majority princely-states acceded to Pakistan while most of the Hindu-majority princely states joined India. However, the decisions of some of the princely-states would shape the Pakistan-India relationship considerably, in the years to come.

Junagadh Dispute

Junagadh was a state on the southwestern end of Gujarat, with the principalities of Manavadar, Mangrol and Babriawad. The Arabian Sea stood between it and Pakistan. The state had an overwhelming Hindu population which constituted more than 80% of its citizens, while the ruler of the state was a Muslim. On August 15 1947, the ruler of the state, Nawab of Junagadh Mahabat Khan acceded to Pakistan. Pakistan confirmed the acceptance of the accession in September 1947. India did not accept the accession as legitimate.

The Indian point of view was that since Junagadh was a state with a predominantly Hindu population it should be a part of India. Additionally, since the state was encircled by Indian territory it should have been a part of India. Indian politicians also stated that by giving Pakistan a predominantly Hindu region to govern, the basis of the two nation theory was contradicted.

The Pakistani point of view was that since Junagadh had a ruler and governing body who chose to accede to Pakistan, they should be allowed to do so. Junagadh, having a coastline, could have maintained maritime links with Pakistan. Additionally, Pakistani politicians stated that the two nation theory did not necessarily mean a clear division of land and absolute transfer of populations as the sheer magnitude of such a proceeding would wreak havoc upon millions.

Neither of the ten states were able to resolve this issue amicably and it only added fuel to an already charged environment.

Sardar Patel, India's then Home Minister, felt that if Junagadh was permitted to go to Pakistan, it would create communal unrest across Gujarat. The government of India gave Pakistan time to void the accession and hold a plebiscite in Junagadh to pre empt any violence in Gujarat. Samaldas Gandhi formed a government-in-exile, the *Arzi Hukumat* of the people of Junagadh. Patel ordered the annexation of Junagadh's three principalities.

Kashmir Dispute

Kashmir was a princely state, ruled by a Hindu, Hari Singh. The Maharaja of Kashmir was equally hesitant to join either India–

, because he knew his Muslim subjects would not like to join a Hindu-based and Hindu-majority nation–, or Pakistan– which as a Hindu he was personally averse to. Pakistan coveted the Himalayan kingdom, while Indian leader Mahatma Gandhi and Indian PM Jawaharlal Nehru hoped that the kingdom would join India. Hari Singh signed a *Standstill Agreement* (preserving status quo) with Pakistan, but did not make his decision by August 15, 1947.

Rumours spread in Pakistan that Hari Singh was trying to accede Kashmir to India. Alarmed by this threat, a team of Pakistani forces were dispatched into Kashmir, fearing an Indian invasion of the region. Backed by Pakistani paramilitary forces,Pashtuns invaded Kashmir in September 1947. Kashmir's security forces were too weak and ill-equipped to fight against Pakistan. Troubled by the deteriorating political pressure that was being applied to Hari Singh and his governance, the Maharaja asked for India's help. However, the Constitution of India barred the Indian Armed Forces' intervention since Kashmir did not come under India's jurisdiction. Desperate to get India's help and get Kashmir back in his own control, the Maharaja acceded Kashmir to India (which was against the will of the majority of Kashmiris), and signed the Instrument of Accession. By this time the raiders were close to the capital, Srinagar. On October 27, 1947, the Indian Air Force airlifted Indian troops into Srinagar and made an intervention. The Indian troops managed to seize parts of Kashmir which included Jammu, Srinagar and the Kashmir valley itself, but the strong and intense fighting, flagged with the onset of winter, made much of the state impassable. After weeks of intense fighting between Pakistan and India, Pakistani leaders and the Indian Prime Minister Nehru declared a ceasefire and sought U.N. arbitration with the promise of a plebiscite. Sardar Patel had argued against both, describing Kashmir as a bilateral dispute and its accession as justified by international law. In 1957, north-western Kashmir was fully integrated into Pakistan, becoming Azad Kashmir (Pakistan-administered Kashmir), while the other portion was acceded to Indian control, and the state of Jammu and Kashmir (Indian-administered Kashmir) was created. In 1962, China occupied Aksai Chin, the northeastern region bordering Ladakh. In 1984, India launched Operation Meghdoot and captured more than 80% of the Siachen Glacier.

Pakistan maintains Kashmiris' rights to self-determination through a plebiscite in accordance with an earlier Indian statement and a UN resolution. Pakistan also points to India's failure of not understanding its own political logic and applying it to Kashmir, by taking their opinion on the case of the accession of Junagadh as an example (that the Hindu majority state should have gone to India even though it had a Muslim ruler), that Kashmir should also rightfully and legally have become a part of Pakistan since majoirity of the people were Muslim, even though they had a Hindu ruler. Pakistan also states that at the very least, the promised plebiscite should be allowed to deçide the fate of the Kashmiri people.

India on the other hand asserts that the Maharaja's decision, which was the norm for every other princely state at the time of independence, and subsequent elections, for over 40 years, on Kashmir has made it an integral part of India. This opinion has often become controversial, as Pakistan asserts that the decision of the ruler of Junagadh also adhered to Pakistan. Due to all such political differences, this dispute has also been the subject of wars between the two countries in 1947 and 1965, and a limited conflict in 1999. The state/province remains divided between the two countries by the Line of Control (LoC), which demarcates the ceasefire line agreed upon in the 1947 conflict.

Other Territorial Disputes

Pakistan is locked in other territorial disputes with India such as the Siachen Glacier and Kori Creek. Pakistan is also currently having dialogue with India regarding the Baglihar Dam being built over the River Chenab in Jammu and Kashmir.

Bengal Refugee Crisis

In 1949, India recorded close to 1 million Hindu refugees, who flooded into West Bengal and other states from East Pakistan (Now Bangladesh), owing to communal violence, intimidation and repression from authorities. The plight of the refugees outraged Hindus and Indian nationalists, and the refugee population drained the resources of Indian states, which were unable to absorb them. While not ruling out war, Prime Minister Nehru and Sardar Patel invited Liaquat Ali Khan for talks in Delhi. Although many Indians termed this appeasement, Nehru signed a pact with Liaquat Ali Khan that pledged both nations to the protection of minorities and creation of minority commissions.

Although opposed to the principle, Patel decided to back this Pact for the sake of peace, and played a critical role in garnering support from West Bengal and across India, and enforcing the provisions of the Pact. Khan and Nehru also signed a trade agreement, and committed to resolving bilateral disputes through peaceful means. Steadily, hundreds of thousands of Hindus returned to East Pakistan, but the thaw in relations did not last long, primarily owing to the Kashmir dispute.

Bangladesh Liberation War (1971)

Pakistan, since independence, was geo-politically divided into two major regions, West Pakistan and East Pakistan. East Pakistan was occupied mostly by Bengali people. In December 1971, following a political crisis in East Pakistan, the situation soon spiralled out of control in East Pakistan and India intervened in favour of the rebelling Bengali populace. The conflict, a brief but bloody war, resulted in an independence of East Pakistan. In the war, the Pakistani army swiftly fell to India, forcing the independence of East Pakistan, which separated and became Bangladesh. The Pakistani military, being a thousand miles from its base and surrounded by enemies, was forced to give in.

Shimla Agreement

Since the 1971 war, Pakistan and India have made only slow progress towards the normalisation of relations. In July 1972, Indian Prime Minister Indira Gandhi and Pakistani President Zulfikar Ali Bhutto met in the Indian hill station of Shimla. They signed the Shimla Agreement, by which India would return all Pakistani personnel (over 90,000) and captured territory in the west, and the two countries would "settle their differences by peaceful means through bilateral negotiations." Diplomatic and trade relations were also re-established in 1976.

Afghanistan Crisis

After the 1979 Soviet war in Afghanistan, new strains appeared in Indo-Pakistani relations. Pakistan actively supported the Afghan resistance against the Soviet Union, which was a close ally of India, which brought opposing political opinions. The Taliban regime in Afghanistan was strongly supported by Pakistan-one of the few countries to do so-before the September 11 attacks. India, on the other hand, firmly opposed the Taliban and criticised Pakistan for supporting it.

Agreements, Talks and Confidence Building Measures

In the following eight years, India voiced increasing concern over Pakistani arms purchases, U.S. military aid to Pakistan, and a clandestine Pakistan's nuclear weapons programme. In an effort to curtail tensions, the two countries formed a joint commission to examine disputes. In December 1988, Prime Ministers Benazir Bhutto and Rajiv Gandhi concluded a pact not to attack each other's nuclear facilities. Agreements on cultural exchanges and civil aviation were also initiated.

In 1997, high-level Indo-Pakistan talks resumed after a three-year pause. The Prime Ministers of Pakistan and India met twice and the foreign secretaries conducted three rounds of talks. In June 1997, the foreign secretaries identified eight "outstanding issues" around which continuing talks would be focused. The dispute over the status of Kashmir, an issue since Independence, remains the major stumbling block in their dialogue. India maintains that the entire former princely state is an integral part of the Indian union, while Pakistan insists that UN resolutions calling for self-determination of the people of the state/province must be taken into account. It however refuses to abide by the previous part of the resolution, which calls for it to vacate all territories occupied.

In September 1997, the talks broke down over the structure of how to deal with the issues of Kashmir, and peace and security. Pakistan advocated that the issues be treated by separate working groups. India responded that the two issues be taken up along with six others on a simultaneous basis. In May 1998 India, and then Pakistan, conducted nuclear tests. After Manmohan Singh become prime minister of India the Punjab provincial Government declared it would develop Gah, his place of birth, as a model village in his honour and name a school after him. There is also a village in India named Pakistan, despite occasional pressure over the years to change its name the villagers have resisted.

Earthquake of Pakistan (2005)

India offered generous aid to Pakistan in response to the 2005 Earthquake. Indian and Pakistani High Commissioners consulted with one another regarding cooperation in relief work. India sent 25 tonnes of relief material to Pakistan including food, blankets and medicine. Large Indian companies such as Infosys have offered aid up to $226,000. On October 12, an Ilyushin-76 cargo plane ferried across seven truckloads (about 82 tons) of army medicines, 15,000 blankets and 50 tents and returned to New Delhi. A senior airforce official also stated that they had been asked by the Indian government to be ready to fly out another similar consignment. On October 14, India dispatched the second consignment to relief material to Pakistan, by train through the Wagah Border. The consignment included 5,000 blankets, 370 tents, 5 tons of plastic sheets and 12 tons of medicine.

A third consignment of medicine and relief material was also sent shortly afterwards by train.. India also pledged $25 million as aid to Pakistan. India opened the first of three points at Chakan Da Bagh, in Poonch, on the Line of Control (LoC) between India and Pakistan for the 2005 Kashmir earthquake relief work. Such generous gestures signalled a new age in confidence, friendliness and cooperation between both India and Pakistan.

Samjhauta Express Bombings (2007)

The 2007 Samjhauta Express bombings was a terrorist attack targeted on the Samjhauta Express train on the 18th of February.

Mumbai Attacks (2008)

The 2008 Mumbai attacks by ten terrorists killed over 173 and wounded 308. India blamed the Lashkar-e-Taiba, a Pakistan-based militant group, for planning and executing the attacks. Islamabad resisted the claims and demanded evidence. India provided evidence in the form of interrogations, weapons, candy wrappers, Pakistani Brand Milk Packets, and telephone sets. Indian officials demanded Pakistan extradite suspects for trial. They also said that, given the sophistication of the attacks, the perpetrators "must have had the support of some official agencies in Pakistan".

Terrorism in Kashmir

Terrorism in Jammu and Kashmir

Terrorist attacks on Jammu & Kashmir State Assembly: A car bomb exploded near the Jammu and Kashmir State Assembly on October 1, 2001, killing 27 people on an attack that was blamed on Kashmiri separatists. It was one of the most prominent attacks against India apart from on the Indian Parliament in December 2001. The dead bodies of the terrorists and the data recovered from them revealed that Pakistan was solely responsible for the activity.

- 1997 Sangrampora massacre: On March 21, 1997, 7 Kashmiri Pandits were killed in Sangrampora village in the Budgam district.
- Wandhama Massacre: In January 1998, 24 Kashmiri Pandits living in the city Wandhama were killed by Islamic terrorists.
- Qasim Nagar Attack: On July 13, 2003, armed men believed to be a part of the Lashkar-e-Toiba threw hand grenades at the Qasim Nagar market in Srinagar and then fired on civilians standing nearby killing twenty-seven and injuring many more.
- Assassination of Abdul Ghani Lone: Abdul Ghani Lone, a prominent All Party Hurriyat Conference leader, was assassinated by an unidentified gunmen during a memorial rally in Srinagar. The assassination resulted in wide-scale demonstrations against the Indian occupied-forces for failing to provide enough security cover for Mr. Lone.
- July 20, 2005 Srinagar Bombing: A car bomb exploded near an armoured Indian Army vehicle in the famous

Church Lane area in Srinagar killing four Indian Army personnel, one civilian and the suicide bomber. Terrorist group Hizbul Mujahideen, claimed responsibility for the attack.

- Budshah Chowk attack: A terrorist attack on July 29, 2005 at Srinigar's city centre, Budshah Chowk, killed two and left more than 17 people injured. Most of those injured were media journalists.
- Murder of Ghulam Nabi Lone: On October 18, 2005 suspected Army man killed Jammu and Kashmir's then education minister Ghulam Nabi Lone. No Terrorist group claimed responsibility for the attack.

Terrorist Activities Elsewhere

The attack on the Indian Parliament was by far the most dramatic attack carried out by Pakistani terrorists. India blamed Pakistan for carrying out the attacks, an allegation which Pakistan strongly denied and one that brought both nations to the brink of a nuclear confrontation in 2001-02. However, international peace efforts ensured the cooling of tensions between the two nuclear-capable nations.

Apart from this, the most notable was the hijacking of Indian Airlines Flight IC 814 en route New Delhi from Kathmandu, Nepal. The plane was hijacked on December 24, 1999 approximately one hour after take off and was taken to Amritsar airport and then to Lahore in Pakistan. After refueling the plane took off for Dubai and then finally landed in Kandahar, Afghanistan. Under intense media pressure, New Delhi complied with the hijackers' demand and freed Maulana Masood Azhar from its captivity in return for the freedom of the Indian passengers on the flight. The decision, however, cost New Delhi dearly. Maulana, who is believed to be hiding in Karachi, later became the leader of Jaish-e-Mohammed, an organisation which has carried out several terrorist acts against Indian Security Forces in Kashmir.

On December 22, 2000, a group of terrorists belonging to the Lashkar-e-Toiba stormed the famous Red Fort in New Delhi. The Fort houses an Indian military unit and a high-security interrogation cell used both by the Central Bureau of Investigation and the Indian Army. The terrorists successfully breached the security cover around the Red Fort and opened fire at the Indian military personnel on duty killing two of them on spot. The attack was significant because it was carried out just two days after the declaration of the ceasefire between India and Pakistan.

Two Kashmiri terrorists belonging to Jaish-e-Mohammed raided the Swami Narayan temple complex in Ahmedabad, Gujarat killing 30 people, including 18 women and five children. The attack was carried out on September 25, 2002, just few days after state elections were held in Jammu and Kashmir. Two identical letters found on both the terrorists claimed that the attack was done in retaliation for the deaths of thousands of Muslims during the Gujarat riots. Two car bombs exploded in south Mumbai on August 25, 2003; one near the Gateway of India and the other at the famous Zaveri Bazaar, killing at least 48 and injuring 150 people. Though no terrorist group claimed responsibility for the attacks, Mumbai Police and RAW suspected Lashkar-e-Toiba's hand in the twin blasts. In an unsuccessful attempt, six terrorists belonging to Lashkar-e-Toiba, stormed the Ayodhya Ram Janmbhomi complex on July 5, 2005. Before the terrorists could reach the main disputed site, they were shot down by Indian security forces. One Hindu worshipper and two policemen were injured during the incident.

Alleged Human Rights Violations by India

A report by the Human Rights Watch, stated two main reasons for the improving human rights condition in the region: First, sincere efforts were made by the new Jammu and Kashmir state government headed by Mufti Muhammad Sayeed to investigate cases of human rights abuses in the state and to punish those guilty including Indian soldiers. More than 15 Indian army soldiers were convicted by the Indian government in 2004 for carrying out human rights abuses in the state. Second, the decrease in cross-border infiltration into India by armed insurgents.

Developments Since 2004

Violent activities in the region declined in 2004. There are two main reasons for this: warming of relations between New Delhi and Islamabad which consequently lead to a ceasefire between the two countries in 2003 and the fencing of the LOC being carried out by the Indian Army. Moreover, coming under intense international pressure, Islamabad was compelled to take actions against the militants' training camps on its territory. In 2004, the two countries also agreed upon decreasing the number of troops present in the region.

Under pressure, Kashmiri militant organisations have made an offer for talks and negotiations with New Delhi, which India has welcomed. India's Border Security Force blamed the Pakistani military for providing cover-fire for the terrorists whenever they infiltrated into Indian territory from Pakistan. In 2005, Pakistan's information minister, Sheikh Rashid, was alleged to have run a terrorist training camp in 1990 in N.W. Frontier, Pakistan. The Pakistani government dismissed the charges against its minister as an attempt to hamper the ongoing peace process between the two neighbours.

Both India and Pakistan have launched several mutual confidence-building measures (CBMs) to ease tensions between the two. These include more high-level talks, easing visa restrictions, and restarting of cricket matches between the two. The new bus service between Srinagar and Muzaffarabad has also helped bring the two sides closer. Pakistan and India have also decided to cooperate on economic fronts.

A major clash between Indian Security Forces and militants occurred when a group of insurgents tried to infiltrate into the Indian-administered Kashmir from Pakistan in July 2005. The same month also saw a Kashmiri militant attack on Ayodhya and Srinagar. However, these developments had little impact on the peace process.

Some improvements in the relations are seen with the re-opening of a series of transportation networks near the India–Pakistan border, with the most important being bus routes and railway lines.

An Indian man held in Pakistani prisons since 1975 as an accused spy walked across the border to freedom March 3, 2008, an unconditional release that Pakistan said was done to improve relations between the two countries.

In 2006, a "Friends Without Borders" scheme began with the help of two British tourists. The idea was that Indian and Pakistani children would make pen pals and write friendly letters to each other. The idea was so successful in both countries that the organisation found it "impossible to keep up". The World's Largest Love Letter was recently sent from India to Pakistan.

Re-evaluation

The insurgents who initially started their movement as a pro-Kashmiri independence movement, have gone through a lot of change in their ideology. Most of the insurgents portray their struggle as a religious one.

Indian analysts allege that by supporting these insurgents, Pakistan is trying to wage a proxy war against India while Pakistan claims that it regards most of these insurgent groups as "freedom fighters" rather than terrorists

Internationally known to be the most deadly theatre of conflict, nearly 10 million people, including Muslims, Hindus, and Buddhists, have been fighting a daily battle for survival. The *cross-border firing* between India and Pakistan, and the terrorist attacks combined have taken its toll on the Kashmiris, who have suffered poor living standards and an erosion of human rights.

Kargil Crisis

Attempts to restart dialogue between the two nations were given a major boost by the February 1999 meeting of both Prime Ministers in Lahore and their signing of three agreements.

These efforts have since been stalled by the intrusion of Pakistani forces into Indian territory near Kargil in Jammu and Kashmir in May 1999. This resulted in intense fighting between Indian and Pakistani forces, known as the Kargil conflict. Backed by the Indian Air Force, the Indian Army successfully regained Kargil. A subsequent military coup in Pakistan that overturned the democratically elected Nawaz Sharif government in October of the same year also proved a setback to relations.

In 2001, a summit was called in Agra; Pakistani President Pervez Musharraf turned up to meet Indian Prime Minister Atal Behari Vajpayee. The talks fell through.

On June 20, 2004, with a new government in place in India, both countries agreed to extend a nuclear testing ban and to set up a hotline between their foreign secretaries aimed at preventing misunderstandings that might lead to a nuclear war.

As of early 2005, both countries are committed to a process of dialogue to solve all outstanding issues. Baglihar Dam issue was a new issue raised by Pakistan in 2005.

India – Sri Lanka Relations

Bilateral relations between the Democratic Socialist Republic of Sri Lanka and the Republic of India have been generally friendly, but were controversially affected by the Sri Lankan civil war and by the failure of Indian intervention during the war. India is the only neighbour of Sri Lanka, separated by the Palk Strait; both nations occupy a strategic position in South Asia and have sought to build a common security umbrella in the Indian Ocean. The two largest ethnic groups of Sri Lanka are Sinhala and Tamil.

Development of Bilateral Relations

India and Sri Lanka established diplomatic relations when the latter gained its independence in 1948. Both nations proceeded to establish extensive cultural, commercial, strategic and defence ties to establish a common sphere of influence in the region, adopting nonalignment to control Western and Soviet influence. The close relationship between the then-Indian Prime Minister Indira Gandhi and then-Sri Lankan Prime Minister Sirimavo Bandaranaike led to the development of strong bilateral relations. In 1971, Indian armed forces helped squash a Communist rebellion against the Sri Lankan government.

Indian Intervention in the Sri Lankan Civil War

In the 1980s, private entities and elements in the state government of Tamil Nadu were believed to be encouraging the funding and training for the Liberation Tigers of Tamil Eelam, a separatist insurgent force..In 1987, faced with growing anger amongst its own Tamils, and a flood of refugees, India intervened directly in the conflict for the first time after the Sri Lankan government attempted to regain control of the northern Jaffna region by means of an economic blockade and military assaults, India supplied food and medicine by air and sea. After subsequent negotiations, India and Sri Lanka entered into an agreement. The peace accord assigned a certain degree of regional autonomy in the Tamil areas with Eelam People's Revolutionary Liberation Front (EPRLF) controlling the regional council and called for the Tamil militant groups to lay down their arms. Further India was to send a peacekeeping force, named the IPKF to Sri Lanka to enforce the disarmament and to watch over the regional council.

Even though the accord was signed between the governments of Sri Lanka and India, with the Tamil Tigers and other Tamil militant groups not having a role in the signing of the accord, most Tamil militant groups accepted this agreement, the LTTE rejected the accord because they opposed the candidate, who belonged to another militant group named Eelam Peoples Revolutionary Liberation Front (EPRLF), for chief administrative officer of the merged Northern and Eastern provinces. Instead the LTTE named three other candidates for the position. The candidates proposed by the LTTE were rejected by India. The LTTE subsequently refused to hand over their weapons to the IPKF.

The result was that the LTTE now found itself engaged in military conflict with the Indian Army, and launched their first attack on an Indian army rations truck on October 8, killing five Indian para-commandos who were on board by strapping burning tires around their necks. The government of India then decided that the IPKF should disarm the LTTE by force, and the Indian Army launched number of assaults on the LTTE, including a month-long campaign dubbed *Operation Pawan* to win control of the Jaffna peninsula from the LTTE. When the IPKF engaged the LTTE, the then president of Sri Lanka, Ranasinghe Premadasa, began supporting LTTE and funded LTTE with arms. During the warfare with the ltte IPKF was also alleged for human rights violation against the civilians. Notably, IPKF was alleged to have perpetrated Jaffna teaching hospital massacre which was the killing of over 70 civilians including patients, doctors and nurses. The ruthlessness of this campaign, and the Indian army's subsequent anti-LTTE operations made it extremely unpopular amongst many Tamils in Sri Lanka. The conflict between the LTTE and the Indian Army left over 1,000 Indian soldiers dead.

The Indo-Sri Lankan Accord, which had been unpopular amongst Sri Lankans for giving India a major influence, now became a source of nationalist anger and resentment as the IPKF was drawn fully into the conflict. Sri Lankans protested the presence of the IPKF, and the newly-elected Sri Lankan president Ranasinghe Premadasa demanded its withdrawal, which was completed by March 1990. On May 21, 1992, Rajiv Gandhi was assassinated and the LTTE was alleged to be the perpetrator. As a result India declared the LTTE to be a terrorist outfit in 1992. Bilateral relations improved in the 1990s and India supported the peace process but has resisted calls to get involved again. India has also been wary of and criticised the extensive military involvement of Pakistan in the conflict, accusing the latter of supplying lethal weaponry and encouraging Sri Lanka to pursue military action rather than peaceful negotiations to end the civil war.

Commercial Ties

India and Sri Lanka are member nations of several regional and multilateral organisations such as the South Asian Association for Regional Cooperation (SAARC), South Asia Co-operative Environment Programme, South Asian Economic Union and BIMSTEC, working to enhance cultural and commercial ties. Since a bilateral free trade agreement was signed and came into effect in 2000, Indo-Sri Lankan trade rose 128% by 2004 and quadrupled by 2006, reaching USD 2.6 billion. Between 2000 and 2004, India's exports to Sri Lanka in the last four years increased by 113%, from USD 618 million to $1,319 million while Sri Lankan exports to India increased by 342%, from $44 million to USD $194 million. Indian exports account for 14% of Sri Lanka's global imports. India is also the fifth largest export destination for Sri Lankan goods, accounting for 3.6% of its exports. Both nations are also signatories of the South Asia Free Trade Agreement (SAFTA). Negotiations are also underway to expand the free trade agreement to forge stronger commercial relations and increase corporate investment and ventures in various industries.

India's National Thermal Power Corp (NTPC) is also scheduled to build a 500 MW thermal power plant in Sampoor (Sampur). The NTPC claims that the this plan will take the Indo-Srilankan relationship to new level.

Fishermen Issue

There have been several incidents of firing on Indian fishermen fishing in Palk Bay.Indian Government has always taken up the issue of safety of Indian fishermen on a priority basis with the Government of Sri Lanka. Presently there is no bona fide Indian fisherman in the Sri Lankan custody. A Joint Working Group (JWG) has been constituted to deal with the issues related to Indian fishermen straying in Sri Lankan territorial waters, work out modalities for prevention of use of force against them and the early release of confiscated boats and explore possibilities of working towards bilateral arrangements for licensed fishing. The JWG last met in Jan 2006.

Development Cooperation

India is active in a number of areas of development activity in Sri Lanka. About one-sixth of the total development credit granted by GOI is made available to Sri Lanka.

Lines of credit: In the recent past three lines of credit were extended to Sri Lanka: US$ 100 million for capital goods, consumer durables, consultancy services and food items, US$ 31 million for supply of 300,000 MT of wheat and US$ 150 million for purchase of petroleum products. All of these lines of credit have been fully utilized. Another line of credit of US$ 100 million is now being made available for rehabilitation of the Colombo-Matara railway.

A number of development projects are implemented under 'Aid to Sri Lanka' funds. In 2006-07, the budget for 'Aid to Sri Lanka' was Rs 28.2 Crs.

Small Development Projects: A MoU on Cooperation in Small

Development Projects has been signed. Projects for providing fishing equipments to the fishermen in the East of Sri Lanka and solar energy aided computer education in 25 rural schools in Eastern Sri Lanka are under consideration.

Health Projects: We have supplied medical equipments to hospitals at Hambantota and Point Pedro, supplied 4 state of the art ambulances to the Central Province, implemented a cataract eye surgery programme for 1500 people in the Central Province and implemented a project of renovation of OT at Dickoya hospital and supplying equipment to it. The projects under consideration are: Construction of a 150-bed hospital at Dickoya, upgradation of the hospital at Trincomalee and a US$ 7.5 million grant for setting up a Cancer Hospital in Colombo.

Education Projects: Upgradation of the educational infrastructure of the schools in the Central province including teachers' training, setting up of 10 computer labs, setting up of 20 e-libraries (Nenasalas), Mahatma Gandhi scholarship scheme for +2 students and setting up of a vocational training centre in Puttalam. India also contributes to the Ceylon Workers Education Trust that gives scholarships to the children of estate workers.

Training: A training programme for 465 Sri Lankan Police officers has been commenced in Dec 2005. Another 400 Sri Lankan Police personnel are being trained for the course of 'Maintenance of Public Order'.

Bibliography

Ahmad, Imtiaz: *State and Foreign Policy: India's Role in South Asia,* New Delhi, Vikas, 1993.

Appleby, Paul H.: *Policy and Administration*, Birmingham, AL: University of Alabama Press, 1949.

Ashton, S.R.: *British Policy Towards the Indian States, 1905-1939*, London, Curzon, 1982.

Austin, Granville: *The Indian Constitution: Cornerstone of a Nation*, Oxford, Clarendon Press, 1966.

Ayesha, Jalal: *Nationalism, Democracy, and Development: State and Politics in India*, Delhi; New York: Oxford University Press, 1997.

Baldwin, David, *Economic Development and American Foreign Policy, 1943-1966,* Chicago, 1966.

Basu, Prahlad K.: *Governance and Public Administration for Poverty Reduction*, Salvador, Brazil, 1997.

Behari, Madhuri: *Indian Trade since Independence: Chronology of Events,* Delhi, D.K. Publications, 1983.

Bemis, Samuel Flagg, *American Foreign Policy and the Blessings of Freedom,* New Haven, 1962.

Bhatta, Sitesh: *Agricultural Price Policy and Production in India,* Delhi, Konark, 1991.

Blau, M.: *Bureaucracy in Modern Society,* New York, Random House, 1956.

Carl J. Friedrich: *Constitutional Government and Democracy,* Boston, Ginn, 1950.

Charnovitz, Steve: *Trade law and global governance,* London, Cameron May, 2002.

Desai, Vasant: *A Study of Rural Economics: A Systems Approach*, Bombay, Himalaya, 1983.

Feis, Herbert, *Foreign Aid and Foreign Policy*, NY, 1964.

Giersch, H. : *Trade Policy and Demand Management*, Tübingen, J.S.B.Muhr, 1973.

Hauft, Ottomar: *Distribution of Stock of Money*, Effingham, London, 1892.

Henken, Louis, *Foreign Affairs and the Constitution*, NY, 1972.

Kegan, K. : *Money and the Mechanism of Exchange*, MacMillan, London, 1890.

Ottomar, H.: *Distribution of Stock of Money*, Effingham, London, 1892.

Kenneth C. Wheare: *Federal Government*, New York, Oxford University Press, 1953.

Lucian W. : *Asian Power and Politics: the Cultural Dimensions of Authority*, Cambridge, Belknap Press, 1985.

Max Beloff: *Foreign Policy and the Democratic Process*, Baltimore, Johns Hopkins University Press, 1955.

Michael Stewart: *Modern Forms of Government: A Comparative Study*, New York, Frederick A. Praeger, 1961.

Norman, Uphoff: *Local Organizations: Intermediaries in Rural Development*, Ithaca, Cornell University Press, 1984.

Raj, K.N.: *New Economic Policy*, Delhi, Oxford University Press, 1986.

Sullivan, Ezra N.: *Bureaucrats and Policy Making*, New York, Holmes & Meier, 1984.

Uphoff, N.: *Local Organizations: Intermediaries in Rural Development*, Ithaca, Cornell University Press, 1984.

Whitakar, A. C. : *Foreign Exchange. Appleton*, New York, 1920.

Index

O

P

R

S

T

U

W

□□□